UNDERSTANDING AND USING

English Grammar

FIFTH EDITION
WORKBOOK

Betty S. Azar
Stacy A. Hagen
Geneva Tesh
Rachel Spack Koch

Understanding and Using English Grammar, Fifth Edition Workbook

Pearson Education, 221 River Street, Hoboken, NJ 07030

Azar Associates: Sue Van Etten, Manager

Staff credits: The people who made up the *Understanding and Using English Grammar Fifth Edition, Workbook* team, representing content creation, design, manufacturing, project management, publishing, rights management, and testing, are Pietro Alongi, Rhea Banker, Stephanie Bullard, Warren Fischbach, Nancy Flaggman, Gosia Jaros-White, Amy McCormick, Brian Panker, Lindsay Richman, Robert Ruvo, Paula Van Ells, and Joseph Vella.

Contributing Editors: Jennifer McAliney, Janice Baillie

Text composition: Aptara

Illustrations: Don Martinetti–pages 148, 150 (bottom), 183, 207, 225; Chris Pavely–pages 4, 5, 46, 52, 66, 71, 89, 135, 136, 137, 146, 150 (top), 153, 164, 170, 186, 191

Photo Credits—page 1: Nataliia Pyzhova/Fotolia; 13: Olly/Fotolia; 24: Samott/Fotolia; 35: Syda Productions/Fotolia; 43: JStone/Shutterstock; 50: RTimages/Fotolia; 63: Markop/Fotolia; 69: Blackday/Fotolia; 75: Sean Pavone/123RF; 83: Goku/Fotolia; 96: Chee Onn Leong/Fotolia; 107 (left): Enrico Della Pietra/Fotolia; 107 (right): Thomas Cockrem/Alamy Stock Photo; 108: Shock/Fotolia; 117: Dolgachov/123RF; 118: Sam Spiro/Fotolia; 129: Aigarsr/Fotolia; 139: Storergv/Fotolia; 151: Julief514/Fotolia; 159: Georgejmclittle/Fotolia; 170: Sushytska/Fotolia; 176: Oksana Kuzmina/Fotolia; 188: Jan Wlodarczyk/Alamy Stock Photo; 201: Bonzami Emmanuelle/Alamy Stock Photo.

ISBN 10: 0-13-427544-6
ISBN 13: 978-0-13-427544-4

Printed in the United States of America
3   18

Contents

The titles listed below refer to section names, not practice titles. In general, one section has multiple exercises. The chart numbers refer to the grammar explanations in the *Understanding and Using English Grammar* Student Book.

Preface

The *Understanding and Using English Grammar Workbook* is a self-study textbook. It is keyed to the explanatory grammar charts found in *Understanding and Using English Grammar, Fifth Edition,* a classroom teaching text for English language learners, as well as in the accompanying *Chartbook,* a reference grammar with no exercises. Students can use the *Workbook* independently to enhance their understanding of English structures. Students can choose from a variety of exercises that will help them use English meaningfully and correctly.

This *Workbook* is also a resource for teachers who need exercise material for additional classwork, homework, testing, or individualized instruction.

The answers to the practices can be found in the *Answer Key* in the back of the *Workbook.* Its pages are perforated so that they can be detached to make a separate booklet. However, if teachers want to use the *Workbook* as a classroom teaching text, the *Answer Key* can be removed at the beginning of the term.

A special *Workbook* section called *Phrasal Verbs,* not available in the main text, is included in the *Appendix.* This section provides a reference list of common phrasal verbs along with a variety of exercises for independent practice.

Present and Past;
Simple and Progressive

PRACTICE 1 ▸ Preview.
Read the passage. Underline the 11 verbs.

Indoor Plants

Many people <u>keep</u> indoor house plants for their natural beauty, but these plants also create a healthier living space. While scientists at NASA (National Aeronautics and Space Administration) were researching air quality in space stations, they discovered that common indoor house plants actually clean the air. The plants absorb carbon dioxide and release oxygen. NASA scientists found that plants also eliminate harmful chemicals in the air. In 1989, NASA published the first results of the NASA Clean Air Study. Today, scientists are still learning about the many benefits of houseplants.

1. Write the six verbs in the simple present tense.

   _____*keep,*_____

2. Write the three verbs in the simple past tense.

   _____

3. Write the verb in the present progressive tense.

   _____

4. Write the verb in the past progressive tense.

   _____

PRACTICE 2 ▸ The simple present and the present progressive. (Chart 1-1)
Complete the sentences. Write the simple present or the present progressive form of the verbs in parentheses.

1. a. The sun (*set*) _____*sets*_____ in the west every evening.

   b. Look! The sun (*set*) _____*is setting*_____ behind the mountain now. How beautiful!

2. a. Bring an umbrella. It (*rain*) _____.

   b. It (*rain*) _____ a lot in the spring.

3. a. I (*listen*) _____ to the weather report every morning.

   b. I (*listen*) _____ to the weather report right now.

4. a. Hurricanes usually (*form*) _____ in tropical areas.

   b. A hurricane (*form*) _____ today off the coast of Florida.

5. a. Snow (*melt*) _____ as the temperature rises.

   b. The kids want to build a snowman. They need to hurry. The snow

   (*melt*) _____ .

PRACTICE 3 ▸ The simple present and the present progressive. (Chart 1-1)
Choose the correct completions.

1. a. Because of the force of gravity, objects (fall)/ are falling   down and not up.

   b. It's autumn! The leaves   fall / are falling,   and winter will soon be here.

2. a. Coffee   grows / is growing   in mountainous areas, not in deserts.

   b. Oh, you   grow / are growing   so fast, Johnny! Soon you'll be taller than your dad.

3. a. Near the Arctic Circle, the sun   shines / is shining   for more than 20 hours a day at the beginning of the summer.

   b. It's a beautiful day! The sun   shines / is shining   and the birds   sing / are singing.

4. a. A human heart   beats / is beating   about 100,000 times a day.

   b. This movie is scary! My heart   beats / is beating   rapidly.

5. a. Most people   sleep / are sleeping   seven to eight hours a night.

   b. It's already noon! Scott   sleep / is sleeping   very late today.

PRACTICE 4 ▸ The simple present and present progressive: affirmative, negative, question forms. (Chart 1-2)
Complete the questions with **Do, Does, Is,** or **Are.**

1. _____Does_____ the sun rise early?

2. _____Is_____ the earth revolving around the sun right now?

3. _____ bears live in caves?

4. _____ it raining today?

5. _____ water freeze at 32 degrees Fahrenheit (0 degrees Celsius)?

6. _____ bees make honey nearby?

7. _____ bees making honey nearby?

PRACTICE 5 ▸ The simple present and present progressive: affirmative, negative, question forms. (Chart 1-2)
Write a correct affirmative or negative statement from the questions in Practice 4.

1. The sun _____doesn't rise_____ in the evening.

2. The earth _____is revolving_____ around the sun right now.

3. Bears _____ in caves.

4. It _____ today.

5. Water _____ at 32 degrees Fahrenheit.

6. Bees _____ honey nearby.

7. Bees _____ honey nearby.

PRACTICE 6 ▸ Non-progressive verbs. (Chart 1-3)

Choose the correct completions.

1. There you are! Behind the tree. I _____ you.
   a. see   b. am seeing

2. My mother's hearing has been getting worse for several months. She _____ a specialist right now.
   a. see   b. is seeing

3. Do you see that man? I _____ him. He was my high school English teacher.
   a. recognize   b. am recognizing

4. My favorite actor _____ at the Paramount Theater.
   a. currently appears   b. is currently appearing

5. A: Is my voice loud enough?

   B: Yes, I _____ you.
   a. hear   b. am hearing

6. A: Aren't you having any coffee?

   B: No, I _____ tea.
   a. prefer   b. 'm preferring

7. A: What's on your mind?

   B: I _____ about my family.
   a. think   b. am thinking

8. A: Did you make a decision yet?

   B: No, I _____ your opinion.
   a. need   b. 'm needing

9. A: Why are you staring at me?

   B: You _____ your mom so much.
   a. resemble   b. are resembling

10. A: There's Dr. Jones on a motorcycle! Do you believe it?

    B: Yeah, he _____ several.
    a. owns   b. is owning

PRACTICE 7 ▸ The present progressive to describe a temporary state.
(Chart 1-3, footnote)

Choose the correct completions. If a situation describes a temporary state, choose the present progressive.

1. My husband and I are short, but our children _____.
   a. are tall   b. are being tall

2. Jane's an intelligent woman, but she won't see a doctor about those headaches she has.

   She _____.
   a. is foolish   b. is being foolish

3. The teacher spoke harshly to the children because they were too noisy, so now they _____.
   a. are quiet   b. are being quiet

4. Don't eat that chocolate dessert. It _____.
   a. is not healthy   b. is not being healthy

5. Timmy! Those are bad words you're saying to Mr. Hawkes. You _____.
   a. are not polite   b. are not being polite

6. I'm worried about Jeff. He has pneumonia. He _____.
   a. is very ill   b. is being very ill

PRACTICE 8 ▸ Regular and irregular verbs. (Chart 1-4)

Part I. Read the passage. <u>Underline</u> the eight past tense verbs.

> **Sputnik**
>
> History <u>changed</u> on October 4th, 1957 when the Soviet Union successfully launched *Sputnik I*. The world's first artificial satellite was about the size of a beach ball (58 cm., or 22.8 in.), weighed only 83.6 kg., or 183.9 pounds, and took about 98 minutes to orbit the Earth on its elliptical path. That launch ushered in new political, military, technological, and scientific developments. While the *Sputnik* launch was a single event, it marked the start of the space age and the space race between the U.S. and the Soviet Union.

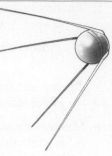

Part II. Answer the questions. Choose "T" if the statement is true. Choose "F" if the statement is false.

1. The Soviet Union launched the first artificial satellite.   (T)   F
2. The first satellite was about the size of a golf ball.   T   F
3. The first orbit around the Earth took about an hour and a half.   T   F
4. *Sputnik* went into space several times.   T   F
5. This first launch was the beginning of the space age and space race.   T   F

PRACTICE 9 ▸ Regular and irregular verbs. (Chart 1-4)

Complete the sentences. Write the simple past of the verbs in blue.

Part I. Regular verbs: The simple past ends in *–ed*.

1. It rains every afternoon in the summer. Yesterday it _____*rained*_____ all afternoon and all night too.
2. It snows a lot in Denver in the winter. Last January it _____ nearly every day.
3. I listen to the weather report every morning. Yesterday I _____ to the weather report several times.

Part II. Irregular verbs: The simple past does not end in *–ed*.

1. Lightening sometimes hits trees in this area. Last week a lightning bolt _____ my neighbor's tree and split it in half.
2. I usually wake up at 6:00 every morning, but today I _____ up at 4:00 because of a loud thunderstorm.
3. The sun rises in the morning. The sun _____ at 6:45 yesterday morning.
4. The sun sets in the evening. The sun _____ at 7:55 yesterday evening.

PRACTICE 10 ▸ Irregular verbs. (Chart 1-4)

Complete the sentences. Write the simple past tense of the verbs in blue.

1. Joe runs in marathons. Last year he _____*ran*_____ in the New York Marathon.
2. Athletes need to drink a lot of water. Joe _____ 12 glasses of water a day when he trained for the marathon.
3. Nowadays, I occasionally swim for exercise when I have time, but I _____ every day when I was a child.
4. Our basketball team doesn't win many games, but we _____ last Friday night.

5. Our soccer team didn't lose a single game this season until last night. Last night we _____ because we played so poorly.

6. Rhonda doesn't take many exercise classes now, but when she was younger she _____ karate and gymnastics classes.

7. The dance class usually begins at noon, but today the teacher was late. The class _____ ten minutes late.

8. Janice teaches a yoga class on Saturdays. Last Saturday she _____ two classes.

9. Harry goes to professional basketball games often. Last month he _____ to a Chicago Bulls game.

10. I always buy fresh vegetables on the weekend. Last Saturday I _____ fresh asparagus.

11. This year corn costs a lot more than it _____ last year.

12. Scott usually eats a salad for lunch. Yesterday he _____ a spinach salad.

13. Vanessa often gives me tomatoes from her garden. Last week she _____ me two baskets of tomatoes.

14. Margaret usually makes eggs for breakfast, but yesterday she _____ pancakes instead.

15. Yesterday I _____ sick, but today I feel much better.

PRACTICE 11 ▸ Irregular verbs. (Chart 1-4)
Write the simple past form of the verbs.

1. sell __*sold*__	11. come _____	21. speak _____
2. buy _____	12. lose _____	22. go _____
3. begin _____	13. sleep _____	23. pay _____
4. have _____	14. build _____	24. forget _____
5. catch _____	15. fight _____	25. write _____
6. quit _____	16. understand _____	26. fall _____
7. find _____	17. spend _____	27. feel _____
8. make _____	18. let _____	28. leave _____
9. take _____	19. see _____	29. upset _____
10. break _____	20. teach _____	30. fly _____

PRACTICE 12 ▸ Irregular Verbs. (Chart 1-4)
In this exercise, a police reporter interviews the victim of a theft. The victim answers the questions, using a past tense verb. Write the victim's words.

1. REPORTER: So, a thief broke into your home last night?

   VICTIM: Yes, a thief _____*broke*_____ into my home last night.

2. REPORTER: Did he steal anything?

   VICTIM: Yes, he _____ some things.

3. REPORTER: Did you know he was in your apartment?

   VICTIM: Yes, I _____ he was in my apartment.

4. REPORTER: Did you hear him come in?

   VICTIM: Yes, I _____ him come in.

5. REPORTER: Did the police come?

   VICTIM: Yes, the police _____ .

6. REPORTER: Did your hands shake when you called the police?

   VICTIM: Yes, my hands _____ when I called them.

7. REPORTER: Did he hide in your garden?

   VICTIM: Yes, he _____ in my garden.

8. REPORTER: Did the police find him?

   VICTIM: Yes, the police _____ him.

9. REPORTER: Did they fight with him?

   VICTIM: Yes, they _____ with him.

10. REPORTER: Did he run away?

    VICTIM: Yes, he _____ away.

11. REPORTER: Did they shoot at him?

    VICTIM: Yes, they _____ at him.

12. REPORTER: Did they catch him?

    VICTIM: Yes, they _____ him.

PRACTICE 13 ▶ Simple past of irregular verbs. (Chart 1-4)

Complete the sentences. Write the simple past of the irregular verbs in the box. Pay special attention to spelling.

✓ bite	catch	hold	pay	sting
blow	feel	mean	quit	swim

1. I broke a tooth when I _____*bit*_____ into a piece of hard candy.
2. The little boy _____ his mother's hand as they walked toward the school bus.
3. Maria promised to help us. I hope she _____ what she said.
4. Arthur _____ out all of the candles on his birthday cake.
5. We both _____ eating fried foods months ago, and we already feel much better.
6. Douglas _____ the outside of his pocket to make sure his wallet was still there.
7. A bee _____ me on the hand while I was working in the garden.
8. Matthew Webb was the first person who _____ across the English Channel.
9. Paul _____ much more for his bike than I spent for mine.
10. Rita threw the ball high in the air. Daniel _____ it when it came down.

PRACTICE 14 ▸ Simple past of irregular verbs. (Chart 1-4)

Complete the sentences. Write the simple past form of the irregular verbs in the box. Pay special attention to spelling.

bet	fly	lead	sink	spin
choose	freeze	ring	✓ spend	weep

1. Dr. Perez _____ *spent* _____ ten hours in the operating room performing delicate surgery.

2. On my first day at the university, my English teacher _____ the class to our classroom. We all followed him.

3. Sally and I made a friendly bet. I _____ her that my grade on the math test would be higher than hers.

4. I _____ when I heard the tragic news. Everyone else cried too.

5. When I threw a piece of wood from the shore, it floated on top of the water.

   When I threw a rock, it _____ immediately to the bottom of the lake.

6. In 1927, Charles Lindbergh _____ from New York to Paris in 33 hours and 30 minutes.

7. When the children _____ around and around, they became dizzy.

8. The telephone _____ several times and then stopped before I could answer it.

9. William had trouble deciding which sweater he liked best, but he finally _____ the blue one.

10. The cold temperature _____ the water in the pond, so we can go ice-skating today.

PRACTICE 15 ▸ The simple past and the past progressive. (Chart 1-5)

Complete the sentences. Write the correct form of the verbs in parentheses.

1. Maria (call) _____ *called* _____ me as soon as she got the good news.

2. Last night at about nine o'clock we (watch) _____ TV when someone knocked at the door.

3. During the study period in class yesterday, it was hard for me to concentrate because the student next to me (hum) _____ .

4. When Harry (meet) _____ Janice, he immediately fell in love with her.

5. Jack was rushing to catch the bus when I (see) _____ him.

6. Last Saturday while Sandy (clean) _____ out the attic, she found her grandmother's wedding dress.

7. It started to rain while I (drive) _____ to work this morning. I didn't have an umbrella with me. I (get) _____ very wet when I stepped out of my car.

8. When we looked outside during the storm, we saw that the wind (blow) _____ very hard, and the trees (bend) _____ over in the wind.

9. When the teacher came into the room, most of the children (play) _____ together nicely. But over in the corner, Luke (pull) _____ Annie's hair. The teacher quickly ran over and pulled Luke away from Annie.

PRACTICE 16 ▶ The simple past and the past progressive. (Chart 1-5)
Write "1" before the action that started first. Write "2" before the action that started second.

1. When the alarm clock rang, I was sleeping.

   _2_ The alarm clock rang.

   _1_ I was sleeping.

2. When I saw Dr. Jarvis yesterday evening, he was waving at me.

   _____ I saw Dr. Jarvis yesterday evening.

   _____ He was waving at me.

3. When I saw Dr. Jarvis yesterday evening, he waved at me.

   _____ I saw Dr. Jarvis yesterday evening.

   _____ He waved at me.

4. I closed the windows when it was raining.

   _____ I closed the windows.

   _____ It began to rain.

5. I was closing the windows when it began to rain.

   _____ I was closing the windows.

   _____ It began to rain.

6. The server brought the check when we were eating our desserts.

   _____ The server brought the check.

   _____ We were eating our desserts.

7. When the doorbell rang, Sam went to the door. "Who is it?" he asked.

   _____ The doorbell rang.

   _____ Sam went to the door.

8. Sam was going to the door when the doorbell rang. "I'm coming, Bob," he said. "I saw you walking up the sidewalk."

   _____ The doorbell rang.

   _____ Sam was already going to the door.

PRACTICE 17 ▶ The simple past and the past progressive. (Chart 1-5)
Choose the correct completions.

1. We (had)/ were having   a wonderful dinner last night to celebrate our 25th wedding anniversary.

2. We   had / were having   a wonderful time when suddenly the electric power went out.

3. When Richard   stopped / was stopping   his car suddenly, the groceries   fell / were falling   out of the grocery bags and   spilled / were spilling   all over the floor of the car.

4. When I was a child, my mother always   served / was serving   cookies and milk to my friends and me when they   came / were coming   home with me after school.

5. When we   looked / were looking   in on our baby last night, he   slept / was sleeping.   I think he   dreamt / was dreaming   about something nice because he   smiled / was smiling.

6. A: Why is Henry in the hospital?

   B: He   worked / was working   on his car in the garage when the gas tank

   exploded / was exploding.

7. A: Oh! What   caused / was causing   the explosion?

   B: Henry   dropped / was dropping   a match too near the gas tank.

PRACTICE 18 ▸ Unfulfilled intentions. (Chart 1-6)
Complete each sentence with a logical phrase from the list. Write the letter of the phrase.

   a. it rained
   b. she didn't want to upset her
   c. I overslept this morning
   d. my battery died
   e. he was out of town
   f. her dinner guest is allergic to seafood
   g. there was no lettuce in the fridge
   h. it was too crowded

1. I was going to go to the library before class, but ___c___ .

2. Jill was planning to invite Jeff to see a movie, but _____ .

3. Susie was going to tell her sister the bad news, but _____ .

4. Scott and Jeff were going to play baseball, but _____ .

5. I was going to text you, but _____ .

6. Lesley was going to make a salad, but _____ .

7. Joy was going to cook lobster, but _____ .

8. We were going to go to the new restaurant, but _____ .

PRACTICE 19 ▸ Unfulfilled intentions. (Chart 1-6)
Check (✓) the sentences that you can rewrite with **was planning** for the underlined words.

1. a. __✓__ I was going to wash my car, but it started to rain.

   b. _____ I was washing my car when it began to rain.

   c. _____ I was going to the store when I remembered that my wallet was at home.

2. a. _____ We were going to visit our cousins, but Jack got sick.

   b. _____ We were going to see them tomorrow.

   c. _____ We were going to our cousins, but we had car trouble.

3. a. _____ Were you going to come to the meeting?

   b. _____ Were we meeting at 1:00?

   c. _____ Were you going home after the meeting?

PRACTICE 20 ▶ Chapter review.

Underline the verbs. Decide which of the following phrases best describes the action of each sentence. Write the appropriate number.

1. actions occurring now or today
2. habitual / everyday actions
3. actions completed in the past (non-progressive)
4. one action in progress when another occurred

1. __2__ I take the bus to school when it rains.

2. __4__ I was riding the bus when I heard the news on my radio.

3. _____ I am riding the bus because my friend is repairing my bike.

4. _____ I rode the bus home yesterday because you forgot to pick me up.

5. _____ Dennis was having coffee this morning when a bird crashed into his kitchen window.

6. _____ Dennis had a big breakfast, but his wife didn't eat anything.

7. _____ Dennis is having a big breakfast this morning.

8. _____ Dennis generally has coffee with breakfast.

9. _____ My mother and I celebrate our birthdays together because they are just a few days apart.

10. _____ We were working when you called on our birthdays last week.

11. _____ One year we celebrated our birthdays apart because my mom was away on business.

PRACTICE 21 ▶ Chapter review.

Complete the crossword puzzle. Use the clues under the puzzle. Write the correct form of the verbs in parentheses.

Across

2. Shhh. I'm (*listen*) _____ to the radio.

5. Good idea! I (*think*) _____ your suggestion is great.

7. What was that? I just (*hear*) _____ a loud noise.

8. I am (*think*) _____ about going home early today.

Down

1. We (*go*) _____ to Mexico last year.

3. I was in my room (*study*) _____ when you called.

4. I (*eat*) _____ lunch with friends yesterday.

6. This is fun. I'm (*have*) _____ a great time here.

7. I only (*have*) _____ a little money right now.

PRACTICE 22 ▸ Chapter review.

Complete the sentences with the correct form of the verbs in parentheses.

A hurricane (*be*) ___*is*___ a huge tropical storm. It brings very strong winds and
1

heavy rain. Hurricanes (*form*) _____ over large bodies of warm water.
2

They (*gather*) _____ heat and energy from warm water. Hurricanes
3

(*rotate*) _____ around the center of the storm, called the "eye." The eye of
4

a hurricane (*be*) _____ the calmest part of the storm. A hurricane usually
5

(*last*) _____ for over a week and (*move*) _____ 10–20 miles
6   7

per hour over the open water. Hurricanes typically (*grow*) _____ weak over land,
8

but when they first touch land, the heavy rain and strong winds (*damage*) _____
9

buildings and trees. These storms sometimes (*destroy*) _____ coastal towns.
10

One of the most damaging hurricanes to hit the United States was Hurricane Katrina in

August, 2005. Hurricane Katrina (*form*) _____ over the Bahamas. Then it
11

(*move*) _____ to Florida and crossed the Gulf Coast. It (*cost*) _____
12   13

billions of dollars in property damage. It especially (*cause*) _____ damage to the city of
14

New Orleans. By the end of the storm, about 80% of the city (*be*) _____ underwater.
15

While the storm (*approach*) _____, many residents (*try*) _____
16   17

unsuccessfully to leave the city. It (*be*) _____ one of the deadliest and costliest hurricanes in
18

U.S. history.

There is still a lot to learn about hurricanes. Today scientists (*study*) _____
19

ways to better predict a hurricane's path. City planners (*learn*) _____ more about
20

preparation for hurricanes. Architects and engineers (*discover*) _____ better ways
21

to design stronger homes and buildings. Better preparation is the best protection against these deadly

storms.

There is one verb error in each sentence. Correct the error.

1. Carole ~~visit~~ *visits* India every year.

2. In the past, no one was caring about air pollution.

3. Today we are knowing that air pollution is a serious health and environmental problem.

4. I move to Houston two years ago.

5. I was eating dinner when you call.

6. The students taking a test right now.

7. Judy felt on the slippery floor.

8. I was going to transferred to another university, but I decided to stay here.

Perfect and Perfect Progressive Tenses

PRACTICE 1 ▶ Preview.

Part I. Read the passage.

> ### Ride-Sharing Companies
>
>
>
> Ride-sharing companies have become some of the world's largest taxi companies, but they don't own any actual taxis. When customers need a driver, they submit their request through the company's app. The drivers use their own cars. Uber is one example of a ride-sharing company. Uber first began in San Francisco in 2009. By 2012, the company had expanded into several major U.S. cities, such as New York, Chicago, and Washington, D.C. Since that time, it has been expanding internationally. Today, people in countries all over the world use ride-sharing companies. While many people have praised these companies, others have expressed concerns over the safety of the ride-sharing system.

1. Write the 7 verbs in the simple present tense.

   _____

2. Write the 3 verbs in the present perfect tense.

   _____

3. Write the verb in the present perfect progressive tense.

   _____

4. Write the verb in the simple past tense.

   _____

5. Write the verb in the past perfect tense.

   _____

Part II. Answer the questions. Choose "T" if the statement is true. Choose "F" if the statement is false.

1. The world's largest taxi companies don't have traditional taxis.   T   F

2. Uber expanded into New York in 2009.   T   F

3. Uber had drivers in Chicago before it expanded internationally.   T   F

4. Customers use an app to find drivers.   T   F

PRACTICE 2 ▸ Irregular verbs. (Charts 2-1 and 2-2)
Complete the chart.

Simple Form	Simple Past	Past Participle
1.	shut	
2. bring		
3.		heard
4.	lost	
5. teach		
6.		begun
7. sing		
8.	ate	
9. see		
10.	threw	
11. become		
12. go		

PRACTICE 3 ▸ The present perfect. (Chart 2-3)
Complete each sentence with *for* or *since*.

1. I haven't seen Elvira …
   a. _____ several years.
   b. _____ a long time.
   c. _____ the holiday last year.
   d. _____ she was in college.
   e. _____ more than a month.
   f. _____ she got married.
   g. _____ she became famous.

2. Mehdi and Pat have been friends …
   a. _____ they were in college.
   b. _____ about 20 years.
   c. _____ 2005.
   d. _____ a long time.
   e. _____ they began to work together.
   f. _____ they met.
   g. _____ their entire adult lives.

PRACTICE 4 ▸ The present perfect with *since, for,* and *ago.* (Chart 2-3)
Complete the sentences with the correct time expression.

1. Today is the 21st of April. I started this job on April 1st. I started this job
   _____ *three weeks* _____ ago. I have had this job since _____ *April 1st* _____.
   I have had this job for _____ *three weeks* _____.

2. I made a New Year's resolution on January 1st: I will get up at 6:00 A.M. every day instead
   of 7:00 A.M. Today is March 1st, and I have gotten up every morning at 6:00 A.M. I made
   this resolution _____ ago. I have gotten up at 6:00 A.M. since
   _____. I have gotten up at 6:00 A.M. for _____.

3. Today is February 28th. Valentine's Day was on February 14th. I sent my girlfriend some
   chocolates on Valentine's Day, and she texted me a "Thank you." After that, I did not hear from her
   again. I have not heard from her for _____. I have not heard from her
   since _____.

4. Today is January 27th, 2016. Sue works for Senator Brown. She began to work for him right after she
   first met him in January, 2010. She began to work for Senator Brown _____
   ago. Sue has worked for Senator Brown for _____. She has worked for
   Senator Brown since _____.

PRACTICE 5 ▸ The present perfect with *since* and *for.* (Chart 2-3)
Rewrite the sentences using ***since*** and ***for***.

1. We know Mrs. Jones. We met her last month.
   a. for _____ *We have known Mrs. Jones for one month.* _____
   b. since _____

2. They live in New Zealand. They moved there in 2014.
   a. for _____
   b. since _____

3. I like foreign films. I liked them five years ago.
   a. since _____
   b. for _____

4. Jack works for a software company. He started working there last year.
   a. for _____
   b. since _____

PRACTICE 6 ▸ The present perfect. (Charts 2-3 and 2-4)

Complete the sentences using the present perfect tense. Write the correct past participle of the verbs in blue.

1. I often eat Thai food. I have _____ Thai food three times this week.

2. I sometimes visit my cousins on weekends. I have _____ them twice this month.

3. I work at the Regional Bank. I have _____ there for eleven years.

4. I like card games. I have _____ card games since I was a child.

5. I know Professor Blonsky. She's my next-door neighbor. I have _____ her all my life.

6. I wear glasses. I have _____ glasses since I was ten years old.

7. I take piano lessons. I have _____ piano lessons for several years.

8. I go to Unisex Haircutters once a month. I have _____ to the same shop for twenty years.

PRACTICE 7 ▸ The present perfect. (Charts 2-3 and 2-4)

Complete the sentences with the present perfect tense of the appropriate verb in the box. Use each verb only once. Include any words in parentheses.

✓ eat	know	ride	sweep	win
improve	make	start	swim	write

1. A: How about more pie?

   B: No, but thanks. I can't swallow another bite. I (already) _____*have already eaten*_____ too much.

2. Our football team is having a great season. They _____ all but one of their games so far this year and will probably win the championship.

3. Jane is expecting a letter from me, but I (not) _____ to her yet. Maybe I'll call her instead.

4. Jack is living in Spain now. His Spanish used to be terrible, but it _____ greatly since he moved there.

5. A: Let's hurry! I think the movie is beginning!

   B: No, the movie (not) _____ yet. They're just showing previews of the coming attractions.

6. A: I hear your parents are coming to visit you. Is that why you're cleaning your apartment?

   B: You guessed it! I (already) _____ the floor, but I still need to dust the furniture. Want to help?

7. A: I understand Tom is a good friend of yours? How long (you) _____ him?

   B: Since we were kids.

8. Everyone makes mistakes in life. I _____ lots of mistakes in my life. The important thing is to learn from one's mistakes. Right?

9. A: I (never) _____ on the subways in New York City. Have you?

   B: I've never even been to New York City.

10. A: (you, ever) _____ in the Atlantic Ocean?

    B: No, only the Pacific — when I was in Hawaii. I even went snorkeling when I was there.

PRACTICE 8 ▸ The present perfect. (Charts 2-2 → 2-4)
Choose the correct sentence.

1. a. Scott has always wanted to go scuba diving. He's been snorkeling, but he hasn't tried scuba diving yet.
   b. Scott has always wanted to go scuba diving. He's been snorkeling, but he hasn't tried scuba diving never.

2. a. Kevin is jittery. He's yet had seven cups of coffee this morning. He should avoid drinking any more caffeine today.
   b. Kevin is jittery. He's already had seven cups of coffee this morning. He should avoid drinking any more caffeine today.

3. a. Vanessa has tried on five different dresses, but she still hasn't found the right one.
   b. Vanessa has tried on five different dresses, but she already hasn't found the right one.

4. a. I wish our professor would give us a break. This is only the third week of class, and we've ever written five essays.
   b. I wish our professor would give us a break. This is only the third week of class, and we've already written five essays.

5. a. We need to write twelve essays this semester. We've wrote only five so far.
   b. We need to write twelve essays this semester. We've written only five so far.

6. a. I haven't had time to finish my research paper yet.
   b. I haven't have time to finish my research paper yet.

7. a. Have you ever been to Shanghai?
   b. Haven't you never been to Shanghai?

8. a. I've ever been to China, but I hope I can go there some day.
   b. I've never been to China, but I hope I can go there some day.

9. a. I wish I could get over this cold. I've had it ever since the beginning of the semester.
   b. I wish I could get over this cold. I've had it never since the beginning of the semester.

10. a. I've gone to the doctor twice, but I didn't get better yet.
    b. I've gone to the doctor twice, but I haven't gotten better yet.

11. a. I've never tried homeopathic medicine, but my neighbor says it's great.
    b. I haven't never tried homeopathic medicine, but my neighbor says it's great.

12. a. I hope I didn't fail my chemistry test. It was the most difficult exam I've ever taken.
    b. I hope I didn't fail my chemistry test. It was the most difficult exam I've still taken.

PRACTICE 9 ▸ Is vs. has. (Chart 2-5)
In spoken English, *is* and *has* can both be contracted to *'s*. Decide if the verb in the contraction is *is* or *has*.

Spoken English	Written English
1. He's absent.	_____
2. Sue's been a nurse for a long time.	_____
3. Her brother's in the hospital.	_____
4. He's not happy.	_____
5. He's felt bad this past week.	_____
6. Here is a newspaper. Take one. It's free.	_____
7. The manager's taken some money.	_____
8. Mira's taking a break.	_____
9. Mira's taken a break.	_____

PRACTICE 10 ▸ The present perfect and the simple past. (Chart 2-6)
Choose the correct completions.

1. a. Botswana   became / has become   an independent country in 1966.

   b. Botswana   was / has been   an independent country for more than 40 years.

2. a. It's raining. It   was / has been   raining since noon today.

   b. It's raining. It's the rainy season. It   rained / has rained   every day since the first of the month.

3. a. I grew up in Scotland until I moved to Argentina with my family. I was 12 then. Now I am 21.
   I   lived / have lived   in Scotland for 12 years.

   b. Now I live in Argentina. I   lived / have lived   in Argentina for 9 years.

4. a. Claude and Pierre worked together at the French restaurant for 30 years. They retired three
   years ago. They   worked / have worked   together for 30 years.

   b. Claude and Pierre   didn't work / haven't worked   for the last three years.

PRACTICE 11 ▸ The present perfect and the simple past. (Chart 2-6)
Complete the sentences with the correct form of the verbs in parentheses.

1. (*know*) I _____*knew*_____ Tim when he was a child, but I haven't seen him for many
   years. I _____*have known*_____ Larry, my best friend, for more than 20 years.

2. (*agree*) The company and its employees finally _____ on salary raises
   two days ago. Since then, they _____ on everything, and the rest of the
   negotiations have gone smoothly.

3. (*take*) Mark _____ a trip to Asia last October. He _____
   many trips to Asia since he started his own import-export business.

4. (*play*) Ivan _____ the violin at several concerts with the London Symphony
   since 1990. Last year he _____ Beethoven's violin concerto at one of the
   concerts.

5. (*call*) When she was in college, Julia _____ her parents a few times a week.
   Now she has a job and is living in Chicago. In the last month she _____ her
   parents only three times.

6. (*send*) Our university _____ 121 students to study in other countries last
   year. In total, we _____ 864 students abroad over the last ten years.

7. (*fly*) Masaru is a pilot for JAL. He _____ nearly 8 million miles during the
   last 22 years. Last year he _____ 380,000 miles.

8. (*oversleep*) Mark missed his physics examination this morning because he _____.
   He _____ a lot since the beginning of the semester. He needs to buy a new
   alarm clock.

PRACTICE 12 ▶ The present perfect and the present perfect progressive. (Chart 2-7)
Choose the correct completions.

1. Sam and Judy began talking on the phone at 9:00 P.M. Now it is 11:00 P.M., and they are still talking. They   have talked / have been talking   for two hours.

2. Sam and Judy speak to each other on the phone several times a day. They are speaking on the phone now, and they might speak again later. Today they   have spoken / have been speaking   to each other on the phone at least seven times.

3. England   has won / has been winning   the World Cup only once since 1930.

4. How long   have you sat / have you been sitting   here in the sun? You're very red. You need to get out of the sun.

5. The chair in the president's office is very special. Sixteen presidents   have sat / have been sitting   in it.

PRACTICE 13 ▶ The present perfect and the present perfect progressive. (Chart 2-7)
Complete the sentences. Write either the present perfect or the present perfect progressive of the verbs in parentheses.

1. The kids are at the park. They (*play*) _____*have been playing*_____ ball for the last two hours, but they don't seem tired yet.

2. Jim (*play*) _____*has played*_____ soccer only a couple of times, so he's not very good at it. He's much better at tennis.

3. Karl (*raise*) _____ three children to adulthood. Now they are educated and working in productive careers.

4. Katie is falling asleep at her desk. Dr. Wu (*lecture*) _____ since ten o'clock, and it's now past noon.

5. Jenna is a law student. Ever since she enrolled in law school, she

   (*miss, never*) _____ a class because of illness.

6. Tim (*sleep*) _____ in the downstairs bedroom only once. He usually sleeps upstairs in the bedroom he shares with his brother.

7. A: How much longer until we arrive at the Singapore airport?

   B: Let me see. It's about 9:15. We (*fly*) _____ for almost six hours. We will be there in another couple of hours.

8. Janice (*sleep*) _____ for almost eleven hours. Do you want me to wake her up?

9. A: Is the rescue crew still looking for survivors of the plane crash?

   B: Yes, they (*search*) _____ the area for hours, but they haven't found anybody else.

PRACTICE 14 ▸ Simple past vs. the present perfect progressive. (Chart 2-7)
Look at the information about Janet and write sentences with the given words. Use the simple past or present perfect progressive as necessary.

In 1998, Janet received her English teaching degree. Here is what happened to Janet after that:

1999	2000	2001	now

move to Canada   join Lingua Schools   become a teacher   be a teacher
as a teaching assistant

1. (move to Canada) _____ *In 1999, Janet moved to Canada.* _____

2. (join Lingua Schools) _____

3. (be a teacher) _____

4. (teach her own class) _____

5. (work at Lingua Schools) _____

PRACTICE 15 ▸ The present perfect, the present perfect progressive, and the past perfect. (Charts 2-3 → 2-8)
Read the two reviews for a smart phone. Choose the correct completions.

***** Best phone ever!

1. Before I purchased this item, I   have / have had   the same phone for over five years. I

   had been thinking / am thinking   about upgrading for years, but I really liked my old phone. I had

   also   been worried / worry   about learning to use such complicated technology. Actually, I had

   nothing to worry about. This phone is so easy to use! I   've had / 've been having   it for only three

   weeks, and I've already learned how to use all the major features. I've installed several apps, and the

   phone still has a lot of memory. I have a terrible sense of direction, and the built-in GPS

   has been / had been   a lifesaver. My favorite feature is the camera. I've already   took / taken

   hundreds of pictures. The picture quality is amazing. This is the best purchase I've ever made!

***** Buyers beware!

2. The price is right. That is the only good thing I can say about this phone. My friends

   had warned / have been warning   me that you get what you pay for, but I didn't listen. Now I have

   a piece of junk. For the past two months it   has given / gave   me nothing but problems. Ever

   since I installed my favorite photo-editing software, the phone   is crashing / has been crashing

   daily. When I try to open more than two apps, the screen freezes. It has been driving me crazy!

   The camera on this phone is terrible. I   've taken / 'd taken   better pictures on my old phone.

   There are much better products available.

PRACTICE 16 ▸ The simple past and the past perfect. (Charts 1-5 and 2-8)

Underline each event. Write "1" over the event that happened first and "2" over the event that happened second.

                      1   *2*

1. <u>We had driven only two miles</u> when <u>we got a flat tire</u>.

2. Alan told me that he had written a book.

3. By the time we arrived at the airport, the plane had already left.

4. The dog had eaten the entire roast before anyone knew it was gone.

5. We didn't stand in line for tickets because we had already bought them by mail.

6. Carl played the guitar so well because he had studied with a famous guitarist.

7. By the time the movie ended, everyone had fallen asleep.

8. After the professor had corrected the third paper, he was exhausted from writing comments on the students' papers.

9. I had just placed an order at the store for a new camera when I found a cheaper one online.

PRACTICE 17 ▸ The past perfect. (Chart 2-8)

Complete the sentences. Write the correct form of the past perfect.

1. Yesterday, John got 100% on a math exam. Before yesterday, he (*get, not*) _____ 100%.

2. Last week, Sonya met her fiancé's parents. Before that, she (*meet, not*) _____ them.

3. Caroline went to a Japanese restaurant today. Before today, she (*try, never*) _____ sushi.

4. A few days ago, Bakir cooked a frozen dinner. Before that, he (*eat, not*) _____ a frozen dinner.

5. Last week, I had to have a tooth pulled. Until then, I (*have, not*) _____ any problems with my teeth.

PRACTICE 18 ▸ The simple past and the past perfect. (Charts 1-5 and 2-8)

Complete the sentences with the simple past or past perfect form of the verb. Write the letter of the correct verb.

1. By the time Jason arrived to help, we _____ moving everything.
   a. already finished   b. had already finished

2. The apartment was hot when I got home, so I _____ the air conditioner.
   a. turned on   b. had turned on

3. The farmer's barn caught on fire some time during the night. By the time the firefighters arrived, the building _____ to the ground. It was a total loss.
   a. burned   b. had burned

4. The dinner I had at that restaurant was expensive! Until then, I ____ so much on one meal.
   a. never spent   b. had never spent

5. When I saw that Mike was having trouble, I ____ him. He was very appreciative.
   a. helped   b. had helped

6. My wife and I went to Disneyland when we visited Los Angeles last spring. Before that time, we

   ____ such a big amusement park. It was a lot of fun.
   a. never visited   b. had never visited

7. My flight to Australia took a long time. I ____ on airplanes for fairly long distances before, but not as long as that trip.
   a. traveled   b. had traveled

PRACTICE 19 ▸ The simple past and the past perfect. (Charts 1-5 and 2-8)
Write the simple past or the past perfect of the verbs in parentheses. In some cases, both forms are correct.

1. Yesterday I (*go*) _____*went*_____ to my daughter's dance recital.

   I (*be, never*) _____*had never been*_____ to a dance recital before.

   I (*take, not*) _____*didn't take*_____ dancing lessons when I (*be*) _____*was*_____ a child.

2. Last night, I (*eat*) _____ four servings of food at the "all-you-can-eat" special

   dinner at The Village Restaurant. Until that time, I (*eat, never*) _____ so much in

   one meal. I've felt miserable all day today.

3. A: I (*see*) _____ you in the school play last night. You (*do*) _____ a

   terrific acting job. (*you, act, ever*) _____ in a play before this one?

   B: Yes. I (*start*) _____ acting when I was in elementary school.

PRACTICE 20 ▸ The present perfect progressive and the past perfect progressive.
                    (Charts 2-7 and 2-10)
Choose the correct completions.

1. I'm studying English. I   have been studying / had been studying   English for several years now.

2. I came from Malaysia to live in New Zealand in 2002. I   have been studying / had been studying

   English for three years before that.

3. Shhh! I want to see the end of this TV show! I   have been waiting / had been waiting   to find out

   who the murderer is.

4. Laura finally called me last night. I hadn't heard from her in four months. I

   have been waiting / had been waiting   for that call for a long time!

5. Before Ada became a veterinarian last year, she   has been working / had been working

   as a veterinarian's assistant while she was in school.

6. Li is going to quit his job. He   has been working / had been working   too many hours for too little

   money in this job. He is probably going to resign next week.

PRACTICE 21 ▸ The present perfect progressive and the past perfect progressive.
(Charts 2-7 and 2-10)

Complete the sentences. Write the present perfect progressive or the past perfect progressive form of the verbs in parentheses.

1. Anna (*listen*) _____*had been listening*_____ to loud rock music when her friends arrived, but she

   turned it off so all of them could study together. When they finished, she turned it back on, and

   now they (*dance*) _____*have been dancing*_____ and (*sing*) _____*singing*_____ for two hours.

2. We (*wait*) _____ for Ali for the last two hours, but he still hasn't

   arrived.

3. We (*wait*) _____ for Ali for over three hours before he finally

   arrived yesterday.

4. Oscar (*train*) _____ for the Olympics for the last three years and

   wants to make the national team next year.

5. The marathon runner (*run*) _____ for almost two hours when

   he collapsed on the pavement. He received immediate medical attention.

6. Tom had a hard time finding a job. He (*try*) _____ to get a new

   job for six months before he finally found a position at a local community college. Now he has a

   two-year contract. He (*teach*) _____ there for only a few weeks,

   but he likes his new job very much.

7. Dr. Sato (*perform*) _____ specialized surgery since she began

   working at the university hospital ten years ago. She still does many operations each year, but now her

   work is very famous, and she travels all over the world lecturing to other surgeons on her technique.

PRACTICE 22 ▸ Chapter review.

There is one verb error in each sentence. Correct the error.

1. *Citizen Kane* is a great classic movie. I've been seeing it ten times.

2. *War and Peace* is a long novel. I'm reading it for two months, and I am still not finished with it!

3. Our guests have left yesterday.

4. We were studying all night. Let's take a break now.

5. Let's not leave yet. I'd been having such a wonderful time at this party.

6. By the time I got home, the rest of the family has eaten.

7. I was late for my nine o'clock class, so I had run all the way from my dorm to my class.

8. Mrs. Wang isn't in the hospital anymore. She had left early this morning.

9. I was born on February 29th in 1960, a leap year. February 29th occurs only once every four years.

   So by the time the 21st century began, I celebrated only ten birthdays!

10. A: Are you still on the phone? Are you holding on for someone?

    B: Yes, I am. I am still holding for the technical support department. I am holding for more than

    half an hour!

PRACTICE 1 ▶ Preview.

Part I. Read the passage. <u>Underline</u> the seven verb forms with **will**.

Yellowstone National Park

Welcome to your ski vacation at Yellowstone National Park! According to the weather forecast, you will have plenty of fresh snow to enjoy this weekend. Before you begin your ski adventure, you need to be aware of possible dangerous situations.

First, make sure you dress appropriately. Temperatures can rise and fall dramatically. Dressing in layers will help you avoid hypothermia and frostbite. A light inner layer of clothing will keep you comfortable and dry. A middle layer will help your body stay warm, and a waterproof outer layer will protect you against rain or snow.

Second, you may encounter wild animals on the trails, but do not approach or try to feed them. You will scare them, and they may become aggressive. In general, animals won't bother you if you don't bother them.

Finally, study a trail map of the ski area so you don't get lost. Stay safe and enjoy your time here!

Part II. Answer the questions. Choose "T" if the statement is true. Choose "F" if the statement is false.

1. The weather forecast predicts good conditions for skiing.   T   F

2. You won't need to dress in layers if the temperature is high.   T   F

3. Animals won't become aggressive if you feed them.   T   F

4. Most animals are always aggressive even if you don't approach them.   T   F

5. Trail maps help you stay safe.   T   F

PRACTICE 2 ▶ Simple future: *be going to.* (Chart 3-1)

Complete the sentences with the correct form of ***be going to*** and the verbs in parentheses.

1. Vanessa and Ben (*travel*) _____ to France next summer.

2. They (*tour*) _____ Paris.

3. They (*visit*) _____ the Louvre, the Eiffel Tower, and the Arc de Triomphe.

4. Ben (*take*) _____ an intensive French class at a language school in Paris.

5. He (*study*) _____ French five hours a day for three weeks.

6. Vanessa is a doctor. She (*do*) _____ volunteer work for the French Red Cross for two weeks.

7. They (*return*) _____ home at the end of the summer.

PRACTICE 3 ▸ Simple future: *will* and *be going to*. (Chart 3-1)

Complete the sentences in two ways. Write sentence "a." with ***will*** and sentence "b." with ***be going to***. Use the correct verb in the box.

arrive	bloom	buy	end	rain	set	take

1. a. The sun rose at 5:46 this morning, and it _____ at 6:52 tonight.

   b. The sun rose at 5:46 this morning, and it _____ at 6:52 tonight.

2. a. The flight left Bangkok at noon today, and it _____ in Mumbai at midnight.

   b. The flight left Bangkok at noon today, and it _____ in Mumbai at midnight.

3. a. There are dark clouds over the mountain. It _____ later today.

   b. There are dark clouds over the mountain. It _____ later today.

4. a. We planted the flowers in March, and they _____ in June.

   b. We planted the flowers in March, and they _____ in June.

5. a. Our semester began in January, and it _____ in May.

   b. Our semester began in January, and it _____ in May.

6. a. When _____ you _____ a new computer?

   b. When _____ you _____ a new computer?

7. a. I _____ not _____ a vacation this year. Maybe next year.

   b. I _____ not _____ a vacation this year. Maybe next year.

PRACTICE 4 ▸ Simple future: *will* and *be going to*. (Chart 3-1)

Part I. Read the message from a history professor to her students.

> The History 101 final exam will be next Friday from 9:00 till 11:00. You need to study the first 12 chapters of the textbook. You do not need to study Chapters 13 and 14. Please review the first part of Chapter 15. The rest of that chapter is not important for your exam. Be prepared to answer a total of 50 multiple-choice questions. Unlike your other exams, you will not have any essay questions on the final. Grades will be available a week after the exam.

Part II. Complete the sentences with ***is, isn't, are, aren't, will,*** or ***won't***.

1. The students in History 101 _____ going to take a final exam next week.

2. The students _____ have two hours to take the exam.

3. The exam _____ going to cover the first 12 chapters and part of Chapter 15.

4. Chapters 13 and 14 _____ going to be on the exam.

5. The second part of Chapter 15 _____ going to be on the exam.

6. The test _____ going to consist of multiple-choice questions.

7. There _____ be any essay questions.

8. Students _____ get their grades a week after the exam.

PRACTICE 5 ▸ Will vs. be going to. (Chart 3-2)

Check (✓) the box that describes each sentence.

	Prediction	Prior Plan	Willingness
1. I'll help you change your tire, Ms. Olsen.			✓
2. It's going to rain tomorrow.			
3. It will rain tomorrow.			
4. Louise is going to help us next week.			
5. Wait. I'll help you carry your luggage.			
6. We're going to see a movie tonight.			

PRACTICE 6 ▸ Will vs. be going to. (Chart 3-2)

Choose "a." if the meaning describes a prior plan. Choose "b." if the meaning describes a decision of the moment.

1. I can't have lunch with you on Friday because I'm going to meet with my professor at noon.
   a. prior plan   b. decision of the moment

2. My computer just crashed. I'll call the technical support department to fix it right now.
   a. prior plan   b. decision of the moment

3. It's very icy and slippery on my street this morning. I'll go out and clear the sidewalk.
   a. prior plan   b. decision of the moment

4. Roberto and Sandy are going to get married next Saturday.
   a. prior plan   b. decision of the moment

5. Jimmy is going to have a tonsillectomy on Monday. The doctors are going to take out his tonsils.
   a. prior plan   b. decision of the moment

6. Look at the price of the airport limousine. It's too much money. We'll go by bus.
   a. prior plan   b. decision of the moment

PRACTICE 7 ▸ Will vs. be going to. (Chart 3-2)

Choose the correct response(s) to the questions or statements. More than one response may be correct.

1. A: What about Dominick? Doesn't he want to come with us?

   B: Nobody knows!   I'll call / I'm going to call   him tonight to find out.

2. A: Jessica practices her violin for ten hours a day!

   B: I know!   She's going to be / She'll be   a famous violinist some day.

3. A: How about dinner and a movie on Friday?

   B: Sorry, I can't.   I'm going to fly / I'll fly   to London on Friday evening.

4. A: Do you and Paul have tickets for any of the hockey games this season?

   B: Yes, we do.   We're going to go to the game / We'll go to the game   tomorrow night.

5. A: I can't open this jar!

   B: Give it to me.   I'm going to open it / I'll open it   for you.

6. A: So you're leaving to go to another university, Professor Hu!

   B: Yes,   I'm going to teach / I will teach   at Emory University. They've made me a great offer.

PRACTICE 8 ▸ Will vs. be going to. (Chart 3-2)

Complete the sentences with *will* or *be going to*. Include any words in parentheses.

1. A: Excuse me, waiter! This isn't what I ordered. I ordered a chicken salad.

   B: Sorry, sir. I _____*will*_____ take this back and get your salad.

   A: Thank you.

2. A: Would you like to join Linda and me tomorrow? We _____*are going to*_____ visit the natural history museum.

   B: Sure. I've never been there.

3. A: Where's the mustard?

   B: In the refrigerator, on the middle shelf.

   A: I've looked there.

   B: OK. I _____ get it for you.

4. A: What's all this paint for? (*you*) _____ paint your house?

   B: No, we _____ paint my mother's house.

5. A: Paul, do you want to go to the mall with me?

   B: No thanks. I already have plans. I _____ wash my car and then clean out the basement.

6. A: Someone needs to take this report to Mr. Day's office right away, but I can't leave my desk.

   B: I _____ do it.

   A: Thanks.

7. A: Who'll pick up Uncle Jack at the airport?

   B: I _____ .

8. A: Why is Carlos wearing a suit and tie? He usually wears jeans to class.

   B: He _____ give a speech at the faculty lunch today.

9. A: Let me ask you something, Toshi.

   B: Sure. What's up, Andy?

   A: I _____ interview for a job this afternoon, and ... well, do I need a tie? I don't have a decent one.

   B: Yes, you need a tie. I _____ lend you one of mine.

   A: Thanks.

10. A: You're going out?

    B: Yes. I _____ stop at the grocery store for some fruit and some rice. Can you think of anything else we need?

    A: How about getting some chocolate-covered nuts?

    B: Good idea! I _____ get some of those too.

PRACTICE 9 ▸ Expressing the future in time clauses. (Chart 3-3)
Complete the sentences with the correct form of the verbs in parentheses.

1. Grandma and Grandpa are planning to travel often when they (*retire*) _____.

2. I'll wake up tomorrow morning when the alarm clock (*ring*) _____.

3. The students will relax after they (*finish*) _____ their final exams.

4. You'll feel a lot better after you (*take*) _____ this medicine.

5. The residents of the coastal areas will prepare for the hurricane before it (*arrive*) _____.

6. Mark will work in a law firm as soon as he (*graduate*) _____ from law school.

7. We'll have dinner as soon as the rice (*be*) _____ ready.

8. I'll tell you as soon I (*hear*) _____ any news.

9. Before we (*leave*) _____ on vacation, we'll stop our newspaper delivery.

10. We'll start our newspaper delivery again after we (*get*) _____ back from vacation.

PRACTICE 10 ▸ Expressing the future in time clauses. (Chart 3-3)
Complete each sentence with the correct clause from Column A or Column B.

	Column A	**Column B**
1. When I see Irina later, _*b*_ .	a. I give her the news	b. I'll give her the news
2. I'll call you tomorrow _____ .	a. after I talk to Rita	b. after I will talk to Rita
3. As soon as I hear from Tom, _____ .	a. I call you	b. I'll call you
4. We'll all be very happy _____ .	a. when you get here	b. when you will get here
5. I'll save my files _____ .	a. before I shut down my computer	b. before I will shut down my computer
6. The passengers will get off the plane _____ .	a. after it lands	b. after it is going to land
7. My cell phone won't work _____ .	a. until I unlock it	b. until I will unlock it
8. After the party is over tonight, _____ .	a. we call a taxi to go home	b. we'll call a taxi to go home
9. I'm not going to pay for the refrigerator _____ .	a. until they fix the broken door	b. until they will fix the broken door
10. I'll take this new medicine _____ .	a. before I go to bed tonight	b. before I will go to bed tonight

PRACTICE 11 ▸ Expressing the future in time clauses. (Chart 3-3)
Complete the sentences with the following: the simple present, the future with **will**, or the future with a form of **be going to**. In some sentences, both **will** and **be going to** may be possible.

1. The strike has been going on for over two months now. The strikers (*return, not*)

   _____will not / are not going to return_____ to work until they (*get*) ___get___ a raise and the

   benefits they are demanding.

2. When Rita (*get*) _____ her driver's license next week, she

   (*be*) _____ able to drive to school every day.

3. A: Mr. Jackson called. He'll be here at the garage to pick up his car in a few minutes. He

   (be, not) _____ very happy when he (learn) _____ about the

   bill for repairs on his car. Do you want to talk to him when he (come) _____ in

   and (ask) _____ about his bill?

   B: Not especially, but I will.

4. After Ali (return) _____ to his country next month, he

   (work) _____ at the Ministry of Agriculture.

5. According to the newspaper, the Department of Transportation

   (build) _____ a new four-lane highway into the city

   next year. In my opinion, it (be) _____ outdated before they

   (complete) _____ it. We need a six-lane highway.

6. A: Have you heard any news about Barbara since her car accident?

   B: No, I've heard nothing. As soon as I (hear) _____ something, I

   (let) _____ you know.

7. A: I see you're reading *The Silk Road*.

   B: I (lend) _____ it to you as soon as I (finish) _____ it.

   A: Really? Thanks!

8. A: Relax. The plumber is on his way. He (be) _____ here before long to

   fix that leak in the pipe under the kitchen sink.

   B: Oh, good. I (be) _____ happy to get that pipe fixed.

PRACTICE 12 ▸ Using the present progressive and the simple present to express future time. (Chart 3-4)

Complete the second sentence with a form of the present progressive to express the same meaning as the first sentence.

1. I'm going to see the dentist tomorrow. I _____*'m seeing*_____ the dentist tomorrow.

2. Jada will have her baby in July. She _____ her baby in July.

3. The new store will open in September. It _____ in September.

4. Most employees are going to work late tonight. They _____ late tonight.

5. We're going to have a graduation party for Miriam on Saturday. We _____ a

   graduation party for Miriam on Saturday.

6. Shelley and Sue are going to attend the conference in New York next April. They

   _____ the conference in New York next April.

PRACTICE 13 ▸ Using the present progressive and the simple present to express future time. (Chart 3-4)

Choose all the possible completions for each sentence.

1. We have tickets for a concert today. It _____ at 7:00 P.M.
   a. starts
   b. is starting
   c. is going to start

2. Look at those black clouds! Pretty soon it ____.
   a. rains
   b. is raining
   c. is going to rain

3. This afternoon I'm having lunch with a friend. After that, we ____ her aunt.
   a. are going to visit
   b. are visiting
   c. visit

4. I'm hurrying to catch a plane. It ____ in an hour!
   a. leaves
   b. is going to leave
   c. is leaving

5. Sorry I can't meet with you tomorrow, Helen. I have an important appointment. I ____ with the president at noon.
   a. 'm meeting
   b. 'm going to meet
   c. will meet

6. A: Nobody has volunteered to bring the drinks for the festival Saturday night. Olga, how about you? Harry, how about you? Please ... can somebody help us out?

   B: OK, OK. I ____ it.
   a. 'll do
   b. 'm doing
   c. 'm going to do

PRACTICE 14 ▸ Using the present progressive to express future time. (Chart 3-4)
Change the verbs in *italics* to a form of the present progressive for a planned event or definite intention.
If no change is possible, write "NC."

1. A: The package needs to be there tomorrow. Will it get there in time?

   B: Don't worry. *I'm going to send* it by express mail.

       I'm sending it by express mail.

2. A: What's the weather report?

   B: *It is going to rain* tomorrow morning.

       NC

3. A: Would you like to have dinner with me tonight, Pat?

   B: Thanks, but *I'm going to have* dinner with my sister and her husband.

   _____

4. A: What *are you going to do* this evening?

   _____

   B: *I'm going to study* at the library.

   _____

5. A: Oh, I spilled my coffee on the floor.

   B: *I'll help* you clean it up.

   _____

6. A: Did you know that Kathy and Paul are engaged?

   B: No. That's great! When *are they going to get* married?

   A: In September.

_____

7. A: *You're going to laugh* when I tell you what happened to me today!

   B: Oh? What happened?

_____

8. A: Have you lived here long?

   B: No, not long. Only about a year. But *we're going to move* again next month. My father's company has reassigned him to Atlanta, Georgia.

_____

9. A: I tried to register for Professor Stein's economics class, but it's full. *Is he going to teach* it again next semester?

   B: I think so.

_____

10. A: Son, *I'm not going to send* you any money this month. You're spending far too much. You need to learn to be more careful.

_____

   B: But Dad ... !

   A: Just do the best you can. *I am going to visit* you next month. We can talk about it then.

_____

PRACTICE 15 ▶ Future progressive. (Chart 3-5)
Complete the sentences. Write the future progressive form of the verbs in blue.

1. Every night at 7:00 I read a book. Tomorrow at 7:10, I

   _____ a book.

2. We fly to Italy tomorrow night. Tomorrow night at this time, we

   _____ over the Atlantic Ocean.

3. On Sunday mornings, I sleep late. Next Sunday morning at 9:00 A.M., I

   _____ .

4. It always snows in December in Moscow. We're going to Moscow in December. At that time, it

   _____ in Moscow.

5. Ellen always watches late movies on TV. I'm sure that tonight she

   _____ an old movie on TV around 2:00 A.M.

PRACTICE 16 ▶ Future progressive. (Charts 3-3 and 3-5)
Complete the sentences with the future progressive or the simple present form of the verbs in parentheses.

1. Just relax, Antoine. As soon as your sprained ankle (*heal*) _____*heals*_____, you can play soccer again. At this time next week, you (*play*) _____*will be playing*_____ soccer again.

2. I'll meet you at the airport tomorrow. After you (*go*) _____ customs, look for me just outside the gate. I (*stand*) _____ right by the door.

3. Ingrid and Ruth won't be at this school when classes (*start*) _____ next semester. They (*attend*) _____ a new school in Taiwan.

4. Please come and visit today when you (*have*) _____ a chance. I (*shop*) _____ from 1:00 to about 3:00, but I'll be home after that.

5. I won't be here next week, students. I (*attend*) _____ a seminar out of town. Ms. Gomez will be the substitute teacher. When I (*return*) _____, I will expect you to be ready for the midterm examination.

PRACTICE 17 ▸ Future perfect and future perfect progressive. (Chart 3-6)

Complete the sentences with the future perfect or the future perfect progressive form of the verbs in the box. Include any words in parentheses. Use each verb only once.

drink	fly	land	listen	ride	✓ rise	save	teach

1. By the time I get up tomorrow morning, the sun (*already*) _____*will already have risen*_____.

2. This is a long trip! By the time we get to Miami, we _____ on this bus for over 15 hours.

3. We're going to be late. By the time we get to the airport, my brother's plane (*already*) _____.

4. He's never going to stop talking. In 15 more minutes, we _____ to him lecture for three solid hours. I don't even know what he's saying anymore.

5. I drink too much coffee. I have already had two cups this morning, and I will probably have two more cups. This means that before lunch, I _____ four cups of coffee.

6. This is the longest flight I have ever taken. By the time we get to New Zealand, we _____ for 13 hours. I'm going to be exhausted.

7. Douglas has been putting some money away every month to prepare for his trip to South America next year. By the end of this year, he _____ enough.

8. Can you believe it? According to our grammar teacher, by the end of this semester, she _____ more than 3,000 students from 42 different countries. She has been teaching for nearly 20 years — and she still loves it!

PRACTICE 18 ▸ Chapter review.

These sentences describe typical events in a day in the life of a woman named Kathy. The sentences are in the past, but all of these things will happen in Kathy's life tomorrow. Change all of the sentences to the future. Use *will*.

1. When Kathy got up yesterday morning, the sun was shining. The same thing will happen tomorrow. When Kathy _____*gets*_____ up tomorrow morning, the sun _____*will be shining*_____.

2. Yesterday she brushed her teeth and showered. Then she made a light breakfast. Tomorrow will be the same. She _____ her teeth and _____. Then she _____ a light breakfast.

3. After she ate breakfast yesterday, she got ready to go to work. And tomorrow after she _____ breakfast, she _____ ready to go to work.

4. By the time she got to work yesterday, she had drunk three cups of coffee. Tomorrow she'll do the same. By the time she _____ to work, she _____ three cups of coffee.

5. Between 8:00 and 9:00, Kathy answered her email and planned her day. She has the same plans for tomorrow. Between 8:00 and 9:00, Kathy _____ her email and _____ her day.

6. By 10:00 yesterday, she had called three new clients. Tomorrow, by 10:00, she _____ three new clients.

7. At 11:00 yesterday, she was attending a staff meeting. She plans to do the same tomorrow. At 11:00, she _____ a staff meeting.

8. She went to lunch at noon and had a sandwich and a bowl of soup. Tomorrow she _____ to lunch at noon and _____ a sandwich and a bowl of soup.

9. After she finished eating, she took a short walk in the park before she returned to the office. Tomorrow she'll do the same. After she _____ eating, she _____ a walk in the park before she _____ to the office.

10. She worked at her desk until she went to another meeting in the middle of the afternoon. And tomorrow she _____ at her desk until she _____ to another meeting in the middle of the afternoon.

11. By the time she left the office, she had attended three meetings. Tomorrow she'll follow the same schedule. By the time she _____ the office, she _____ three meetings.

12. When Kathy got home, her children were playing in the yard, and Grandma was watching them from the porch. Tomorrow will be the same. When Kathy _____ home, her children _____ in the yard, and Grandma _____ them from the porch.

13. The children had been playing since 3:00 in the afternoon. And tomorrow they _____ since 3:00 in the afternoon.

14. The family had dinner together and talked about their day. Tomorrow will be the same. They _____ dinner together, and they _____ about their day.

15. They watched television for a while, and then Kathy and her husband put the kids to bed. The same thing will happen tomorrow. They _____ television for a while, and then they _____ the kids to bed.

16. By the time Kathy went to bed yesterday, she had had a full day and was ready for sleep. Tomorrow will be the same for Kathy. By the time she _____ to bed, she _____ a full day and _____ ready for sleep.

PRACTICE 19 ▶ Chapter review.
There is one verb error in each sentence. Correct the error.

1. Next month, I'm travel to Europe with my sister.
2. My sister is going to attends an academic conference in Amsterdam.
3. While she is attending the conference, I'll touring the city.
4. After Amsterdam, we are going go to Ibiza.
5. When I'll be there, I'm going to swim in the Mediterranean.
6. My sister and I are going to visit a few other cities in Spain before we'll go to Lisbon.
7. By the end of our trip, we'll have been travel for two weeks.
8. When I return home, I'll have visit three European countries.
9. It's going be an awesome vacation.

Review of Verb Tenses

PRACTICE 1 ▸ Verb tense review. (Chapters 1 → 3)
Read the passage. <u>Underline</u> the 16 verbs.

Cooking Class

Central Market is offering two classes this month. If you are curious about Indian Food, then Tandoori Nights is the class for you. This class will meet every Friday night 6:00–8:00. Instructor Elaine Adams had owned a small café in India for several years before she returned to the United States last year. She is going to focus primarily on chicken and vegetarian dishes from northern India. For Spanish food enthusiasts, we are offering Spanish Style Slow Cooking. This class meets Saturday afternoons 2:00–4:00. Instructor Ruben Reyes has been teaching classes at Central Market for nearly twenty years. He has written three cookbooks on Spanish and Mediterranean cuisine. His newest book explores the art of slow cooking. His class introduces students to several main dishes. If you haven't registered, there is still time, but classes are getting full.

---

1. Write the six verbs in the simple present tense.

   _____

2. Write the two verbs in the present progressive tense.

   _____

3. Write the verb in the simple past tense.

   _____

4. Write the two verbs in the simple future tense.

   _____

5. Write the two verbs in the present perfect tense.

   _____

6. Write the verb in the present perfect progressive tense.

   _____

7. Write the verb in the past perfect tense.

   _____

PRACTICE 2 ▸ Verb tense review. (Chapters 1 → 3)
Complete the sentences with the correct form of the verbs in parentheses.

1. A: I'm going to ask you some questions so that we can practice verb tenses. What do you do every day before you come to class? Name one thing.

   B: I (*eat*) _____*eat*_____ breakfast.

2. A: What did you do last night? Name three separate activities.

   B: Last night I (*eat*) _____ dinner. Then I (*visit*) _____ some friends, and later I (*write*) _____ a couple of letters.

3. A: What are you doing right now? What activity is in progress right now, at this exact moment?

   B: Right now I (*talk*) _____ to you. I (*answer*) _____ your questions.

4. A: Think about this exact time yesterday. What activity was in progress then?

   B: Let me see. At this time yesterday, I was at the library. I (*study*) _____ for a test.

5. A: How many questions have I asked since we began this exercise?

   B: I think you (*ask*) _____ me five or six questions since we began this exercise.

6. A: What have you been doing for the past five minutes? In other words, what activity began five minutes ago and has been in progress from then until now?

   B: I (*talk*) _____ to you for the past five minutes. I started talking to you five minutes ago, and I am still talking to you.

7. A: Where will you be tomorrow morning?

   B: I (*be*) _____ in class tomorrow morning.

8. A: What will you be doing at this exact time tomorrow? In other words, what activity will be in progress at this exact same time tomorrow?

   B: Right now I am sitting in the classroom. And at this exact time tomorrow, I (*sit*) _____ in the classroom.

PRACTICE 3 ▸ Verb tense review. (Chapters 1 → 3)
Choose the correct completions.

1. My grandfather   has never flown / had never flown   in an airplane, and he has no plans to ever fly.

2. Jane isn't here yet. I   am waiting / have been waiting   for her since noon, but she still didn't arrive / hasn't arrived.

3. In all the world, there   have been / are   only 14 mountains that   reach / are reaching   above 8,000 meters (26,247 feet).

4. When my parents were teenagers, people   hadn't owned / didn't own   computers. By the time I was a teenager, I   was owning / had owned   a computer for several years.

5. Right now we   are having / have   a heat wave. The temperature   is / has been   in the upper 90s Fahrenheit (30s Celsius) for the last six days.

6. I have a long trip ahead of me tomorrow, so I think I'd better go to bed. Let me say good-bye now because I won't see you in the morning. I   will leave / will have left   by the time you   get / will get   up.

7. Last night I   went / was going   to a party. When I   get / got   there, the room was full of people. Some of them   danced / were dancing   and others   talked / were talking.   One young woman   was standing / has been standing   by herself. I   have never met / had never met   her before, so I   introduced / was introducing   myself to her.

8. About three o'clock yesterday afternoon, Jessica   was sitting / had sat   in bed reading a book. Suddenly, she   heard / was hearing   a loud noise and   got / was getting   up to see what it was. She   has looked / looked   out the window. A truck   has just backed / had just backed   into her new car!

PRACTICE 4 ▶ Verb tense review. (Chapters 1 → 3)
Choose the correct completions.

1. Next month I have a week's vacation. I   take / am taking   a trip. I   leave / left   on Saturday, July 2nd. First, I   've gone / 'm going   to Madison, Wisconsin, to visit my brother. After I   will leave / leave   Madison, I   am going to go / have gone   to Chicago to see a friend who   is studying / will have studied   at the university there. She   has lived / lives   in Chicago for three years, so she   knows / knew   her way around the city. She   has promised / will be promising   to take me to many interesting places. I   had never been / have never been   to Chicago, so I   am looking / have looked   forward to going there.

2. The weather is beautiful today, but until this morning, it   has been raining / had been raining   steadily for almost a week. A week ago, the temperature suddenly   was dropping / dropped,   and after that we had bad weather for a week. Now the weather forecaster says that tomorrow it   is going to be / is   very warm. The weather certainly   was changing / changes   quickly here. I never know what to expect. Who knows? When I   wake / will wake   up tomorrow morning, maybe it   snows / will be snowing.

PRACTICE 5 ▶ Verb tense review. (Chapters 1 → 3)
Complete the sentences with the verbs in parentheses. Use any appropriate tense.

On June 20th, I returned home. I (be) _____ away from home for two years. My
                                                1
family (meet) _____ me at the airport with kisses and tears. They (miss) _____ me
              2   3
as much as I had missed them. I (be) _____ very happy to see them again.
                                      4

When I (get) _____ the chance, I (take) _____ a long look at them. My
              5   6
little brother (be) _____ no longer little. He (grow) _____ a lot. He
                    7   8
(be) _____ almost as tall as my father. My little sister (wear) _____
      9   10
a green dress. She (change) _____ quite a bit too, but she
                            11
(be, still) _____ very curious. She (ask) _____ me a thousand
            12   13
questions a minute, or so it seemed.

My father (*gain*) _____ 14 some weight, and his hair

(*turn*) _____ 15 a little grayer, but otherwise he was just as I had remembered him.

My mother (*look*) _____ 16 a little older, but not much. The wrinkles on her

face (*be*) _____ 17 smile wrinkles.

PRACTICE 6 ▸ Verb tense review. (Chapters 1 → 3)
Complete the sentences with the verbs in the box. Use any appropriate tense.

be	break	do	happen	have	play	recuperate	see

A: Where's Sonia? I (*not*) _____ 1 her lately.

B: She _____ 2 at home from an accident.

A: An accident? What _____ 3 to her?

B: She _____ 4 her arm while she _____ 5 volleyball last week in the

game against South City College.

A: Gosh, that's too bad. I'm sorry to hear that. How _____ 6 she _____ 7 ?

B: OK, I guess. Actually, she _____ 8 a cast on her arm, but she is not in any pain. I

think that she _____ 9 back in class next week.

PRACTICE 7 ▸ Verb tense review. (Chapters 1 → 3)
Complete the sentences with the verbs in parentheses. Use any appropriate tense.

A: Have you ever heard of the Socratic method?

B: No, I haven't. What is it?

A: It's a method of teaching that Socrates (*use*) _____ 1 in ancient Greece more

than two thousand years ago. Some teachers still (*use*) _____ 2 this kind of

method today.

B: Really? What (*it, consist*) _____ 3 of today? How

(*teachers, use*) _____ 4 this method now?

A: Well, the teacher (*not, give*) _____ 5 any information to the students. She

or he just asks a series of questions, but (*not, make*) _____ 6 any statements.

The teacher (*know*) _____ 7 what the important questions to ask the students are.

Then the students have to think about the answers.

B: That (*sound*) _____ 8 good to me! When I was in high school, I had a lot of

teachers who just (*talk*) _____ 9 too much. Sometimes the students even

(*fall*) _____ 10 asleep in class!

A: I (*agree*) _____ 11 with you. You will learn faster after you

(*think*) _____ 12 about something than if you just have to remember facts.

B: That's true. I (take) _____ a philosophy class now with a wonderful
13

professor. She (always, ask) _____ questions! I guess she
14

(use) _____ the Socratic method for the whole semester, and I
15

(not, realize) _____ it!
16

PRACTICE 8 ▶ Verb tense review. (Chapters 1 → 3)
Complete the sentences with the correct form of the verbs in parentheses.

1. Nora is at the hospital because her cousin is having surgery today. The surgery began at 7:00 and is
   expected to end at noon. Nora arrived at the hospital at 8:00 A.M.

   a. It's 8:10 A.M. Nora (wait) _____ in the waiting room.

   b. It is now 9:00 A.M. Nora (wait) _____ for one hour.

   c. By 11:00, the surgery will still be going on, and Nora will still be waiting in the waiting room. At
      that time, Nora (wait) _____ in the waiting room for three hours.

2. Hundreds of passengers are in the security line at the airport. Jaime entered the security line
   at 8:00 A.M.

   a. It's 8:15 A.M. Jaime (stand) _____ in the security line at the airport.

   b. It is now 9:00 A.M. Jaime (stand) _____ in the security line
      for an hour.

   c. Jaime is probably going to be standing in the security line for another hour. By 9:30 A.M., he
      (stand) _____ in the security line for an hour and a half.

   d. Jaime is probably going to be finished standing in the security line by 10:00 A.M. If he is finished
      at 10:00 A.M., he (stand) _____ in line for a total of two hours!

PRACTICE 9 ▶ Verb tense review. (Chapters 1 → 3)
Choose the correct completions.

1. A: Hurry up! We're waiting for you. What's taking you so long?

   B: I ____ for an important phone call. Go ahead and leave without me.
      a. wait   c. have waited
      b. will have waited   d. am waiting

2. A: Robert is going to be famous someday. He ____ in three movies already.

   B: I'm sure he'll be a star.
      a. has been appearing   c. has appeared
      b. had appeared   d. appeared

3. A: Where's Polly?

   B: She ____.
      a. is in her room studying   c. studies in her room
      b. in her room is studying   d. has studied in her room

4. A: What ____ of the new simplified tax law?

   B: It's more confusing than the old one.
      a. are you thinking   c. have you thought
      b. do you think   d. have you been thinking

5. A: When is Mr. Fields planning to retire?

B: Soon, I think. He _____ here for a long time. He'll probably retire either next year or the year

after that.
a. worked   c. has been working
b. had been working   d. is working

6. A: Why did you buy all this sugar and chocolate?

B: I _____ a delicious chocolate cake for dinner tonight.
a. make   c. 'm going to make
b. will make   d. will have made

7. A: Let's go! What's taking you so long?

B: I'll be there as soon as I _____ my keys.
a. find   c. 'm going to find
b. will find   d. am finding

8. Next week when there _____ a full moon, the ocean tides will be higher.
a. is being   c. is
b. will be   d. will have been

9. While I _____ TV last night, a mouse ran across the floor.
a. have watched   c. watched
b. was watching   d. have been watching

10. Fish were among the earliest forms of life. Fish _____ on earth for ages and ages.
a. existed   c. exist
b. are existing   d. have existed

11. The phone _____ constantly since Jack announced his candidacy for president this morning.
a. has been ringing   c. had rung
b. rang   d. had been ringing

12. The earth _____ on the sun for its heat and light.
a. depended   c. was depending
b. depending   d. depends

13. I don't feel good. I _____ home from work tomorrow.
a. 'm staying   c. stay
b. will have stayed   d. stayed

14. Today there are weather satellites that send down information about the earth's atmosphere. In the

last several decades, space exploration _____ great contributions to weather forecasting.
a. is making   c. makes
b. has made   d. made

15. On July 20th, 1969, astronaut Neil Armstrong _____ down onto the moon. He was the first person
ever to set foot on another celestial body.
a. was stepping   c. stepped
b. has stepped   d. has been stepping

16. Mechanical problems delayed the flight. When the tired passengers finally boarded the aircraft,

many were annoyed and irritable because they _____ in the airport for three and a half hours.
a. are waiting   c. have been waiting
b. were waiting   d. had been waiting

17. If rising sea levels continue at the present rate, in another 50 years this town _____ anymore.
a. doesn't exist   c. isn't existing
b. isn't going to exist   d. won't be existing

18. Homestead High School's football team _____ a championship until last season when the new coach led them to win first place in their league.
    a. has never won
    b. is never winning
    c. had never been winning
    d. had never won

19. Nonnative speakers need many years of intensive language study before they can qualify as interpreters. By the end of this year, Chen _____ English for three years, but he will still need more training and experience before he masters the language.
    a. will be studying
    b. has studied
    c. will have been studying
    d. has been studying

PRACTICE 10 ▶ Verb tense review. (Chapters 1 → 3)
Choose the correct completions.

1. A: May I speak to Dr. Paine, please?

   B: I'm sorry, he _____ a patient at the moment. Can I help you?
      a. is seeing
      b. sees
      c. was seeing
      d. has been seeing

2. A: When are you going to ask your boss for a raise?

   B: I _____ to her twice already! I don't think she wants to give me one.
      a. 've talked
      b. was talking
      c. 've been talking
      d. 'd talked

3. A: Do you think Harry will want something to eat after he gets here?

   B: I hope not. It'll probably be after midnight, and we _____ .
      a. are sleeping
      b. will be sleeping
      c. have been sleeping
      d. be sleeping

4. Paul, could you please turn off the stove? The potatoes _____ for at least 30 minutes.
   a. are boiling
   b. boiling
   c. have been boiling
   d. were boiling

5. A: I once saw a turtle that had wings. The turtle flew into the air to catch insects.

   B: Stop kidding. I _____ you!
      a. don't believe
      b. am not believing
      c. didn't believe
      d. wasn't believing

6. A: Is it true that spaghetti didn't originate in Italy?

   B: Yes. The Chinese _____ spaghetti dishes for a long time before Marco Polo brought it back to Italy.
      a. have been making
      b. have made
      c. had been making
      d. make

7. A: Could someone help me lift the lawnmower into the pickup truck?

   B: I'm not busy. I _____ you.
      a. help
      b. 'll help
      c. am helping
      d. am going to help

8. My family loves this house. It _____ the family home ever since my grandfather built it 60 years ago.
   a. was
   b. has been
   c. will be
   d. is

9. Here's an interesting statistic: On a typical day, the average person _____ about 48,000 words. How many words did you use today?
   a. used
   b. was using
   c. is using
   d. uses

10. It's against the law to kill the black rhinoceros. They _____ extinct.
    a. became
    b. have become
    c. are becoming
    d. become

11. After ten unhappy years, Janice finally quit her job. She _____ along with her boss for a long time before she finally decided to look for a new position.
    a. hadn't been getting
    b. isn't getting
    c. didn't get
    d. hasn't been getting

12. The National Hurricane Center is closely watching a strong hurricane over the Atlantic Ocean. When it _____ the coast of Texas sometime tomorrow afternoon, it will bring with it great destructive force.
    a. reaches
    b. will reach
    c. reaching
    d. is reaching

13. At one time, huge prehistoric reptiles dominated the earth. This Age of Dinosaurs _____ much longer than the present Age of Mammals has lasted to date.
    a. lasted
    b. was lasting
    c. had lasted
    d. has lasted

14. Jim, why don't you take some time off? You _____ too hard lately. Take a short vacation.
    a. worked
    b. work
    c. have been working
    d. were working

15. The city is rebuilding its run-down waterfront, transforming it into a pleasant and fashionable outdoor mall. Next summer when the tourists arrive, they _____ 104 beautiful new shops and restaurants.
    a. will found
    b. will be finding
    c. will find
    d. will have found

16. A minor earthquake occurred at 2:07 A.M. on January 3rd. Most of the people in the village _____ at the time and didn't even know it had occurred until the next morning.
    a. slept
    b. had slept
    c. sleep
    d. were sleeping

17. The little girl started to cry. She _____ her doll, and no one was able to find it for her.
    a. has lost
    b. had lost
    c. was lost
    d. was losing

18. According to research, people usually _____ in their sleep 25 to 30 times each night.
    a. turn
    b. are turning
    c. turned
    d. have turned

Subject-Verb Agreement

PRACTICE 1 ▶ Preview.
Read the passage. Choose the correct completions.

10,000 Hours

The key to success   is / are   a lot of practice and hard work.
Malcolm Gladwell, in his book *Outliers*,   explain / explains   the
10,000-hour rule. According to Gladwell, 10,000 hours of
practice   is / are   enough to become an expert in almost any field.
That's about three hours every single day for ten straight years.
Gladwell   provides / provide   several examples.

The Beatles   was / were   one of the most successful musical
groups in history. Before the Beatles became famous, the band
members played near military bases in Germany for eight hours a day, seven days a week. They did
this for a year and a half. They had performed about 1,200 times before they reached commercial
success. That   is / are   more than most bands today perform in their entire career.

Another example   is / are   Bill Gates. Most people   agrees / agree   Gates is a computer genius.
When Gates   was / were   in school in the 1960s, computer programming was not very popular.
Most schools didn't have computer classes or clubs, but Gates   was / were   lucky. He attended a
school that had advanced technology. He began programming in the eighth grade. By the time he
finished high school, he had already completed several hundred hours of computer programming.

Is / Are   there a skill you have practiced for 10,000 hours? What do you think?   Is / Are   10,000 hours
enough to make you an expert?

PRACTICE 2 ▶ Final -s on nouns and verbs. (Chart 5-1)
Look at the words that end in **-s**. Check (✓) the correct columns.

	Noun	**Verb**	**Singular**	**Plural**
1. a. A boat floats.		✓	✓	
b. Boats float.				
2. a. My friend lives in my neighborhood.				
b. My friends live in my neighborhood.				
3. a. Helen eats a donut every morning.				
b. Donuts contain a lot of sugar.				
4. a. Babies cry when they are hungry.				
b. My baby cries every night.				

PRACTICE 3 ▸ Spelling of final -s / -es. (Chart 5-1)
Complete the sentences with **-s** or **-es**.

1. Holly teach_es__ English at a community college.

2. Her class_____ are from 9:00 A.M. till 1:00 P.M. five day_____ a week.

3. She use_____ a lot of song_____ and game_____ in her lesson_____.

4. When she finish_____ work at the college each day, she go_____ to the gym.

5. After she exercise_____, she pick_____ her children up from school.

PRACTICE 4 ▸ Basic subject-verb agreement. (Chart 5-2)
Choose the correct completions.

1. The weather   is / are   cold.

2. Vegetables   is / are   good for you.

3. Each student   has / have   a locker in the gym.

4. A dog   barks / bark.

5. Dogs   barks / bark.

6. Ann   is / are   at home.

7. Ann and Sue   is / are   at home.

8. Every student and teacher   is / are   here today.

9. A student and teacher   is / are   talking in the hallway.

10. Eating vegetables   is / are   good for you.

PRACTICE 5 ▸ Collective nouns. (Chart 5-3)
Complete the sentences with **is** or **are**. Use **is** when possible.

1. a. The faculty _____ forming a new committee.

   b. The committee _____ meeting next month.

   c. Committee members _____ responsible for new policy decisions.

2. a. Our college basketball team _____ the best in the league.

   b. The team members _____ on the cover of a sports magazine this month.

   c. Tonight is the final game of the season. The crowd _____ very excited.

3. a. The school choir _____ performing three concerts this weekend.

   b. Choir members _____ rehearsing today.

PRACTICE 6 ▸ Collective nouns. (Chart 5-3)
Decide if the word in blue refers to a unit or emphasizes the individual members.

1. The team practices five nights a week.	a unit	the individual members
2. The public is still unaware of the situation.	a unit	the individual members
3. The staff are available from 9:00 to 5:00.	a unit	the individual members
4. The family has a reunion every year.	a unit	the individual members
5. The faculty have a semester break this week.	a unit	the individual members
6. The government is passing a new law.	a unit	the individual members

PRACTICE 7 ▸ Subject-verb agreement: using expressions of quantity. (Chart 5-4)
Complete the sentences with *is* or *are*.

1. a. Some of Highway 21 _____ closed due to flooding.

   b. Some of the highways _____ closed due to flooding.

2. a. A lot of that movie _____ full of violence.

   b. A lot of movies _____ full of violence.

3. a. Half of the pizza _____ for you and half _____ for me.

   b. Half of the pizzas _____ vegetarian.

4. a. Most of my friends _____ people I met in school.

   b. Every one of my friends _____ a sports fan.

5. a. The number of desks in that classroom _____ 35.

   b. A number of stores _____ closed today because of the holiday.

PRACTICE 8 ▸ Subject-verb agreement: using expressions of quantity. (Chart 5-4)
Choose the correct completions.

1. A large part of our town   have / has   been badly damaged by a big fire.

2. Most of the houses   was / were   destroyed by the fire.

3. Most of the house   was / were   destroyed by the fire.

4. One of the houses   was / were   destroyed by the fire.

5. Each of the houses   is / are   in ruins.

6. Each house   is / are   in ruins.

7. Every one of the houses   has / have   serious damage.

8. Every house   has / have   serious damage.

9. None of the houses   has / have   escaped damage.

PRACTICE 9 ▸ Subject-verb agreement: using *there + be*. (Chart 5-5)
Choose the correct completions.

1. There   is / are   a cup on the table.

2. There   is / are   some cups on the table.

3. There   is / are   a lot of people in the line for the movie.

4. There   is / are   a snack bar in the lobby of the theater.

5. There   wasn't / weren't   any hurricanes in Florida last year.

6. There   was / were   a terrible tsunami in Asia in 2004.

7. Why   isn't / aren't   there any windows in the classroom?

8. Why   isn't / aren't   there a teacher in the classroom?

9. There   has / have   been an ongoing problem with the color printer.

10. There   has / have   been a lot of problems with the color printer.

Choose the correct completions.

1. States   is / are   political units.

2. The United States   is / are   in North America.

3. The news in that newspaper   is / are   biased.

4. Economics   is / are   an important area of study.

5. Diabetes   is / are   an illness. Mumps   is / are   another kind of illness. Rabies   is / are   a disease you can get from an infected animal.

6. One hundred meters   isn't / aren't   a long distance to travel by car.

7. Five minutes   isn't / aren't   too long to wait.

8. Six and four   is / are   ten.

9. People   is / are   interesting.

10. English   is / are   a common language.

11. The English   is / are   friendly people.

12. The elderly in my country   is / are   given free medical care.

13. Four colorful fish   is / are   swimming in the fish tank.

14. The police   is / are   coming to investigate the accident.

PRACTICE 11 ▶ Subject-verb agreement. (Charts 5-2 → 5-6)
Complete the sentences with the present tense of the appropriate verb in the box. Some verbs may be used more than once.

| be | contain | cost | drive | like | make | remind |

1. There _____ an old barn near our town. The barn has been converted to a bookstore, and its name is The Old Barn Bookstore.

2. It's a very popular place, especially on weekends. People _____ it a lot. They _____ out to the barn on weekends.

3. It's about twenty miles from downtown. Twenty miles _____ a long drive, but the bookstore is worth the drive.

4. A lot of the books in The Old Barn Bookstore _____ not new books. There _____ a lot of used books, old books, and even valuable antique books.

5. There _____ a large number of beautiful art books too. Each one _____ excellent photographs of famous pieces of art. Most of these books _____ quite expensive.

6. One of the books _____ over a hundred dollars because it is very valuable. It has an autograph and an inscription by Ernest Hemingway.

7. There _____ a small café in The Old Barn Bookstore too. The number of food items on the menu _____ very small, but about twenty different kinds of coffee _____ served.

8. Last Sunday I was browsing through some books when I heard a group of people speaking French. I used to understand French, but now French _____ very difficult for me to understand. However, hearing French always _____ me of my days as a student and _____ me feel young again.

PRACTICE 12 ▶ Subject-verb agreement. (Charts 5-2 → 5-6)
Choose the correct completions.

1. Each skater in the competition   has / have   trained since childhood.

2. A convention of English teachers from all over the world   take / takes   place every spring.

3. Some of the new movies   is / are   good, but a lot of them   has / have   too much violence.

4. We saw a film about India last night. Some of the movie   was / were   fascinating, and there   was / were   a lot of beautiful mountain scenes.

5. Three-fourths of the patients who   take / takes   this new medicine report improvement.

6. Almost three-quarters of the surface of the earth   is / are   covered by water.

7. There   is / are   100 senators in the United States Senate. The number of votes necessary for a simple majority   is / are   51.

8. There   has / have   been some encouraging news about pandas in recent years. There   is / are   more pandas living today than there   was / were   ten years ago.

9. The United Arab Emirates   is / are   a country in the Middle East.

10. The *New York Times*   is / are   an important newspaper.

11. Economics   is / are   impossible for me to understand.

12. Diabetes   is / are   an illness. People who   has / have   it must be careful with their diet.

13. Five dollars   is / are   too much to pay for a pencil!

14. The English   speak / speaks   with an accent that is different from the American accent.

15. The handicapped   use / uses   a special entrance in this building.

PRACTICE 13 ▸ Subject-verb agreement. (Chapters 1–5)
Complete the sentences with the correct form of the verbs in parentheses. Use any appropriate tense.

1. Nearly 90% of the people in our town always (*vote*) _____ in local elections.

2. In recent years, a number of students (*participate*) _____ in language programs abroad.

3. The number of students who knew the answer to the last question on the exam (*be*) _____ very low.

4. Every one of the boys and girls in the school (*know*) _____ what to do if the fire alarm rings.

5. A lot of people in the United States (*speak*) _____ and (*understand*) _____ Spanish.

6. Why (*be*) _____ the police standing over there right now?

7. Why (*broadcast*) _____ most of the television stations _____ news at the same hour every night?

8. Some of the most important books for my report (*be*) _____ not available in the school library, so I'll have to look for information on the Internet.

9. Recently there (*be*) _____ times when I have seriously considered dropping out of school.

10. Not one of the women in my office (*receive*) _____ a promotion in the past two years. All of the promotions (*go*) _____ to men.

11. The news on the radio and TV stations (*confirm*) _____ that a serious storm is approaching our city.

12. Geography (*be*) _____ fascinating. Mathematics (*be*) _____ fascinating. I love those subjects!

13. Mathematics and geography (*be*) _____ my favorite subjects.

14. By law, every man, woman, and child (*have*) _____ the right to free speech. It is guaranteed in our constitution.

15. (*Be, not*) _____ sugar and pineapple the leading crops in Hawaii now?

16. Why (*be*) _____ there a shortage of qualified school teachers at the present time?

17. How many states in the United States (*begin*) _____ with the letter "A"?*

18. The United States (*consist*) _____ of 50 states.

19. What places in the world (*have*) _____ no snakes?

20. Politics (*be*) _____ a constant source of interest to me.

21. (*Be*) _____ there ever any doubt in your mind about the outcome of the election? You were sure that Garcia was going to win, weren't you?

---

*See the Answer Key for the answer to this question.

PRACTICE 14 ▸ Chapter review.

Correct the errors in the use of singular and plural forms of nouns and verbs. Do not add any new words.

1. My mother wear~s~ glasses.

2. Elephants is large animals.

3. Your heart beat faster when you exercise.

4. Healthy hearts needs regular exercise.

5. Every child in the class know the alphabet.

6. Some of the magazine at the dentist's office are two year old.

7. A number of the students in my class is from Mexico.

8. One of my favorite subject in school is algebra.

9. There's many different kind of insects in the world.

10. Writing compositions are difficult for me.

11. The United States have a population of over 300 million.

12. Most of the movie take place in Paris.

13. Most of the people in my factory division likes and gets along with one another, but a few of the worker doesn't fit in with the rest of us very well.

CHAPTER 6

Nouns

PRACTICE 1 ▶ Preview.
Read the passage. Answer the questions.

> **The Green Exchange Program**
>
> The "Green Exchange Program" in Curitiba, Brazil allows people
> to exchange <u>household</u> trash for food. Residents of the city take
> cardboard, glass, metal, and paper to a recycling center. In exchange,
> they get fresh food, such as fruit, vegetables, and eggs. People can also
> exchange their trash for <u>bus</u> tickets. <u>Curitiba's</u> recycling program is very
> effective. Ninety percent of its residents recycle about two-thirds of their
> trash every day.
>
>

1. Which word in blue is a singular count noun?

   _____

2. Which three words in blue are plural count nouns?

   _____

3. Which five words in blue are noncount nouns?

   _____

4. Which <u>underlined</u> word shows possession?

   _____

5. Which two <u>underlined</u> words are nouns used as adjectives?

   _____

PRACTICE 2 ▶ Regular and irregular plural nouns. (Chart 6-1)
Write the plural forms of the given nouns.

1. one car, two _____

2. one woman, two _____

3. one match, two _____

4. one mouse, two _____

5. one city, two _____

6. one donkey, two _____

7. one half, two _____

8. one chief, two _____

9. one class, two _____

10. one foot, two _____

11. one hero, two _____

12. one piano, two _____

13. one video, two _____

14. one basis, two _____

15. one bacterium, two _____

16. one series, two _____

PRACTICE 3 ▶ Regular and irregular plural nouns. (Chart 6-1)

Complete the sentences with the correct plural form of the nouns in the box. Use each word once.

belief	fish	monkey	species	thief
child	kilo	✓ potato	stereo	tooth

1. I had my favorite vegetable for dinner: delicious fried _____*potatoes*_____.

2. At the zoo, we saw a lot of _____ jumping around in the trees.

3. The police caught the two _____ who had stolen over 100 _____ from people's cars.

4. The shopping mall has a playground for _____.

5. Our baby got two new _____ this week!

6. The two families found that they hold the same _____; they believe in the same things.

7. Some people think that whales are a species of _____, but they are not; they are mammals.

8. The adult male of some _____ of bears weighs about 600 _____.

PRACTICE 4 ▶ Final -s / -es. (Chart 6-1)

Add final **-s** / **-es** where necessary. Do not change, add, or omit any other words in the sentences.

1. A bird care*s* for its feather*s* by cleaning them with its beak.

2. There are many occupation in the world. Doctor take care of sick people. Pilot fly airplane. Professor teach class. Farmer raise crop.

3. An architect design building. An archeologist dig in the ground to find object from past civilizations.

4. The first modern computer were developed in the 1930s and 1940s. Computer were not commercially available until the 1950s.

5. There are several factory in my hometown. The glass factory employ many people.

6. Kangaroo are Australian animal. They are not on any of the other continent, except in zoo.

7. Mosquito are found everywhere in the world, including the Arctic.

8. At one time, many people believed that tomato were poisonous.

PRACTICE 5 ▶ Nouns as adjectives. (Chart 6-2)

Complete the sentences with the nouns in parentheses. Use the singular or plural form as appropriate.

1. (*project*) Julie manages _____*projects*_____ for her company. She's a _____*project*_____ manager.

2. (*grocery*) They sell _____ at that store. It is a _____ store.

3. (*tomato*) I like _____ salads. I like salads that contain _____.

4. (*picture*) A friend gave us a wooden frame for _____. It's a very attractive wooden _____ frame.

5. (*flower*) I have a _____ garden. I grow several different kinds of _____.

6. (*drug*) Some people are addicted to _____. They are _____ addicts.

7. (*egg*) This carton holds one dozen _____. It's an _____ carton.

8. (*two + lane*) We drove down an old, narrow highway that had only _____. We drove down a _____ highway.

9. (*five + minute*) I gave a _____ speech in class. My speech lasted for _____.

10. (*sixty + year + old*) The Watkins family lives in a _____ house. Any house that is _____ usually needs a lot of repairs.

11. (*truck*) You need a special license to drive a _____. Ed has been a _____ driver for twenty-five years.

12. (*computer*) Susan programs _____. There are good jobs for _____ programmers everywhere.

13. (*peanut*) Emily has a _____ allergy. She is allergic to _____.

PRACTICE 6 ▸ Nouns as adjectives. (Chart 6-2)
Choose the correct completions.

1. A table in a kitchen is a _____.
   a. kitchen table   b. table kitchen   c. kitchen's table

2. The two tables in my bedroom are my _____.
   a. bedrooms tables   b. tables bedroom   c. bedroom tables

3. Scott has an office at his home. It's a _____.
   a. office home   b. home office   c. office of home

4. A lot of people have offices in their homes. They have _____.
   a. home offices   b. homes offices   c. homes office

5. I am out of food for my dog. I need a bag of _____.
   a. dogs food   b. dog food   c. food dog

6. There is a sink in the kitchen and one in each bathroom. We have two bathrooms. So we have one kitchen sink and two _____.
   a. bathrooms sinks   b. bathroom sink   c. bathroom sinks

7. In the back of our house, we grow vegetables in a garden. It's a _____.
   a. vegetable garden   b. vegetables garden   c. garden vegetables

8. We have two trees that grow cherries. They are _____.
   a. tree cherries   b. cherry trees   c. cherries trees

9. Joy and Don have a house by the beach. They have a _____.
   a. beach house   b. house beach   c. beaches house

10. That store sells chargers for phones. It sells _____.
    a. charger phone   b. phones charger   c. phone chargers

PRACTICE 7 ▸ Nouns as adjectives. (Chart 6-2)
Complete the sentences. Write the correct phrase using the two nouns in blue.

1. That handbook is for students. It is a _____ *student handbook* _____.

2. There was a party to celebrate Lynn's birthday. There was a _____ for Lynn.

3. The retirees receive checks from the government every month. They receive a

_____ every month.

4. The seats in the airplane are very small. The _____ are very small.

5. The pajamas are made of cotton. They are _____.

6. There were no rooms in the local hotels that were available. There were no available

_____.

7. Their baby is ten months old. They have a _____.

8. Our trip lasted for three days. We took a _____.

9. Their apartment has three rooms. It is a _____.

10. The professor asked us to write a paper of five pages. She asked us to write a

_____.

11. Luigi is a singer. He sings in operas. He's a famous _____.

12. A convention for people who collect stamps is being held at City Center. My uncle is a collector.

He has been a _____ since he was a boy.

PRACTICE 8 ▶ Possessive nouns. (Chart 6-3)
Answer the questions.

1. My parents' house is over 100 years old.

   a. What is the possessive noun? _____

   b. How many parents are there, one or more than one? _____

   c. What two nouns does the possessive (s') connect? _____ + _____

2. Safety is a parent's concern.

   a. What is the possessive noun? _____

   b. How many parents are there, one or more than one? _____

   c. What two nouns does the possessive ('s) connect? _____ + _____

3. Cats' eyes shine in the dark.

   a. What is the possessive noun? _____

   b. How many cats are there, one or more than one? _____

   c. What two nouns does the possessive (s') connect? _____ + _____

4. My cat's eyes are big and green.

   a. What is the possessive noun? _____

   b. How many cats are there, one or more than one? _____

   c. What two nouns does the possessive ('s) connect? _____ + _____

5. Do you know Mary's brother?

   a. What is the possessive noun? _____

   b. What belongs to Mary? _____

   c. What two nouns does the possessive ('s) connect? _____ + _____

6. Do you know Mary's brothers?

   a. What is the possessive noun? _____

   b. What belongs to Mary? _____

   c. What two nouns does the possessive ('s) connect? _____ + _____

7. My brothers' team won the game.

   a. What is the possessive noun? _____

   b. How many brothers do I have, one or more than one? _____

   c. What two nouns does the possessive (s') connect? _____ + _____

8. My brother's team won the game.

   a. What is the possessive noun? _____

   b. How many brothers do I have, one or more than one? _____

   c. What two nouns does the possessive ('s) connect? _____ + _____

PRACTICE 9 ▸ Possessive nouns. (Chart 6-3)

Check (✓) the correct number for the words in blue.

1. The teacher's office is down the hall.	☐ one	☐ more than one
2. The teachers' office is down the hall.	☐ one	☐ more than one
3. My sisters' clothes are all over my bed.	☐ one	☐ more than one
4. I visited the boy's house.	☐ one	☐ more than one
5. I agree with the judges' decision.	☐ one	☐ more than one
6. The customer service representative must listen to the customers' complaints.	☐ one	☐ more than one
7. The professor discussed the student's assignment.	☐ one	☐ more than one
8. The flight attendant put the passenger's bags in the overhead compartment.	☐ one	☐ more than one

PRACTICE 10 ▸ Possessive nouns. (Chart 6-3)

Make the *italicized* nouns possessive by adding apostrophes and final **-s** / **-es**. Delete and change a letter if necessary.

1. a. He put the mail in his *secretary* _'s_____ mailbox.

   b. There are three secretaries in our office. The *secretary* _ies'_____ mailboxes are in the hallway.

2. a. Tom has two cats. The *cat* _____ food and water dishes are on a shelf in the laundry room.

   b. I have one cat. My *cat* _____ feet are white, but the rest of her is black.

3. a. My *supervisor* _____ names are Ms. Anderson and Mr. Gomez.

   b. Your *supervisor* _____ name is Ms. Wright.

4. a. My twin *baby* _____ eyes are dark blue, just like their father's eyes.

   b. My *baby* _____ eyes are dark blue, just like her father's eyes.

5. a. Olga's *child* _____ name is Olaf.

   b. José and Alicia's *children* _____ names are Pablo and Gabriela.

6. a. All of the performers in the play did well. The audience applauded the *actor* _____ excellent performances.

   b. An *actor* _____ income is uncertain.

PRACTICE 11 ▶ Possessive nouns. (Chart 6-3)
Choose the correct completions.

1. My   mother's / mothers'   name is Maria.

2. Both my   grandmother's / grandmothers'   names were Maria too.

3. The   teacher's / teachers'   class is so big that the students in the back of the room can't hear her when she talks.

4. My   bosses' / boss'   name is Carl.

5. An   employee's / employees'   wallet was found under a table at the   employee's / employees' cafeteria yesterday.

6. Here's the directory for the department store: the   mens' / men's   department is on the first floor; the   women's / womens'   department is on the second floor; the   children's / childrens' department is on the third floor. On the third floor, the   girl's / girls'   clothes are on the right side, and the   boy's / boys'   clothes are on the left side.

PRACTICE 12 ▶ More about expressing possession. (Chart 6-4)
Choose the correct sentence.

1. a. I was 20 minutes late for yesterday's chemistry class.
   b. I was 20 minutes late for the chemistry class of yesterday.

2. a. I knew I had made a big mistake when I saw my professor's face.
   b. I knew I had made a big mistake when I saw the face of my professor.

3. a. I missed important information about next week's final exam.
   b. I missed important information about the final exam of next week.

4. a. I was late because I had run into an old teacher. She is now the history department's chair.
   b. I was late because I had run into an old teacher. She is now the chair of the history department.

5. a. She told me about a job opening for an office's assistant in the history department.
   b. She offered me a job opening for an office assistant in the history department.

6. a. I'm interested in the job. I will fill out the application's form later today.
   b. I'm interested in the job. I will fill out the application form later today.

7. a. I also need to copy my classmate's chemistry notes today.
   b. I also need to copy the chemistry notes of my classmate today.

PRACTICE 13 ▶ Count and noncount nouns. (Chart 6-5)
Look at the *italicized* nouns. Write "C" above the count nouns and "NC" above the noncount nouns.

1. We bought a lot of *food*. We bought some *eggs*, *bread*, *milk*, *coffee*, and *bananas*.

food = NC, *eggs* = C, *bread* = NC, *milk* = NC, *coffee* = NC, *bananas* = C

2. I get a lot of *mail*. I get some *letters*, *magazines*, *catalogs*, and *bills* almost every day.

3. *Euros*, *pounds*, and *dollars* are different kinds of *money*.

4. Alma doesn't wear much *jewelry*. She wears a *ring* and sometimes *earrings*.

5. A *language* consists of *vocabulary* and *grammar*.

6. We need some *furniture* for the patio: a *table*, six *chairs*, and an *umbrella*.

PRACTICE 14 ▸ Count and noncount nouns. (Charts 6-5 → 6-7)
Choose the correct completions.

1. Every day I learn some more new   word / words   in English.

2. Olga knows   an / some   American slang.

3. There are a lot of   car / cars   on the highway at rush hour.

4. We got here so fast! There wasn't   much / many   traffic on the highway.

5. I ate a tuna   sandwich / sandwiches   for lunch.

6. We got only   some / one   good picture on our trip.

7. That website contains   an / some   excellent information.

8. That is   a very / very   good news!

PRACTICE 15 ▸ Count and noncount nouns. (Charts 6-5 → 6-7)
Add final *-s* / *-es* to the nouns in *italics* if necessary. Do not add, omit, or change any other words. Some sentences have no errors.

1. Jackie has brown *hair* and gray *eye*ₛ.

2. My parents gave me some good *advice*.

3. I always drink *water* when I'm hot and thirsty.

4. Do winning athletes need *luck*?

5. Our country has made a lot of *progress* in the last 25 years.

6. How many *class* are you taking this semester?

7. There are some *message* in my voicemail. I need to check them.

PRACTICE 16 ▸ Count and noncount nouns. (Charts 6-5 → 6-7)
Choose the correct completions.

1. It takes   courage / a courage   to be an astronaut.

2. We bought   some / a   new clothing.

3. The baby needs a new pair of   shoe / shoes.

4. The garbage truck comes on Monday, Wednesday, and Friday mornings to pick up the
   garbage / garbages.

5. I ordered twelve   glass / glasses   from a site on the Internet. When they arrived, one
   glass / glasses   was broken.

6. Many people need to wear   glass / glasses   to see better. The lenses should be made of
   glass / glasses   that doesn't break easily.

7. I filled out a report for   some / a   lost luggage at the airport, but I'm not optimistic. I wonder if
   they find   much / many   lost suitcases.

8. Would you like to go out tonight? I don't have   much / many   homework, and I'd like to go out
   and have   some / a   fun.

9. Ireland is famous for its beautiful green   hill / hills.   Ireland has   a lovely / lovely   scenery, but it often has   a damp / damp   weather.

10. The four-leaf clover is a symbol of   a good / good   luck in Ireland.

PRACTICE 17 ▶ Expressions of quantity with count and noncount nouns. (Chart 6-8)
Cross out the expressions that <u>cannot</u> be used to complete the sentences. Item 1 has been started for you.

1. Isabel did _____ work last Saturday.

   a. ~~three~~
   b. ~~several~~
   c. some
   d. a lot of
   e. too much
   f. too many
   g. a few
   h. a little
   i. a number of
   j. a great deal of
   k. hardly any
   l. no

2. Zach is planning _____ projects for next month.

   a. three
   b. several
   c. some
   d. a lot of
   e. too much
   f. too many
   g. a few
   h. a little
   i. a number of
   j. a great deal of
   k. hardly any
   l. no

PRACTICE 18 ▶ Expressions of quantity with count and noncount nouns. (Chart 6-8)
Complete the sentences with **much** or **many**. Also write the plural forms of the nouns as necessary. In some sentences, you will need to circle the correct verb in blue.

1. How ____*many*____ ~~computer~~ *computers* are there in the language lab?

2. How ____*much*____ equipment is there in the language lab?

3. How ____*many*____ ~~child~~ *children*   is /(are) in Ms. Thompson's class?

4. How _____ tooth do babies usually have when they're born?

5. Ellen and Rick have traveled widely. They've visited _____ country.

6. I don't know _____ American slang.

7. Enrique hasn't made _____ progress in learning to play the piano. That's because he doesn't spend _____ time practicing.

8. How _____ apps do you usually download a month?

9. My hair is frizzy today. There   is / are   too _____ humidity in the air.

10. I haven't done _____ reading lately.

11. There   is / are   so _____ smog in Los Angeles yesterday that you couldn't see any of the hills or mountains from the city.

12. I didn't know _____ grammar before I took this course.

13. How _____ active volcano   is / are   there in the world today?

14. Politicians give _____ speech during their careers

PRACTICE 19 ▸ Expressions of quantity with count and noncount nouns. (Chart 6-8)
Choose all the correct completions for each sentence.

1. Pat bought a few _____ at the art show.
   a. pictures
   b. photographs
   c. art
   d. ceramic bowls

2. Mike bought some _____ at the supermarket.
   a. milk
   b. orange
   c. magazines
   d. flashlight battery

3. There were several _____ on the plane.
   a. child
   b. people
   c. babies
   d. passenger

4. There was a little _____ on the table.
   a. food
   b. cream
   c. coffee
   d. sandwiches

5. We have plenty of _____ for everyone.
   a. food
   b. pizza
   c. drinks
   d. hot dog

6. Can you bring a couple of _____ with you when you come to the party?
   a. ice
   b. hamburger
   c. bottles of soda
   d. water

7. I don't have many _____ about this.
   a. thoughts
   b. knowledge
   c. ideas
   d. information

8. Do Charlie and Kate have much _____?
   a. problems
   b. children
   c. fun
   d. work

9. I know a number of _____ .
   a. people
   b. things
   c. professors
   d. news

10. They don't have a great deal of _____ .
    a. intelligence
    b. information
    c. facts
    d. education

PRACTICE 20 ▸ Using *a few* and *few*; *a little* and *little*. (Chart 6-9)
In each pair of sentences, check (✓) the sentence that has the *bigger quantity* of something.

1. a. We have a little money. __✓__

   b. We have little money. _____

2. a. They know few people. _____

   b. They know a few people. _____

3. a. She has very little patience. _____

   b. She has a little patience. _____

4. a. I speak some Spanish. _____

   b. I speak little Spanish. _____

5. a. Marta asked few questions. _____

   b. Marta asked a few questions. _____

PRACTICE 21 ▸ Using *a few* and *few*; *a little* and *little*. (Chart 6-9)
Choose the correct completions.

1. Belinda learned to skate very quickly. At first, she fell down _____ times, but now she very rarely

   falls down.
   a. few   b. a few   c. a little

2. The police didn't have a good description of the bank robber. _____ witnesses actually saw his face.
   a. Few   b. A few   c. Little

3. Please pass the cream. I like _____ cream in my coffee. It tastes better.
   a. a few   b. a little   c. very few

4. You'd better know the answers when Professor Simpson calls on you in class tomorrow. He has _____

   patience with students who are not prepared.
   a. very little   b. very few   c. a little

5. Before the hurricane, the stores were crowded with people buying supplies. By the time I got to a

   store, _____ flashlight batteries were left, and _____ bottled water was available.
   a. very little / very few   b. very little / very little   c. very few / very little

6. Come over to our house tonight. Peter is bringing his guitar. He'll play _____ folk music, and we'll

   sing _____ old songs.
   a. few / little   b. a few / a little   c. a little / a few

7. To make this sauce, first cook _____ onions in _____ oil.
   a. few / little   b. a few / a little   c. little / few

PRACTICE 22 ▸ Using *a few* and *few*; *a little* and *little*. (Chart 6-9)
Without changing the meaning of the sentences, replace the *italicized* words with **a few**, **few**,
a little, or **little**.

1. If you put ~~some~~ *a little* sugar on those berries, they will taste sweeter.

2. Many people live to be more than 100 years old, but only ~~some~~ *a few* people live to be 110 years old.

3. Many cities in the world have a population of over a million, and *some* cities have a population

   of more than ten million.

4. You might reach your goal if you put forth *some* more effort.

5. The professor lectured very clearly. At the end of the class, *not many* students had questions.

6. I have to go to the post office because I have *some* letters to mail.

7. Every day Max goes to his mailbox, but it is usually empty. He gets *almost no* mail.

8. My friend arrived in the United States *some* months ago.

9. I think you could use *some* help. Let me give you *some* advice.

10. Margaret likes sweet tea. She usually adds *some* honey to her tea. Sometimes she adds *some* milk too.

PRACTICE 23 ▸ Singular expressions of quantity: *one, each, every.* (Chart 6-10)
Choose the correct word in the box. Write the correct singular or plural form. Some words may be used more than once.

child	goose	neighbor	✓ state
chimpanzee	man	puppy	woman

1. There is only one _____*state*_____ in the United States that is completely surrounded by water: Hawaii.

2. One of the _____*states*_____ in the United States that shares a border with Canada is Vermont.

3. Our dog had six puppies. I wanted to keep them all, but I couldn't. I kept one of the _____, but I gave away the other five.

4. There were six puppies. One _____ was black and white, and five were all black.

5. The children enjoyed the zoo. One of the _____ wandered away from the group, but she was quickly found at the snack bar.

6. The children particularly liked watching the chimpanzees. One _____, a boy named Kevin, seemed to be having a conversation with one of the _____.

7. One of our _____ gave a welcoming party for a new family who had just moved to our neighborhood from Ecuador.

8. There were several men riding on motorcycles together. One _____ seemed to be their leader. He was riding in front of the group.

9. The geese are flying in a V-formation. One _____ is at the point of the V, apparently leading the whole flock.

10. Our book club consists of 15 women. One of the _____ was just elected mayor of our town.

PRACTICE 24 ▸ Singular expressions of quantity: *one, each, every.* (Chart 6-10)
Correct the errors in the *italicized* words. Not every sentence has an error.

1. According to the Constitution of the United States, *every persons* has certain rights.

2. One of *rights* is the right to vote.

3. Each of *states* is represented by two senators in the U.S. Senate.

4. *Each of* senator is elected for a six-year term.

5. The number of representatives in the House of Representatives depends on the population of *each state*.

6. For example, Nevada, one of the very *small state*, has only three representatives, but New York, a populous state, has 29 representatives.

7. Every one of *citizen* is eligible to vote for president, but not every *citizen* exercises this right.

8. In some countries, voting is compulsory. Every *citizens* must vote.

PRACTICE 25 ▶ Using *of* in expressions of quantity. (Chart 6-11)
Complete the sentences with *of* or **Ø**.

1. Several _____ my colleagues are going to the lecture at the library tonight.

2. I have several _____ colleagues who have Ph.D's.

3. Many _____ the houses in New Orleans were lost to the floods that occurred after Hurricane Katrina.

4. These days, _____ new houses are being built with stronger materials to withstand hurricanes.

5. A few _____ children are born with exceptional musical talent.

6. Some _____ the children in Mr. McFarlane's music class are playing in a recital.

7. Most _____ people like to hear compliments.

8. My cousin won a million _____ dollars on a game show.

9. Many _____ places in the world use wind as a source of energy. Some _____ these places supply energy to thousands _____ homes and businesses.

10. There was hardly any _____ rain this spring. As a result, hardly any _____ my flowers bloomed.

11. To form the plural of most _____ the words in English, we add an *-s* or *-es* at the end. Not every word forms its plural in this way, however. Some _____ words have irregular endings.

PRACTICE 26 ▶ Chapter review.
There is one error in each sentence. Correct the error.

1. Last month, my brother and I cleaned out my grandparents attic.

2. We found a lot of old stuffs.

3. There was boxes and boxes of books.

4. We even found a 100-years-old copy of *The Adventures of Tom Sawyer*.

5. My brother was looking for old comic books, but he didn't find much comics.

6. He found a little of my uncle's old toys.

7. It was hard works, but we had a lot of fun.

8. My grandmother was happy to have a clean attic, and I was happy to have some of her old dishes and furnitures.

9. One persons' junk is another person's treasure.

PRACTICE 27 ▶ Chapter review.

Complete the crossword puzzle. Use the clues under the puzzle and the words in the box. All the words in the puzzle are from the charts in Chapter 6. All the sentences are well-known sayings in English.

all	every	many	mice	some
an	man	men	one	two

Across

3. _____ good things must come to an end.

4. You can't make an omelet without breaking _____ eggs.

6. A _____ is known by his friends.

8. _____ cloud has a silver lining.

Down

1. _____ heads are better than one.

2. _____ picture is worth a thousand words.

3. _____ apple a day keeps the doctor away.

5. When the cat's away, the _____ will play.

6. Too _____ cooks spoil the broth.

7. Dead _____ tell no tales.

Articles

PRACTICE 1 ▸ Preview.
Read the passage. Underline the 22 articles (*a*, *an*, *the*).

> **Worry Dolls**
>
> Worry dolls are tiny colorful dolls. They usually come in a group of six to eight dolls in a small wooden box. These dolls are a folk tradition from Guatemala. The dolls are about one-half inch tall. Guatemalan artisans use a short piece of wire to make a frame with legs, arms, a torso, and a head. The artisans wrap yarn around the frame for the shape, and they use pieces of traditional fabric for the costumes. In the folk tradition, children tell a worry to each doll before they go to bed. Then they put the dolls back in the box and close the lid. When the children wake up in the morning, the worries are gone. The dolls have taken away all of the worries.

PRACTICE 2 ▸ Indefinite and definite nouns. (Chart 7-1)
Decide if the nouns in blue are definite or indefinite.

1. I have a friend from Guatemala.	definite	indefinite
2. She makes worry dolls.	definite	indefinite
3. Every year she sells the dolls at a fair.	definite	indefinite
4. The fair is in June.	definite	indefinite
5. Last year I bought some worry dolls.	definite	indefinite
6. The dolls help me sleep at night.	definite	indefinite

PRACTICE 3 ▸ Using *some*. (Chart 7-1)
Insert *some* where possible.

1. Hanna is going to the store. *no change*
2. She's buying _{some} ingredients for a cake.
3. She's making a cake for her roommate's birthday.
4. She invited friends over for a party tonight.
5. They will eat cake and listen to music.
6. Hannah's friend Michael is a photographer. He'll take pictures.

PRACTICE 4 ▸ Articles: indefinite nouns. (Chart 7-1)

Complete the sentences with *a, an,* or *some*.

1. I asked _____*a*_____ question.

2. The students asked _____*some*_____ questions.

3. I got _____*an*_____ answer.

4. I received _____ information.

5. Chess is _____ game.

6. The children played _____ games at the party.

7. I heard _____ news about the hurricane.

8. I read _____ newspaper.

9. My professor wrote _____ letter to the newspaper.

10. I wrote _____ email to my professor.

11. I got _____ mail from the university.

12. Susan left _____ things in her car.

13. Matt bought _____ printer.

14. The printer needs _____ ink.

PRACTICE 5 ▸ Articles: indefinite and definite nouns. (Chart 7-1)

Complete the sentences with *a, an, the,* or *Ø*. Capitalize where necessary.

1. INDEFINITE: I'm shopping for _____*Ø*_____ clothes this weekend.

   DEFINITE: _____*The*_____ clothes in that store are very expensive.

2. INDEFINITE: I need _____ shirt.

   DEFINITE: I will try on _____ shirt before I buy it.

3. INDEFINITE: Does this store have _____ fitting room?

   DEFINITE: _____ fitting room is in the back of the store.

4. DEFINITE: _____ size is too large.

   INDEFINITE: I am looking for _____ different size.

5. DEFINITE: _____ salesclerk is helpful.

   INDEFINITE: Have you seen _____ salesclerk? I need help.

6. DEFINITE: Where is _____ price tag on these shoes?

   INDEFINITE: These shoes do not have _____ price tag.

7. INDEFINITE: I have _____ coupon.

   INDEFINITE: _____ coupon is for 20% off.

PRACTICE 6 ▸ Articles: generic nouns. (Chart 7-2)
Check (✓) if the noun in blue is singular or plural. Also check (✓) the nouns that have a generic meaning.

	Singular	Plural	Generic	Specific
1. a. Dogs need a lot of attention.		✓	✓	
b. I'm taking the dog for a walk.				
2. a. Hamsters are popular house pets.				
b. A hamster is a rodent.				
3. a. A cat can jump up to five times its own height.				
b. The cat jumped onto a table.				
4. a. Animal shelters take stray, lost, or abandoned animals.				
b. I adopted a dog from the animal shelter.				

PRACTICE 7 ▸ Articles: generic nouns. (Chart 7-2)
Choose the correct completions. All of the sentences have a generic meaning.

1. a. The baseball / Baseball   is a popular sport.

   b. Athletes wear   the uniforms / uniforms.

2. a. A data analyst / Data analyst   collects, organizes, and interprets statistical information.

   b. The data collection / Data collection   is important to many businesses.

3. a. The clarinet / Clarinet   is a musical instrument. It is a wind instrument.

   b. The violin / Violin   is a string instrument.

4. a. A pecan / pecan   is a nut.

   b. The pecans / Pecans   grow in Texas.

5. a. A blog / Blog   is a discussion or informational website.

   b. The bloggers / Bloggers   write content for blogs.

6. a. A meme / meme   is a humorous image or video that is copied and spread on the Internet.

   b. The memes / Memes   are popular on social media websites.

PRACTICE 8 ▸ Descriptive information with definite and indefinite nouns. (Chart 7-3)
Check (✓) if the noun in blue is about a definite or specific noun.

1. a. I ordered the book my teacher recommended. __✓__

   b. I like books about historical events. _____

2. a. Vanessa has a job interview at a world-famous hospital. _____

   b. She is nervous about the interview at that hospital. _____

3. a. I get lost easily. Please draw me a map to your house. _____

   b. I didn't get lost. The map to your house really helped. _____

4. a. Rhonda and Caroline met for lunch at a restaurant in Lexington. _____

   b. Do you know of a good restaurant in Lexington? I'm traveling there next week. _____

5. a. There is the store I told you about. _____

   b. There is a new store downtown. _____

6. a. Mariko needs a grammar book. _____

   b. Did Daniel do the homework in the grammar book? _____

PRACTICE 9 ▸ Using articles. (Charts 7-1 → 7-3)
Complete the sentences with *a, an,* or *the*.

1. A: Let's take _____ break. Do you want to go to _____ movie?

   B: That's _____ good idea. Which movie do you want to see?

   A: _____ movie at the Rialto Theater is a comedy. Let's see that one.

2. A: Who knows _____ answer to this question?

   B: I do!

3. A: Professor Li, I have _____ question about the assignment.

   B: What's your question?

4. A: There's _____ spot on my shirt!

   B: Here. Take out _____ spot with this spot remover.

5. A: Listen! I hear _____ noise! Do you hear it?

   B: Yes, I hear something.

6. A: What was _____ noise that you heard?

   B: I think it was _____ mouse.

   A: But we don't have any mice in _____ house!

   B: Well, maybe it was just _____ wind.

PRACTICE 10 ▸ General article usage. (Chart 7-4)
Complete the sentences with *a/an*, *the*, or *Ø*. Capitalize as necessary.

1. ____Ø____ lightning is ____a____ flash of light. It is usually followed by ____Ø____ thunder.

2. Last night we had ____a____ terrible storm. Our children were frightened by ____the____ thunder.

3. _____ circles are _____ round geometric figures.

4. _____ circle with _____ slash drawn through it is an international

   symbol meaning "Do not do this!" For example, _____ circle in

   _____ illustration means "No Smoking."

5. _____ inventor of _____ modern cell phone was Dr. Martin Cooper.

   He made the first call on the first portable handset in 1973 when he was

   _____ employee of the Motorola company.

6. Frank Lloyd Wright is _____ name of _____ famous architect. He is _____ architect who designed the Guggenheim Museum in New York. He also designed _____ hotel in Tokyo. _____ hotel was designed to withstand _____ earthquakes.

7. There was _____ small earthquake in California last year. _____ earthquake caused damage to several buildings, but fortunately, no one was killed.

PRACTICE 11 ▶ General article usage. (Chart 7-4)
Read each conversation. Choose the sentence that explains what the speakers are talking about.

1. A: Where's the teacher? I have a question.

   B: I'm not sure.
      a. Speaker A is asking about any teacher.
      b. Speaker A is asking about a teacher Speaker B is familiar with.

2. A: I put down the phone and now I can't find it.

   B: Oh, no!
      a. Speaker A is referring to a phone Speaker B is familiar with.
      b. Speaker A is referring to any phone.

3. A: Could you pick up some eggs and rice at the store? We'll have the rice for dinner.

   B: Sure.
      a. In the first sentence, *rice* is general. In the second sentence, *rice* is specific.
      b. In both sentences, *rice* is specific.

4. A: Bananas have a lot of potassium.

   B: They're very healthy.
      a. Speaker A is referring to a specific group of bananas.
      b. Speaker A is referring to bananas in general.

5. A: Does Saturn have a moon that orbits it?

   B: I don't know!
      a. Speaker A is talking about a specific moon.
      b. Speaker A is talking about any moon.

6. A: Have you seen the moon tonight?

   B: Yes! It's spectacular.
      a. The speakers are referring to the moon that goes around the Earth.
      b. The speakers are referring to any moon in the solar system.

PRACTICE 12 ▶ Using *the* or Ø with titles and geographic names. (Chart 7-5)
Complete the sentences with *the* or Ø.

1. _____ Doctor Kennedy moved from _____ United States to _____ Switzerland last year.

2. Some day I'll go to _____ Himalayas and climb _____ Mount Everest.

3. Pat and Laura went kayaking on _____ Colorado River.

4. _____ Canada borders three oceans. Canada's west coast is on _____ Pacific Ocean. To the north lies _____ Arctic Ocean. The east coast is on _____ Atlantic Ocean.

5. Jeff and Susanna traveled to _____ Europe for their honeymoon.

6. A: Have you ever been to _____ Caribbean Islands?

   B: Yes. I went scuba diving in _____ Jamaica a few years ago.

7. _____ Professor Bartels speaks Dutch. She is from _____ Netherlands.

8. _____ Austin is the capital city of _____ Texas.

PRACTICE 13 ▶ Chapter review.
Choose the correct completions.

Louis Braille was born in   the / Ø   France in 1809. He lost his eyesight due to   the / an   accident when he was   a / Ø   child. When he was 15 years old, he developed   a / Ø   writing system for the / Ø   blind. The / A   writing system consists of   the / Ø   raised dots. The number and patterns of the / some   dots form characters. The / A   system is called "Braille" after   the / an   inventor. Braille has spread from   the / Ø   France to many countries around   the / Ø   world.

PRACTICE 14 ▶ Chapter review.
Correct the errors.

1. It's beautiful today. Sun is shining and sky is clear.

2. I read good book about globalization.

3. The penguins live in Antarctica. The polar bears don't live in Antarctica.

4. Which is more important — the love or the money?

5. A: What does this word mean?

   B: Do you have dictionary? Look up word in dictionary.

6. A: Watch out! There's a bee buzzing around!

   B: Where? I don't see it. Ouch! It stung me! I didn't see bee, but I felt it!

7. Kevin is going to grocery store. He's getting some ingredients for a pasta dish.

8. Every summer Yoko's family goes camping in Canadian Rockies, but this summer they're going to beach instead.

PRACTICE 1 ▶ Preview.
Read the passage. In the parentheses after the pronoun, write the antecedent.

Selfie Sticks

A selfie stick holds a camera or smartphone on a pole. It enables

people to take a photograph of themselves (_____*people*_____)

1

from wide angles. Selfie sticks have become very popular.

They (_____*selfie sticks*_____) are taking the place of tripods. Many people

2

prefer selfie sticks over tripods because they (_____)

3

are easier to set up. They are also less expensive. The traditional way to take a "selfie," or a picture of

yourself, is to hold the camera yourself. Photography expert Amanda Campbell does not recommend

this method. She (_____) explains that your hands usually shake when you

4

are taking a selfie, so it (_____) will turn out blurry. People often drop and break their

5

(_____) cell phones when they are taking selfies. There are many good benefits to selfie

6

sticks. *Time* magazine called selfie sticks "the greatest invention of 2014."

    However, many opponents do not like selfie sticks. They (_____)

7

do not like to see people constantly posing in front of their own camera. Selfie sticks can also be

dangerous. One man caused an accident when he (_____) used his selfie stick on a

8

roller coaster. Because Disneyland is worried about accidents, it (_____) has banned

9

selfie sticks in its (_____) parks worldwide. Many museums have also banned them

10

(_____). They (_____) do not want visitors to bump into important

11   12

works of art as they (_____) try to take the perfect selfie. The *New York Times* called

13

selfie sticks "the most controversial gift of 2014."

PRACTICE 2 ▶ Personal pronouns. (Chart 8-1)
Draw a circle around each pronoun that has an antecedent. Draw an arrow from the pronoun to its
antecedent.

  1. Bob works for Trans-Ocean Airlines. (He) flies cargo across the Pacific Ocean.

  2. Mr. and Mrs. Nobriega are moving. They have bought a house in the suburbs.

3. There goes my English teacher. Do you know her?

4. The baby just began to walk. She is eleven months old.

5. A new kind of car is being advertised. It runs on a battery.

6. There are two hawks up there on the telephone wire. Do you see them?

7. Sorry, Mr. Frank is not in the office now. Please call him at home.

8. We have a dog and a cat. They are part of our family.

PRACTICE 3 ▸ Personal pronouns. (Chart 8-1)
Choose the correct completions.

1. Sarah and   I / me   are taking a yoga class.

2. I'm going to tell you something, but don't tell anyone. It's just between you and   I / me.

3. Carlos and Julia were at the movies together. I saw   they / them.   They / Them   were holding hands.

4. Where are my papers? I left   it / them   right here on the table.

5. I have   my / mine   problems, and you have   your / yours.

6. Jim and Helena both work from home. He works at   he / his   computer all day, and she works at   her / hers.   At five o'clock sharp they both stop   they / their   work.

7. My aunt is only five years older than I am.   She and I / Her and me   are very close. We are like sisters.   Our / Ours   friends and relatives treat   our / us   like sisters.

8. I studied Latin when I was in high school. Of course, nobody speaks Latin today, but Latin was very useful to   me / I.   Because I understand   it / its   grammar, I can understand grammar in other languages. And my vocabulary is bigger because of   it / its   too.

9. When baby giraffes are born,   they / its   are six feet tall, taller than the average person.   They / It   sometimes grow an inch a day, and they double   its / their   height in one year.

10. Did you know Mauna Kea in Hawaii is actually the tallest mountain in the world? If you measure it from   its / it's   base at the bottom of the Pacific Ocean to   its / it's   peak, it has a height of 33,476 feet 10,203 meters.   Its / It's   taller than Mount Everest.

PRACTICE 4 ▸ Personal pronouns: agreement with generic nouns and indefinite pronouns. (Chart 8-2)
Choose the correct completions. In some sentences, both choices are correct.

1. All students must bring _____ books to class every day.
   a. his   b. their

2. Each girl in the class must bring _____ books to class every day.
   a. her   b. his or her

3. Everyone on the tennis team must leave _____ cell phone number with the coach.
   a. his or her   b. their

4. Everybody on the men's bowling team brings _____ own bowling ball to the bowling alley.
   a. his   b. his or her

5. Everyone should know how to do _____ job.
   a. his or her   b. their

6. Girls, whose keys are these? Somebody left _____ keys on the table.
   a. their   b. her

7. Nobody in the Boy Scout troop failed _____ tests. Everybody passed.
   a. his   b. their

PRACTICE 5 ▸ Personal pronouns: agreement with collective nouns. (Charts 8-2 and 8-3)
Complete the sentences with a word or phrase in the box. You may use an item more than once.

her	his or her	its	them
his	it	their	they

1. Tonight's audience is special. Everyone in _____ is a member of the fire department or the police department. The show is being performed especially for _____.

2. When the play was over, the audience arose from _____ seats and applauded wildly.

3. The actors bowed to the audience's applause. The leading man took _____ bow first, and then the leading lady took _____ bow.

4. The faculty of the philosophy department is very small. In fact, _____ has only two professors. _____ share an office.

5. Well, Mia, I'm sorry you're having problems. Everyone has _____ problems, goodness knows!

6. A notice sent home with each girl on the girls' volleyball team said: "The girls' volleyball team is playing at Cliffside on Friday of this week. This will be _____ final game of the season. Each girl must have a signed consent form for a field trip from _____ mother or father."

7. Instructions on an application for admission to a university said: "Each student must submit _____ application by December 1st. The admissions committee will render _____ final decision before April 1st."

PRACTICE 6 ▸ Reflexive pronouns. (Chart 8-4)
Complete the sentences with the appropriate reflexive pronouns.

1. In our creative writing class, we all had to write short biographies of _____*ourselves*_____.

2. Anna wrote a biography of _____.

3. Tom wrote a biography of _____.

4. Larry and Harry, who are twins, wrote biographies of _____, but surprisingly, they were not similar.

5. I wrote a biography of _____.

6. After our teacher had read them all, he asked us, "Did all of you enjoy writing about _____?"

7. One student replied. He said, "Well, yes, I think we did. But now we would like to know something about you. Will you tell us about _____?"

PRACTICE 7 ▶ Reflexive pronouns. (Chart 8-4)

Complete the sentences with one of the words or phrases in the box, and add a reflexive pronoun.

| feeling sorry for | help | ✓ is angry at | pat |
| fix | introduce | laugh at | talks to |

1. John overslept and missed his plane to San Francisco. Now he

   _____ _is angry at himself_ _____ for not checking his alarm clock before going to bed.

2. I didn't know anyone at the party. I stood alone for a while; then I decided to walk over to an

   interesting-looking person and _____ to him.

3. Sue, please _____ to some more cake. And would you like

   some more coffee?

4. You did a great job, team. You should all _____ on the back for

   playing the game so well.

5. Sabrina is a lonely little girl. She doesn't have any brothers or sisters, or live near any friends.

   Sometimes she _____ or to an imaginary friend.

6. The sink is not going to _____. We have to call a plumber to do it.

7. Come on, Kim. Don't be so hard on yourself. Everyone makes mistakes. We have to

   _____ sometimes and keep a sense of humor!

8. I told Tommy he couldn't buy a new toy today. He's mad at me. He's in his bedroom

   _____ .

PRACTICE 8 ▶ Using *you, one*, and *they* as impersonal pronouns. (Chart 8-5)

Choose the correct completions.

1. People make New Year's resolutions at the beginning of a new year. They promise _____ that they
   will do something to improve their well-being, or to benefit their community or the world.
   a. them   b. oneself   c. themselves

2. One should be honest with _____.
   a. one   b. oneself   c. yourself

3. Parents tell their children, "You should be polite to _____ elders."
   a. your   b. one's   c. their

4. How do _____ start this car?
   a. you   b. one   c. he

5. How does _____ make a complaint in this store? Is there a customer-service department?
   a. you   b. they   c. one

6. If you are a student, _____ can get a discount at shops in the mall.
   a. they   b. you   c. one

7. Students can get discounts at the mall. _____ just have to show their student ID.
   a. They   b. Themselves   c. One

PRACTICE 9 ▶ Forms of *other*. (Chart 8-6)

Choose the correct completions.

1. One of the biggest problems in the world is global warming. _____ problem is AIDS.
   a. Another   b. The another   c. Other

2. Some cities have strict anti-pollution laws, but _____ cities do not.
   a. other   b. others   c. the others

3. New York is a multilingual city. In addition to English, many people speak Spanish. _____ speak French, Chinese, Portuguese, or Russian.
   a. Others   b. Other   c. Another

4. In addition to these languages, there are 40 _____ languages spoken in New York City, according to the U.S. Census Bureau.
   a. other   b. others   c. another

5. Istanbul lies on both sides of the Straits of Bosporus. One side is in Europe, and _____ side is in Asia.
   a. another   b. the other   c. other

6. There are 47 countries in Africa. Of these, 35 countries have coastlines. _____ do not have coastlines; they are landlocked.
   a. Others   b. The other   c. The others

7. There are several countries that have a king or a queen. One is Thailand. _____ is England.
   a. Another   b. The other   c. The another

8. There are a few _____ countries that have a king or a queen, but I can't remember which ones.
   a. others   b. other   c. another

9. Scandinavia consists of four countries. One is Denmark. _____ are Finland, Norway, and Sweden.
   a. The other   b. The others   c. Others

10. Canada has ten provinces. French is the official language of Quebec province. English is the language of _____ provinces.
    a. others   b. another   c. the other

11. Washington is one of the five states of the United States with borders on the Pacific Ocean. What are _____ states?*
    a. other   b. the other   c. the others

PRACTICE 10 ▸ Forms of *other*. (Chart 8-6)
Choose the correct completions.

1. A: How much longer until we get home?

   B: We're almost there. We have   other / another   20 minutes.

2. A: This road is expensive! I see we have to pay more money at the next toll booth.

   B: Right. I think we have to pay   another / others   three dollars.

3. A: So you didn't buy that house way out in the country?

   B: No, it's too far from work. I have to drive ten miles to work now. I don't want to add   another / the another   ten miles to the trip.

4. A: I heard you moved out of your apartment.

   B: That's right. They raised the rent by 100 euros. I didn't want to pay   other / another   100 euros.

5. A: How was the test?

   B: I am sure that I failed. I didn't finish. I needed   other / another   ten or fifteen minutes to finish.

6. A: Who won the game?

   B: The other team. In the last minute of the game, our team scored six points, not enough to win; we needed   another / other   eight points.

*See the Answer Key for the answer to this question.

PRACTICE 11 ▸ Common expressions with *other*. (Chart 8-7)

Complete the sentences in Column A with a phrase from Column B.

Column A

1. John loves Mary and Mary loves John. They love _____.

2. Nobody in my class understands this poem _____ Ron, who seems to understand everything.

3. The discussion group doesn't meet every week; it meets _____ week, that is, twice a month.

4. A tiger is a feline; _____, it's a cat, a big cat.

5. The children jumped into the water one by one, in a line, _____.

6. What? The letter carrier quit his job? I saw him just _____. He seemed happy.

Column B

a. every other

b. one after another

c. the other day

d. each other

e. in other words

f. other than

PRACTICE 12 ▸ Review. (Chapters 6–8)

Read the passage and correct the errors.

Cyber Security

Who are hackers?

Hackers look for weaknesses in a computer system. They use the weaknesses to break into computer systems or computer networks. Some hackers break into computer systems because he enjoys the challenge. The others work for large companies. These companies hire hackers to find weaknesses and point it out. Afterwards, the companies fix the weaknesses. Another hackers have criminal motivations. These hacker create viruses and worms. They steal important informations, such as the passwords and bank account numbers.

What are viruses and worms?

A computer virus is piece of code. Viruses attach themself to files and programs. They copy themself and spread to each computers they come in contact with. They often spread through email messages or Internet downloads. Some viruses slow down computers. Anothers completely disable computers.

Worms are similar to viruses, but they do not need to attach to a files or programs. Worms use networks to send copies of its code to others computers.

How can you protect your devices?

There are much ways to protect your devices. To start with, keep your firewall on. A firewall is software program or piece of hardware. It protects your device from hackers. Second, install anti-virus software. This software finds and removes viruses and worms. Next, keep your operating system up to date. Newer operating systems have fixed a lot of the security problem from the old versions. Finally, don't open an attachments or download anything from a unfamiliar person.

PRACTICE 1 ▸ Preview.
Read the passage. Underline the 10 modal verbs.

Applying to a University

Thank you for your interest in State University. You **must meet** certain entrance requirements before you **can apply** for admission. Each academic department has different requirements. You **should read** the specific requirements for your major. All applicants **must submit** a completed application form, entrance exam results, high school or college transcripts, and an application fee.

You **must submit** your application electronically. All students **must take** at least one entrance exam. Some majors **may require** more than one exam. The testing agency **will send** all entrance exam results directly to the university. Your high school or college **may send** your transcripts electronically or by mail in a sealed envelope. You **may pay** the application fee online with a credit card payment or mail a check or money order to the Office of Admissions.

PRACTICE 2 ▸ Expressing necessity: *must, have to, have got to* (Chart 9-2)
Choose the correct completions. More than one answer may be possible.

1. The application deadline is next week. I _____ to submit my application as soon as possible.
   a. must   b. have got   c. has

2. Sarah and I are taking our entrance exam tomorrow. We _____ arrive at the testing center by 9:00 A.M.
   a. must   b. have got   c. have to

3. We _____ to bring identification, such as a driver's license, to the testing center.
   a. must   b. have got   c. have

4. Sarah doesn't have a driver's license. She _____ bring her passport instead.
   a. must   b. has to   c. have to

5. Have you taken the entrance exam yet, or do you still _____ take it?
   a. must   b. has to   c. have to

PRACTICE 3 ▸ Expressing lack of necessity and prohibition. (Chart 9-3)
Complete the sentences with ***must not*** or ***don't have to***.

1. a. We _____ do tonight's homework. It is extra credit work.

   b. We _____ turn in our homework late. The professor does not accept late work.

2. a. You _____ park in a fire lane. It is prohibited.

   b. You _____ park this far away. There are plenty of open spaces near the building.

3. a. The university does not allow smoking in the campus buildings. You _____ smoke within 25 feet of any campus building.

   b. I can read the "No smoking" signs. You _____ tell me.

4. a. We _____ stay in the library past 10:00. It closes at that time.

   b. The library is open tomorrow, but it is a school holiday. We _____ be on campus.

PRACTICE 4 ▶ Expressing necessity, lack of necessity, and prohibition. (Charts 9-2 and 9-3)
Read the statements. Then check (✓) the box that describes each item.

	Necessity	Lack of Necessity	Prohibition
1. Taxpayers must pay their taxes by April 15th.	✓		
2. You must not touch electrical wires.			
3. Students don't have to register on campus. They can register by computer.			
4. We've got to hurry! We don't want to miss our flight!			
5. You don't have to pay for the car all at once. You can pay month by month.			
6. Passengers must show their boarding passes and their IDs when they go through security.			
7. A person has to be 17 years old to obtain a driver's license in many states.			
8. Doctors have to graduate from medical school and pass special exams before they can practice medicine.			
9. Soldiers must not disobey a superior officer.			
10. Nobody has to come to work tomorrow! The company has given everybody a day off.			

PRACTICE 5 ▶ Expressing necessity, lack of necessity, and prohibition. (Charts 9-2 and 9-3)
Choose the correct completions.

1. Plants _____ have water or they will die.
   a. must   b. don't have to   c. must not

2. A lot of people _____ leave their homes to go to work. They can work from their home offices.
   a. must   b. don't have to   c. must not

3. To stay alive, people _____ breathe oxygen.
   a. must   b. don't have to   c. must not

4. People who have diabetes will have serious health problems if they eat foods with a lot of sugar.

   They _____ eat foods with a lot of sugar.
   a. must   b. don't have to   c. must not

5. A salesperson _____ motivate people to buy his or her product.
   a. has to   b. doesn't have to   c. must not

6. You _____ finish your work on this project before you go on vacation. Your job is in danger.
   a. must   b. must not   c. don't have to

7. My room is a mess, but I _____ clean it before I go out tonight. I can do it in the morning.
   a. have got to   b. must not   c. don't have to

8. I _____ get some help with my statistics course. If I don't, I won't pass it.
   a. have got to   b. must not   c. don't have to

9. Yoko _____ study for her English tests. She understands everything without studying.
   a. has to   b. must not   c. doesn't have to

10. Everywhere in the world, stealing is against the law. People _____ steal.
    a. must   b. must not   c. don't have to

PRACTICE 6 ▶ Advisability: should, ought to, had better. (Chart 9-4)
Choose the sentence with the stronger meaning.

1. a. I should study.
   b. I'd better study.

2. a. You must turn right here.
   b. You should turn right here.

3. a. He's got to get a warmer jacket.
   b. He ought to get a warmer jacket.

4. a. You should get new tires for your car.
   b. You'd better get new tires for your car.

5. a. They shouldn't say those words.
   b. They must not say those words.

6. a. Jane had better not tell anyone about this.
   b. Jane shouldn't tell anyone about this.

7. a. You must not drink the water here.
   b. You shouldn't drink the water here.

8. a. We don't have to vote for John Turner.
   b. We shouldn't vote for John Turner.

PRACTICE 7 ▸ Advisability: *should, ought to, had better*. (Chart 9-4)
Cross out the ideas that are not good advice for each situation, or are not relevant to the situation.
More than one answer may be possible.

1. José wants to lose weight.
   a. He should exercise regularly.
   b. ~~He should eat a lot of sweets.~~
   c. He should go on a diet.

2. Ludmila wants to go to medical school in a few years.
   a. She should study poetry now.
   b. She should take science and math courses now.
   c. She should start saving money for tuition.

3. Ikira is a concert pianist.
   a. He should take good care of his hands.
   b. He should go bowling often.
   c. He should visit his grandmother often.

4. Mia is failing her math class.
   a. She should drink a lot of black coffee.
   b. She should get a tutor to help her.
   c. She should study more.

5. Beth wants her flowers to grow.
   a. She should water them.
   b. She should take a math class.
   c. She should give the flowers plant food as directed.

6. Ira sprained his ankle.
   a. He should practice standing on it.
   b. He should rest his ankle.
   c. He should put ice on it.

PRACTICE 8 ▸ Advisability: *should, ought to, had better*. (Chart 9-4)
Give advice to the people in the following situations. Write the letter of the piece of advice that fits each
situation.

   a. call home and talk to his family quite often
   b. change his clothes before he goes
   c. clean it up right away
   d. get his roommate a set of earphones
   e. join some clubs to meet people with similar interests
   f. make her own decisions about her career
   g. stop for gas as soon as we see a station
   h. take it back now so you won't have to pay any more money

1. Ann would like to make some new friends. She should _____.

2. We're running out of gas! We had better _____.

3. Sam and Tim, both teenagers, have messed up the house, and their parents are coming home soon.

   They had better _____.

4. You are going to have to pay a fine because your library book is overdue. You ought to _____.

5. Ron is wearing jeans. He has to go to a wedding this evening. He had better _____.

6. Mary's parents expect her to work in the family business, a shoe store, but she is an adult and wants

   to be an architect. She should _____.

7. Richard's roommate, Charlie, stays up very late studying. While Charlie is studying, he listens to loud music, and Richard can't get to sleep. Richard ought to _____.

8. Pierre is feeling really homesick these days. He should _____.

PRACTICE 9 ▸ Expectation: *be supposed to*. (Chart 9-5)
Rewrite the sentences with a form of *be supposed to* + *verb*.

1. Allen is expected to arrive at seven o'clock.

   Allen _____ at seven o'clock.

2. I'm expected to go hiking with Beth on Saturday, but I'd really rather sleep late.

   I _____ hiking with Beth on Saturday, but I'd really rather sleep late.

3. The weather is expected to be nice over the weekend.

   It _____ nice over the weekend.

4. The plane was expected to arrive at 6:35, but it didn't.

   The plane _____ at 6:35, but it didn't.

5. I was expecting my friends to come over tonight, but they didn't.

   They _____ tonight, but they didn't.

6. Our dog is very independent. We expect him to run to us when we call his name, but he completely ignores us.

   Our dog _____ to us when we call his name, but he completely ignores us.

PRACTICE 10 ▸ Expectation: *should*. (Chart 9-5)
Rewrite the sentences in blue with *should*.

1. The movie has excellent reviews. **I expect it to be a good movie.**

   _____

2. The movie came out a year ago. **I expect it is available online now.**

   _____

3. It is a comedy. **I expect it to be funny.**

   _____

4. The lead actor appears in a new movie every year. **I expect he will appear in a new movie soon.**

   _____

PRACTICE 11 ▸ Ability: *can, know how to*, and *be able to*. (Chart 9-6)
Part I. Rewrite the sentences using *be able to*.

1. Kevin can speak four languages.

   _____

2. Please speak more loudly. I can't hear you.

   _____

3. Can you arrive early tomorrow?

   _____

4. I can understand your point of view.

   _____

Part II. Rewrite the sentences using **know how to**.

1. Ikuko can create a PowerPoint presentation.

   _____

2. Lucy failed her driving test. She can't parallel park.

   _____

3. Mazzen can code in JavaScript.

   _____

4. Can you fix my computer?

   _____

PRACTICE 12 ▸ Possibility: *can, may, might.* (Chart 9-7)
Complete the sentences with **can, may,** or **might** to express possibility.

1. I have a meeting tonight. I _____ be home late.

2. Joe _____ rent an apartment in the suburbs.

3. Apartments in the city limits _____ be very expensive.

4. Bring an umbrella. It _____ rain this afternoon.

5. I usually dress in layers in the spring. The weather _____ be cool.

PRACTICE 13 ▸ Polite requests with *I* as the subject; polite requests with *you* as the subject. (Chart 9-8)
Complete the sentences with a phrase in the box.

Can I help you	Could you please repeat
Can you hurry	May I borrow
could you help me	Would you please give me

1. A: Oh, no! I've lost my passport. Rick, _____ find it?

   B: OK. I'll be right there.

2. A: Oh, no! I've lost my passport.

   B: _____, Jenny? Maybe I can find it for you.

3. A: I'm sorry. Mr. Robbins isn't in today. Do you want to leave a message on his voicemail?

   B: Well, it's very important. _____ his cell phone number?

4. A: _____ your dictionary, please?

   B: Sure.

5. A: OK, sir. I'll be there sometime today to fix your refrigerator.

   B: _____, please? The frozen food is melting fast!

6. A: Students, do you understand the assignment?

   B: Not really, Dr. Johnson. _____ what you said?

PRACTICE 14 ▸ Polite requests with *Would you mind.* (Chart 9-9)
Complete the sentences with *if I* + the present tense or the *-ing* form of the verb.

1. a. I want you to cook dinner. Would you mind _____*cooking*_____ dinner?

   b. I want to cook dinner. Would you mind _____*if I cooked*_____ dinner?

2. a. We want you to take us to the airport. Would you mind _____ us to the airport?

   b. We want to take you to the airport. Would you mind _____ you to the airport?

3. a. I want to open the windows. Would you mind _____ the windows?

   b. I want you to open the windows. Would you mind _____ the windows?

4. a. We want you to join us for lunch. Would you mind _____ us for lunch?

   b. We want to join you for lunch. Would you mind _____ you for lunch?

5. a. I want you to write a letter to the boss. Would you mind _____ a letter to the boss?

   b. I want to write a letter to the boss. Would you mind _____ a letter to the boss?

PRACTICE 15 ▸ Polite requests with *Would you mind.* (Chart 9-9)
Complete the sentences with the verbs in parentheses. Write *if I* + the past tense or the *-ing* form of the verb. In some sentences, either response is possible, but the meaning is different.

1. A: It's cold in here. Would you mind (*close*) _____*closing*_____ the window?

   B: Not at all. I'd be glad to.

2. A: It's cold in here. Would you mind (*close*) _____*if I closed*_____ the window?

   B: Not at all. Go right ahead. I think it's cold in here too.

3. A: You're going to the library? Would you mind (*take*) _____ this book back to the library for me?

   B: Not at all.

4. A: I'm not feeling well at all. Would you mind (*go*) _____ home now?

   B: Oh, I'm sorry. I hope you can come back when you feel better.

5. A: I'm not feeling well at all. Would you mind (*leave*) _____ now before the visiting hours are over?

   B: Oh, of course not. We shouldn't stay more than a short time for a hospital visit anyway.

6. A: I'll be working late tonight, honey. Would you mind (*cook*) _____ dinner tonight? I'll clean up after dinner.

   B: I'd be happy to. About what time do you think you'll be home?

7. A: We have a lot of chicken left over from dinner last night. Would you mind (*make*) _____ a chicken salad from the leftovers for dinner tonight?

   B: No, that'll be good. You make a great chicken salad.

8. A: I'm exhausted. Chopping wood in the hot sun is hard on me. Would you mind
   (*finish*) _____ the work yourself?

   B: No problem, Grandpa. Why don't you go in and rest? I'll finish up.

9. A: Would you mind (*use*) _____ your name as a reference on this job application?

   B: Not at all. In fact, ask them to call me.

10. A: I'd like to apply for the job as department manager. Would you mind
    (*recommend*) _____ me to the boss?

    B: No. As a matter of fact, I was thinking of recommending you myself.

PRACTICE 16 ▸ Making suggestions: *let's, why don't, shall I / we.* (Chart 9-10)
Choose the correct completions. More than one answer may be possible.

1. _____ we go out for dinner tonight?
   a. Shall   b. Why do   c. Let's   d. Why don't

2. _____ home and watch a movie.
   a. Why not staying   b. Let's stay   c. Why not we stay   d. Shall stay

3. Why _____ the teacher for help?
   a. you not ask   b. don't you ask   c. you ask   d. don't you to ask

4. It's cold in this room. _____ the window?
   a. Why don't I close b. Shall I close   c. Let's closing   d. I shall

5. Why don't we _____ for lunch tomorrow?
   a. meeting   b. meets   c. meet   d. met

6. _____ go out tonight. I have a test in the morning.
   a. Let's don't   b. Let's not   c. Let's no   d. Don't lets

PRACTICE 17 ▸ Chapter review.
Correct the modal verb errors.

1. Our teacher can to speak five languages.

2. Oh, this table is heavy! Jim, may you help me move it?

3. We come to class on weekdays. We are not have to come to class on weekends.

4. Park here. It's free. You must not pay anything.

5. When you speak in front of the judge, you must to tell the truth. You must not tell lies.

6. Pat looks tired. She should gets some rest.

7. I not able to go to the party this weekend.

8. The children are suppose to be in bed by nine o'clock.

9. The Garcias supposed to be here at 7:00, but I think they will be late, as usual.

10. We're going to make chicken for dinner. Why you don't join us?

11. Here's my advice about your diet, Mr. Jackson. You could not eat a lot of sugar and salt.

12. A: This is wonderful music. Will we dance?

    B: No, let's don't dance. Let's just sit here and talk.

CHAPTER 10

Modals, Part 2

PRACTICE 1 ▸ Preview.
Read the passage. Underline the four modals.

A Surprise Victory

Last Friday's soccer match should have been an easy game for the Wildcats. Their team had an undefeated record this season. However, fans couldn't believe it when the Falcons defeated the Wildcats 5-2. It was the first win of the season for the Falcons. The Falcons must have practiced very hard to achieve their surprise victory. The next Falcons game is this Friday at 6:00 P.M. on their home field. It should be an exciting game!

PRACTICE 2 ▸ Repeated action in the past. (Chart 10-1)
Complete the sentences with *would* or *used to* and a verb in the box. Use *would* when possible. Use any words in parentheses.

bring	fall	listen	say	stay	throw
come	have	live	sleep	tell	wipe

1. I'll always remember Miss Emerson, my fifth-grade teacher. Sometimes a student

   _____ asleep in her class. Whenever that happened, Miss Emerson

   _____ a piece of chalk at the student!

2. My father never liked to talk on the phone. Whenever it rang, he

   (*always*) _____, "I'm not here!" Usually, he was only joking and

   _____ to the phone when it was for him.

3. I have fond childhood memories of my Aunt Betsy. Whenever she came to visit, she

   (*always*) _____ me a little present.

4. My uncle Oscar _____ with us when I was a child. He had some strange habits.

   For example, he (*always*) _____ his plate with his napkin whenever

   he sat down to a meal.

5. When I was in college, I _____ some bad habits. I didn't study until the night

   before a test, and then I _____ up all night studying. Then the next day after

   the test, I _____ all afternoon.

6. I'll never forget the wonderful evenings I spent with my grandparents when I was a child. My

   grandmother _____ stories of her childhood seventy years ago, and we

   _____ intently and ask a lot of questions.

PRACTICE 3 ▸ Past tense of *must* and *have to*. (Chart 10-2)
Rewrite the sentences using the past tense.

1. You must use blue ink on the form.

   _____

2. The students have to memorize 100 new words a week.

   _____

3. Sylvia has to cancel her summer vacation plans.

   _____

4. Who do you have to call?

   _____

5. The children must get vaccinations.

   _____

6. The passengers have to fasten their seat belts because of the turbulent weather.

   _____

PRACTICE 4 ▸ The past form of *should*. (Chart 10-2)
Give advice about the situation using the past form of ***should***. Complete each sentence with a verb in the box. Use any words in parentheses.

buy	come	order	take	visit
change	keep	stay	turn	watch

1. A: We're having hamburgers? I thought you were cooking a turkey for the holiday.

   B: I did, but I cooked it for too long. It burned up in the oven! I _____

   it out after three hours, but I forgot.

2. A: Where are we? Are we lost?

   B: I think we are. We _____ left instead of right at the last intersection.

3. A: I'm tired this morning! What time did we finally go to bed last night?

   B: Around 2:00 A.M. We (*not*) _____ that late movie.

4. A: Is Lionel angry at you?

   B: He is. I _____ his mother when she was so sick, but I didn't.

5. A: Beautiful shoes! Where did you buy them?

   B: I bought them at Norwalk's, but I _____ them online. They were

   a lot cheaper there.

6. A: How was dinner at Henri's?

   B: Not so good. I had the fish, but it didn't taste fresh. I _____

   something else.

7. A: Why are you upset with Frank?

   B: He came to work today with a terrible cold, coughing and sneezing all over us! He

   (*not*) _____ to work today.

   He _____ home.

8. A: Are you glad you took the new job?

   B: No, actually, I'm not. I (*not*) _____ jobs.

   I _____ my old job.

PRACTICE 5 ▸ Present and past forms of *should*. (Chart 10-2)

Give advice in each situation. Complete each sentence with the present or past form of ***should*** and the verb in parentheses.

1. Travel teaches us about the world. Everyone (*travel*) _____.

2. We did not travel to Africa when we had the opportunity last year.

   We (*go*) _____ at that time.

3. Our house will look much better with a fresh coat of paint. It will look good in a yellow

   color. I think we (*paint*) _____ our house, and the color

   (*be*) _____ yellow.

4. We painted our house. Now it's white and has beige shutters. It doesn't look good. We

   (*not, paint*) _____ our house in such dull colors.

5. Ernie is allergic to shellfish. Last night he ate shellfish, and he broke out with terrible hives. Ernie

   (*not, eat*) _____ that shellfish.

6. Some people are sensitive to caffeine. They cannot fall asleep at night if they drink coffee in the

   afternoon. These people (*not, drink*) _____ coffee after 12:00 P.M. They

   (*drink*) _____ decaffeinated coffee or tea instead.

7. Years ago, people did not realize that some species were dying off because of human activity. For

   example, many buffalo in North America were killed because of human thoughtlessness. As a result,

   there are few buffalo left in North America. People (*not, kill*) _____

   those buffalo.

8. Today, people are making efforts to save the environment and to save endangered species. We

   (*make*) _____ strong efforts to recycle, conserve our resources, and

   nourish endangered species.

PRACTICE 6 ▸ Past forms of *be supposed to*. (Chart 10-2)

Rewrite the sentences. Use a form of ***be supposed to*** + *verb*.

1. The plane was expected to arrive at 6:35, but it didn't.

   The plane _____ at 6:35, but it didn't.

2. I was expecting my friends to come over tonight, but they didn't.

   They _____ tonight, but they didn't.

3. I was expecting to give a presentation in class today, but we ran out of time.

   I _____ a presentation in class today, but we ran out of time.

4. Weather forecasters expected it to snow today, but it didn't.

It _____ today, but it didn't.

5. Did your teacher expect you to turn in your essay today?

_____ your essay today?

PRACTICE 7 ▶ Ability: *can* and *could*. (Chart 10-3)
Complete the sentences with *can, can't, could,* or *couldn't.*

1. Fish _____ talk.

2. My uncle was a wonderful craftsman. He made beautiful things out of wood. But he

_____ read or write because he never went to school.

3. A bilingual person _____ speak two languages.

4. I _____ get to sleep last night because it was too hot in my room.

5. Why _____ all the nations of the world just get along in peace? Why are there always

wars somewhere on earth?

6. When I was younger, I _____ stay up past midnight and get up at dawn feeling ready

to go. I _____ do that any longer now that I'm middle-aged.

7. I was sitting in the back of the classroom today. I _____ hear the professor.

_____ I borrow your notes?

PRACTICE 8 ▶ Degrees of certainty: present time. (Chart 10-4)
How certain is the speaker when making each of the following remarks? Check (✓) the appropriate box.

	100%	About 95%	About 50% or less
1. Charlotte might be home by now.			✓
2. Phil must be home now.			
3. Mr. Brown's at home now.			
4. Lilly must know the answer to this question.			
5. Fred might have the answer.			
6. Shelley knows the answer.			
7. Those people must have a lot of money.			
8. You may remember me from high school.			
9. We could be related!			
10. Traffic might be heavy on the interstate.			

PRACTICE 9 ▸ Degrees of certainty: present time. (Chart 10-4)

Choose the correct completions. In some sentences, both answers are correct.

1. A: Drive slowly! This is a school zone. Children are crossing the street here.

   B: It ____ be three o'clock. That's the time that school is out.
      a. must   b. might

2. A: Professor McKeon says that we're going to have a very high inflation rate next year.

   B: He ____ be right. He knows more about economics than anyone I know.
      a. must   b. could

3. A: Have you heard anything from Ed? Is he still on safari in Africa?

   B: He ____ be, or he ____ already be on his way home. I'm just not sure.
      a. must ... must   b. may ... may

4. A: Is that a famous celebrity over there in the middle of that crowd?

   B: It ____ be. She's signing autographs.
      a. must   b. might

5. A: Isn't Peter Reeves a banker?

   B: Yes. Why don't you talk to him? He ____ be able to help you with your loan.
      a. must   b. may

6. A: Is Margaret's daughter 16 yet?

   B: She ____ be. I saw her driving a car, and you have to be at least 16 to get a driver's license.
      a. must   b. might

7. A: Overall, don't you think the possibility of world peace is greater now than ever before?

   B: It ____ be. I don't know. Political relationships can be fragile.
      a. must   b. may

8. A: What's the matter with my son, doctor? Why does he cough and sneeze every day?

   B: He's allergic to something. It ____ dust in the house, or certain foods, or pollen in the air, or something else. It's hard to know, so we'll do some tests to find out.
      a. must be   b. may be

9. A: The speedometer on my car is broken. Do you think I'm driving over the speed limit?

   B: I can't tell. It doesn't seem like it, but you ____ .
      a. must be   b. could be

10. A: You've been on the go all day. Aren't you exhausted?

    B: Yes, I ____ . I can't remember when I've ever been this worn out.
       a. am   b. must be

11. A: I thought this movie was a comedy!

    B: Me too, but it ____ sad. Look at the people leaving the theater. A lot of them are crying.
       a. might be   b. must be

12. A: How old do you think Roger is?

    B: I just saw his driver's license. He ____ 33.
       a. could be   b. is

PRACTICE 10 ▶ Degrees of certainty: present time negative. (Chart 10-5)

Complete the sentences with the correct phrase in the box.

> a. can't be him
> b. can't be true
> c. may not be
>
> d. may not speak
> e. must not get
> f. must not like

1. A: I can't hear the singers! That man sitting behind us is snoring in his sleep!

   B: I hear him! He _____ opera.

2. A: Look! Isn't that our history professor over there? In the yellow sweater!

   B: No, that _____. He's in Tokyo this week, giving a presentation.

3. A: This coffee doesn't taste very good. It's supposed to be 100% Arabica.

   B: It _____ 100% Arabica. Maybe they mixed it with something else. Maybe it's a blend.

4. A: Who is that woman standing alone over there? She isn't talking to anyone.

   B: Well, she _____ any English. Or maybe she's very shy. Anyway, let's go over and try to talk to her.

5. A: Jane has been accepted at Harvard, I heard.

   B: No way! That _____. She isn't even a good student.

6. A: Did you see the new pickup truck that Mario's driving?

   B: I sure did. It's very big. It _____ good gas mileage.

PRACTICE 11 ▶ Degrees of certainty: past time. (Chart 10-6)

Choose the sentence that describes the given sentences.

1. The little boy is crying. His knees are scraped and bleeding.
   a. He may have fallen down.
   b. He must have fallen down.

2. Someone called, but I don't know who it was. Maybe it was Alice, but I'm not sure.
   a. It may have been Alice.
   b. It must have been Alice.

3. Nobody's answering the phone at Juan's apartment. I guess he has already left for the airport. He always likes to get to the airport early, you know.
   a. He might have already left for the airport.
   b. He must have already left for the airport.

4. I've lost track of my old friend Lola from high school. Maybe she moved away. Maybe she got married and has a different last name.
   a. She could have moved away.
   b. She must have moved away.

5. Irv looks unhappy today. Maybe his boss criticized him. Maybe he had an argument with his girlfriend. Maybe he lost a lot of money in the stock market.
   a. Irv might have had an argument with his girlfriend.
   b. Irv must have had an argument with his girlfriend.

6. I told Charles — only Charles — about my secret engagement, but now everyone is congratulating me! It's clear that Charles can't keep a secret.
   a. Charles may have told everyone.
   b. Charles must have told everyone.

PRACTICE 12 ▶ Degrees of certainty: past time negative. (Chart 10-6)
Write the past negative of an appropriate modal and the verb in parentheses.

1.   ANN: I've called Howard ten times, I'm sure. He doesn't answer his cell phone.

      SAM: He (*remember*) _____ you were going to call him.

            He's a little forgetful, you know. I'll bet he forgot to turn his phone on.

2.   LAWYER: Mr. Jones, where were you on the night of June 24th?

      MR. JONES: I was at home. I was at home all night.

      LAWYER: You (*be*) _____ at home on that night, Mr. Jones.

            Four witnesses saw you at the victim's apartment.

3.   JIM: Look! There are lights on in the Thompsons' house. Didn't they go away on vacation?

      ANN: They (*leave*) _____ yet. Or maybe they left the automatic

            timer on to deter burglars.

4.   BOB: Hey, you guys! You are not supposed to ride your bikes on the sidewalk! You could crash

            into someone!

      SUE: They (*hear*) _____ you, Bob. Look! They just kept going.

5. Scientists are not sure why the Mayan civilization collapsed. The Mayans

   (*have*) _____ enough to eat, or perhaps their enemies became

   too strong for them.

6. After his voyage on the *Kon Tiki,* Thor Heyerdahl set forth the theory that modern Polynesians

   descended from ancient South Americans. However, later scientists believe this

   (*happen*) _____. They believe it was impossible because of

   recent DNA evidence to the contrary.

PRACTICE 13 ▶ Degrees of certainty: present and past time. (Charts 10-4 → 10-6)
Complete the conversations with *must* and the verb in parentheses. Use the correct present or past
form. Use *not* if necessary.

1. A: You got here in 20 minutes! You (*drive*) _____ really fast. Normally

      it's a 40-minute drive.

   B: No faster than usual.

2. A: Sally gave a speech at her graduation. I think I saw tears in her parents' eyes.

   B: Oh, that is touching. They (*be*) _____ very proud of her.

3. A: That's strange. Oscar didn't come to the meeting. He never misses a meeting.

   B: He (*know*) _____ about it. He was out of town all last week, and

   probably no one told him.

4. A: How old do you think our teacher is?

   B: Well, she was a couple of years ahead of my father in college, so she

   (*be*) _____ around 55 now.

5. A: Uh-oh! I can't find my credit card.

   B: You (*leave*) _____ it at the cash register at the grocery store.

6. A: Have you seen Clark? I can't find him anywhere.

   B: He was feeling terrible. He (*go*) _____ home a while ago.

7. A: Look! Do you see that big bird on top of the tree?

   B: What big bird?

   A: You can't see that? You (*need*) _____ stronger glasses.

8. A: What happened to your knee?

   B: I twisted it very badly in the tennis match.

   A: Oh! That (*hurt*) _____ a lot!

PRACTICE 14 ▸ *Must have* vs. *had to*. (Charts 9-2 and 10-6)
Choose the correct response.

1. ANN: Why didn't you come to the party?
   BOB: a. I had to study.   b. I must have studied.

2. SAM: Where's Sally? She's still not here?
   DAN: a. She must have overslept.   b. She had to oversleep.

3. IRA: Thomas missed an important meeting this morning.
   JAN: I just spoke with him and he's very sick. He told me he . . .
        a. had to go to the doctor's.   b. must have gone to the doctor's.

4. BOB: We're out of coffee again.
   TOM: a. Jane must have forgotten to get some.   b. Jane had to forget to get some.

5. PAT: How were you able to stay awake during that long, boring lecture?
   ONA: It was difficult!
        a. I must have drunk a lot of coffee!   b. I had to drink a lot of coffee!

6. LIL: I can't sleep again!
   MAX: a. You must have drunk too   b. You had to drink too
        much coffee today.   much coffee today.

PRACTICE 15 ▸ Degrees of certainty: future time. (Chart 10-7)
Complete the sentences in Column A with a phrase from Column B.

Column A

1. Keiko has always loved animals. She's in veterinary school now. She should _____ .

2. Most apple trees bear fruit about five years after planting. Our apple tree is four years old. It should _____ next year.

3. Aunt Ella's plane arrived an hour ago. She's taking a taxi, so she should _____ .

4. We could invest this money in a conservative stock fund. If we do that, we should _____ at the end of a year.

5. Ali should _____ . He's been studying hard for it all semester.

6. The little horse is growing very fast. He should _____ in a year.

7. Bake the fish in the oven at 350 degrees. It should _____ in about ten minutes.

8. Take this medicine every morning. You should _____ in about two weeks.

9. Luis is taking a heavy course load. He wants to finish school quickly. He should _____ .

10. The mechanic is fixing the car now. It should _____ .

Column B

a. be here just in time for dinner

b. do very well on the final exam

c. feel better

d. double his weight

e. make a great veterinarian

f. have about 5% more

g. be fixed before five o'clock

h. graduate next June

i. be moist and tender

j. give us some apples

PRACTICE 16 ▸ Degrees of certainty: future time. (Chart 10-7)
Choose the correct completions.

1. Today is Monday. Tomorrow   should / will   be Tuesday.

2. Hello, Jack. This is Arturo in the tech department. I'm working on your computer now. Good news — I can fix it pretty easily and it   should / must   be ready by 5:00 P.M. today.

3. My son's birthday is next month. He   should / will   be two years old.

4. It's ten minutes to four. The next bus   must / should   arrive at four o'clock. The buses usually stop here every hour on the hour.

5. A: Don't be late! They won't let you into the theater after the play begins.
   B: OK. I   will / should   be at the theater at 7:15. I promise.

6. Your husband is resting comfortably, Ms. Robbins. I'm giving him some antibiotics, so the infection   must / should   clear up quickly.

7. A: Look up there. Is that Mars?
   B: I don't think so. Mars isn't visible right now. It   should / must   be Venus. Venus is visible now.

8. A: Who's going to win the tennis tournament?
   B: Well, the Australian is highly rated, and she   must / should   win, but the Serbian is good too. Maybe she'll surprise us and win.

PRACTICE 17 ▸ Progressive forms of modals. (Chart 10-8)
Complete the sentences. Use the appropriate progressive forms of *must*, *should*, or *may* / *might* / *could* and a verb in the box. You may use a verb more than once.

date	fly	hike	kid	sleep	work

1. A: Call Phil. He's at his office now.

   B: Let's email him instead. He _____ on something important at the moment. Or maybe he's with a client.

2. A: When will Betty be back from Italy?

   B: Tonight. She _____ over the Atlantic at this very moment.

3. A: Helga must know the answer to this problem. Shall we call her?

   B: Not now. It's 11:00 P.M. She _____ .

4. A: Listen, I just heard this. Mr. Milner isn't going to be our teacher anymore. He has joined the army.

   B: You _____! That can't be true. Who told you that?

5. A: Sara told me that she had won the lottery, and so she invited us all to dinner at Henri's French restaurant.

   B: Oh, she _____ when she said that. She never plays the lottery!

6. A: What do you think Ann's doing now on her vacation?

   B: Oh, she _____ in the mountains. Or maybe she's relaxing at the pool.

7. A: I was hoping to go out with John, but I heard he's dating Julia.

   B: Well, he (*not*) _____ Julia anymore. I think that they may have broken up.

PRACTICE 18 ▸ Combining modals with phrasal modals. (Chart 10-9)
Complete each sentence with the given words. Write the words in their correct order in the sentences.

1. to \ get \ have

   You _____*have to get*_____ a passport if you are going to travel in other countries.

2. be \ should \ to \ able \ complete

   Everyone _____ this form easily.

3. have \ to \ won't \ stand

   People _____ in the line for a long time. The line is moving quickly.

4. you \ be \ able \ leave \ to \ will

   When _____ here?

5. not \ able \ to \ graduate \ to \ going \ am \ be

   I _____ with my class. I lost a complete semester when I was sick.

6. been \ must \ to \ get \ have \ not \ able

   Mike and Helen haven't arrived yet. They were going to try to get on an earlier flight. They _____ on the earlier flight.

PRACTICE 19 ▸ Expressing preference: *would rather.* (Chart 10-10)
Complete the sentences with a form of ***would rather*** and a verb in the box. Use any words in parentheses.

eat	go	have	sail	say	study

1. I know you want to know, but I (*not*) _____ anything more about this
   topic. I told Marge that I'd keep it a secret.
2. Last night, I _____ home right after dinner at the restaurant,
   but my friends insisted on going back to John's apartment to listen to some music and talk.
3. I _____ history and literature in college than study
   business as I did. I majored in business, and now that's all I know. I might never again have the
   opportunity to learn about history and literature.
4. If you insist, we'll go to the pizza place after the movie, but I
   (*not*) _____ pizza again. I'm tired of it.
5. Do you think that young people _____ a choice about whom to
   marry, or do you think that they prefer their parents to choose a partner for them?
6. I like my work a lot, but my favorite thing is sailing. I love sailing. At this moment, even though I
   have just been promoted to vice-president of my company, I _____
   right now instead of sitting here in my office.

PRACTICE 20 ▸ Chapter review.
Choose the correct completions.

1. A: Where's Angie? Didn't she come back after lunch?

   B: I'm not sure where she is. But she _____ the presentation that Human Resources is giving
      right now.
      a. is attending   b. could attend   c. could be attending

2. A: You're taking Spanish at 8:00 A.M. every day? Why did you choose such an early class?

   B: Because Ms. Cardenas is the teacher. She _____ excellent. I've been in the class for a month
      now, and I don't mind the early hour.
      a. should be   b. must be   c. is

3. A: The meteorologists predicted five major hurricanes for this hurricane season.

   B: They _____ wrong, you know. Sometimes they make mistakes.
      a. must be   b. might be   c. are

4. A: Is this chicken in the refrigerator still good?

   B: I don't think so. It's been in there for over a month! It _____ spoiled by now.
      a. may be   b. must be   c. could be

5. A: Can you tell me if Flight 86 is on time?

   B: It is on time, sir. It _____ at Gate B21 in about five minutes.
      a. might arrive   b. might be arriving   c. should be arriving

6. A: Did you know that Mike got a scholarship to State School of Engineering?

   B: Yes, I know that! I was the first one he told about it. He _____ very happy.
      a. might be   b. must be   c. is

7. A: Did you know that Li received a scholarship to the City School of Music?

   B: No, I didn't. That's great news! He _____ very happy.
   a. might be   b. must be   c. is

8. A: Who's going to win the election?

   B: It's a close call. The senator _____ with all his experience, but the opposition candidate is stronger than anyone expected.
   a. must win   b. must be winning   c. should win

9. A: Where's Harold? He's supposed to be at this meeting. Didn't Jim tell him about it?

   B: Jim _____ to tell him.
   a. must forget   b. must have forgotten   c. should have forgotten

10. A: This soup has an interesting flavor, but there's too much salt in it.

    B: Yes, it is too salty. I _____ so much salt in it.
    a. must not have put   b. shouldn't have put   c. may not have put

PRACTICE 21 ▶ Chapter review.

Write modal sentences for the situations.

1. The plane is late, and we didn't call the airport.

   a. I expect it will arrive soon. _____ *It should arrive soon.* _____

   b. Maybe it took off late. _____ *It may / might / could have taken off late.* _____

   c. It was a good idea to call the airport, but we didn't. _____ *We should have called the airport.*

2. There's a package in the mail. _____

   a. Maybe it's for me. _____

   b. I'm sure it's for me. _____

   c. It's impossible that it's for me. _____

3. Tom didn't respond to my email.

   a. I expected him to respond. _____

   b. Maybe he didn't get it. _____

   c. I'm pretty sure he didn't get it. _____

   d. His email isn't working. It was impossible for him to get it. _____

   _____

4. There's water all over the kitchen floor.

   a. Perhaps the dishwasher is leaking. _____

   b. The dishwasher is new. It's impossible that it's the dishwasher. _____

   c. I'm pretty sure a pipe is broken. _____

   d. It's a good idea for you to call a plumber. _____

   e. It isn't necessary for us to call a plumber. _____

Read the following passage. Choose all of the possible completions in parentheses.

Distracted Drivers

Distracted drivers often cause major traffic accidents. In the past, before the widespread use of smartphones, drivers   would / could / should   be distracted by eating, reading maps, or grooming. These activities   can / could / might   still cause problems, but one of the biggest issues today is cell phone use. People   can / might / must   use their phones to talk, text, engage in social media, play games, use navigation systems, check their bank accounts, write shopping lists, listen to music, or look up information on the Internet.

Joy has become a leading advocate against distracted driving since she had an accident last year. She hit another car and blacked out. She   can't / couldn't / shouldn't   remember anything about the accident. According to her phone records, she   must have been / must be / must have   talking on the phone when the accident occurred. Luckily, no one was injured. It   could have been / must have been / can have been   much worse. She still feels terrible about the accident. She   shouldn't have been using / shouldn't have used / shouldn't used   her phone while she was driving.

Advocates like Joy are calling for stricter distracted-driving laws. Several places have already adopted laws against texting or using a cell phone at all while driving. With more distracted-driving laws, the roads   should / can / may   become much safer.

CHAPTER 11

The Passive

PRACTICE 1 ▸ Preview.
Read the passage. <u>Underline</u> the seven passive voice verbs.

School Closing

The National Weather Service has issued a winter storm warning. Heavy snowfall is expected early this evening. More than a foot of snow is anticipated by tomorrow morning. Because student safety is our top priority, classes have been canceled for the remainder of the day. The university's business offices are also closed. Residence and dining halls will remain open. Tonight's basketball game has been postponed to next Tuesday. Classes will be canceled all day tomorrow. The university is monitoring the weather closely and will notify the campus community with any additional updates. More details can be found on our school website.

PRACTICE 2 ▸ Forming the passive. (Charts 11-1 and 11-2)
Change the active to the passive by writing the correct form of *be*. Use the same tense for *be* in the passive sentence that is used in the active sentence.

Mrs. Bell answered my question. My question _____*was*_____ **answered** by Mrs. Bell.

1. *simple present:*

   Authors write books. .... Books _____ **written** by authors.

2. *present progressive:*

   Mr. Brown is writing that book. .... That book _____ **written** by Mr. Brown.

3. *present perfect:*

   Ms. Lee has written the report. .... The report _____ **written** by Ms. Lee.

4. *simple past:*

   Bob wrote that letter. .... That letter _____ **written** by Bob.

5. *past progressive:*

   A student was writing the report. .... The report _____ **written** by a student.

6. *past perfect:*

   Lucy had written a memo. .... A memo _____ **written** by Lucy.

7. *simple future:*

   Your teacher will write a report. .... A report _____ **written** by your teacher.

8. *be going to:*

   Tom is going to write a letter. ....The letter _____ **written** by Tom.

9. *future perfect:*

   Alice will have written the report. ....The report _____ **written** by Alice.

10. The judges have made a decision. ....A decision _____ **made** by the judges.

11. Several people saw the accident. ....The accident _____ **seen** by several people.

12. Ann is sending the letters. ....The letters _____ **sent** by Ann.

13. Fred will plan the party. ....The party _____ **planned** by Fred.

14. The medicine had cured my illness. ....My illness _____ **cured** by the medicine.

15. The cat will have caught the mouse. ....The mouse _____ **caught** by the cat.

16. Engineers design bridges. ....Bridges _____ **designed** by engineers.

17. The city is going to build a bridge. ....A bridge _____ **built** by the city.

18. A guard was protecting the jewels. ....The jewels _____ **protected** by a guard.

PRACTICE 3 ▶ Active vs. passive. (Charts 11-1 and 11-2)

Underline the subject of each sentence. Circle the complete verb. Then identify the sentences as active (A) or passive (P).

1. a. _A_ Henry (visited) a national park.

   b. _P_ The park (was visited) by over 10,000 people last month.

2. a. ____ Olga was reading the comics.

   b. ____ Philippe has read all of Tolstoy's novels.

   c. ____ *Bambi* has been read by children all over the world.

3. a. ____ Whales swim in the ocean.

   b. ____ Whales were hunted by fishermen until recently.

4. a. ____ The answer won't be known for several months.

   b. ____ I know the answer.

5. a. ____ Two new houses were built on our street.

   b. ____ A famous architect designed the new bank on First Street.

6. a. ____ The Internet was invented before I was born.

   b. ____ The Internet has expanded the knowledge of people everywhere.

7. a. ____ The World Cup is seen on TV all over the world.

   b. ____ Soccer fans all over the world watch the World Cup on TV.

PRACTICE 4 ▸ Forming the passive. (Chart 11-2)
Complete the sentences. Change the verbs in blue from active to passive.

1. Alex writes the book. → The book _____ *is written* _____ by Alex.
2. Alex is writing the book. → The book _____ by Alex.
3. Alex has written the book. → The book _____ by Alex.
4. Alex wrote the book. → The book _____ by Alex.
5. Alex was writing the book. → The book _____ by Alex.
6. Alex had written the book. → The book _____ by Alex.
7. Alex will write the book. → The book _____ by Alex.
8. Alex is going to write the book. → The book _____ by Alex.
9. Alex will have written the book. → The book _____ by Alex.
10. Did Alex write the book? → _____ the book _____ by Alex?
11. Will Alex write the book? → _____ the book _____ by Alex?
12. Has Alex written the book? → _____ the book _____ by Alex?

PRACTICE 5 ▸ Forming the passive. (Chart 11-2)
Part I. Complete the sentences. Change the verbs from active to passive.

1. Picasso painted that picture.

   That picture was _____ *was painted by Picasso* _____.

2. Experienced pilots fly these planes.

   These planes _____.

3. A famous singer is going to sing the national anthem.

   The national anthem _____.

4. Yale University has accepted my cousin.

   My cousin _____.

5. The doctor will examine the patient.

   The patient _____.

6. The defense attorney is questioning a witness.

   A witness _____.

7. A dog bit our mail carrier.

   Our mail carrier _____.

8. The mother bird was feeding the baby bird.

   The baby bird _____.

9. His words won't persuade me.

   I _____.

10. I didn't paint this picture. Did Laura paint it?

    The picture _____.

    Was it _____?

11. Does Mrs. Crane own this restaurant? I know that her father doesn't own it anymore.

Is this restaurant _____?

I know that it _____.

12. I didn't sign these papers. Someone else signed my name.

These papers _____.

My name _____.

Part II. Change each sentence to the active voice. The subject of the new sentence is given. Keep the same tense of the verb.

1. My teeth are going to be cleaned by the dental assistant.

The dental assistant _____.

2. Was that email sent by Mr. Tyrol?

_____ Mr. Tyrol _____?

3. The Fourth of July isn't celebrated by the British.

The British _____.

4. Has your house been sold by the realtor yet?

_____ the realtor _____?

5. The thief hasn't been caught by the police.

The police _____.

6. The carpets are being cleaned by the carpet cleaners.

The carpet cleaners _____.

PRACTICE 6 ▶ Active vs. passive. (Charts 11-1 and 11-2)
Check (✓) the incorrect sentences.

_____ 1. I wasn't surprised by his message.

__✓__ 2. Accidents are happened every day.

_____ 3. The plane was arrived at nine.

_____ 4. Towels are supplied by the hotel.

_____ 5. Jill's essay was published in a magazine.

_____ 6. Are ghosts existed?

_____ 7. Mr. Lee was died last year.

_____ 8. It hasn't been rained lately.

_____ 9. The speech was delivered by a young politician.

_____ 10. The actress has been appeared in three films this year.

_____ 11. The error was noticed by everyone.

_____ 12. The meeting has been postponed until next week.

PRACTICE 7 ▶ Active vs. passive. (Charts 11-1 and 11-2)
Choose the correct completions.

1. We'll let you know about the job. You _____ by my secretary next week.
   a. will notify   b. will be notified   c. will have notified

2. Last night I _____ to lock my front door.
   a. wasn't remembered   b. didn't remember   c. hadn't been remembered

3. This old wooden desk _____ by my grandfather over 40 years ago.
   a. built   b. had built   c. was built

4. Disneyland is a world-famous amusement park in Southern California. It _____ by millions of people every year.
   a. is visited   b. visited   c. has visited

5. I _____ with people who say space exploration is a waste of money. What do you think?
   a. not agree   b. don't agree   c. am not agree

6. Do you really think that we _____ by creatures from outer space in the near future?
   a. will invade   b. be invaded   c. will be invaded

7. Had you already _____ by this university when you heard about the scholarship offer from the other school?
   a. were accepted   b. accepted   c. been accepted

8. When Jason was only ten, his father _____ .
   a. was died   b. died   c. dead

9. Elephants _____ a long time, sometimes for 70 years.
   a. live   b. were lived   c. have been lived

10. The impact of the earthquake yesterday _____ by people who lived hundreds of kilometers from the epicenter.
   a. felt   b. has felt   c. was felt

11. At one time, the entire world _____ by dinosaurs.
   a. ruled   b. was ruled   c. been ruled

12. Some dinosaurs _____ on their hind legs and were as tall as palm trees.
   a. walked   b. were walked   c. have stood

PRACTICE 8 ▶ Using the passive. (Chart 11-3)
Choose the sentence that has the same meaning as the given sentence.

1. In my dream, the monster is being chased.
   a. The monster is chasing someone in my dream.
   b. Someone is chasing the monster in my dream.

2. An airplane was delivered to a cargo facility last week.
   a. The airplane delivered some cargo.
   b. Someone delivered the airplane.

3. Witnesses are going to be asked for information.
   a. Someone will request information from witnesses.
   b. Witnesses will request information from someone.

4. Internet access will be provided free of charge.
   a. The Internet will provide access.
   b. Someone will provide Internet access.

5. All of the participants have been counted.
   a. Someone has finished counting the participants.
   b. The participants have finished counting.

PRACTICE 9 ▶ Using the passive. (Chart 11-3)
Complete each passage with the given verbs. Write the correct form of the verb, active or passive.

1. invent / tell

   The sandwich _____ by John Montagu, an Englishman with the title of
   the Earl of Sandwich. Around 1762, he was too busy to sit down at a regular meal, so he
   _____ his cook to pack his meat inside some bread in order to save him time.

2. attend / establish / give

   Al-Azhar University in Cairo, Egypt, is one of the oldest universities in the world. It
   _____ around the same time as the city of Cairo, in 969 A.D. The first
   lecture _____ in 975 A.D. Students (*still*) _____ the university today.

3. become / kill / know / live / relate / save

   One animal that is famous in the history of the American West is actually a bison, but it
   _____ by the name of *buffalo*. The American buffalo _____
   to a similar animal in Asia, the water buffalo. Buffaloes _____ in parks and
   flat grasslands. At the end of the nineteenth century, they almost _____
   extinct because thousands of them _____ by hunters. Fortunately, they
   _____ by the efforts of naturalists and the government.

4. believe / give / like / originate / treat / use / value

   Garlic _____ in Asia over 6,000 years ago, and it spread throughout Europe
   and Africa. Today, people _____ to use garlic not only for its strong flavor, but
   because it _____ them physical strength and good health. In ancient times,
   garlic _____ so highly that it _____ as money. Injuries
   and illnesses _____ with garlic by the ancient Greeks. Even today, garlic
   _____ to be effective by some people in lowering cholesterol and in treating
   other digestive disorders.

PRACTICE 10 ▶ Active vs. passive. (Charts 11-1 → 11-3)
Write complete sentences with the given words. Use the simple past.

1. the chefs \ prepare \ the food ___*The chefs prepared the food*___.
2. the food \ prepare \ yesterday ___*The food was prepared yesterday*___.
3. the rain \ stop _____.
4. a rainbow \ appear \ in the sky _____.
5. the documents \ send \ to you \ yesterday _____.
6. my lawyer \ send \ the documents to me _____.
7. the winner of the election \ announce \ on TV _____.
8. I \ not agree \ with you about this _____.
9. what \ happen \ yesterday _____?
10. something wonderful \ happen \ to me _____.
11. the trees \ die \ of a disease _____.

12. the trees \ kill \ by a disease _____.

13. a disease \ kill \ the trees _____.

14. I \ accept \ at the University of Chicago _____.

15. I \ recommend \ for a scholarship _____.

PRACTICE 11 ▸ The passive form of modals and phrasal modals. (Chart 11-4)
Choose the correct completions.

1. A language   can't be / couldn't have been   learned only by reading about it. You have to practice speaking it.

2. These jeans   should be washed / should have been washed   before you wear them. The material will be softer and more comfortable.

3. This shirt was washed in hot water, and it shrank. It   should have washed / should have been washed   in cold water.

4. The road is still being fixed. It is supposed   to be finished / to finish   by next month, but I'm not so sure it will be.

5. There's an old house for sale on Route 411. They say that George Washington visited it, so it   must be built / must have been built   in the 1700s.

6. Taxes   have to pay / have to be paid   on or before April 15th. Payments   must be sent / must have been sent   to the government on or before April 15th.

7. The senator has made a good point, but I disagree. May I   permit / be permitted   to speak now?

8. Our kitchen is old and dark. We're going to renovate it. It   ought to be painted / ought to paint   a light shade of green or white to make it look brighter.

PRACTICE 12 ▸ The passive form of modals and phrasal modals. (Chart 11-4)
Complete the sentences with the words in parentheses. Write the appropriate form, active or passive.

1. a. The decision (*should + make*) _____ as soon as possible.

   b. We (*should + make*) _____ our decision right now, without further discussion.

2. a. A decision (*should + make*) _____ before now.

   b. We (*should + make*) _____ our decision weeks ago.

3. a. I agree with you completely. Truer words (*couldn't + speak*) _____.

   b. They say that Einstein (*couldn't + speak*) _____ until he was four years old.

4. a. All vehicles (*must + register*) _____ with the Department of Motor Vehicles of this state.

   b. You (*must + register*) _____ your car with the Department of Motor Vehicles.

5. a. This bill (*have to + pay*) _____ by tomorrow.

   b. I (*have to + pay*) _____ this bill online. I can't mail a check, or it won't get there in time.

6. a. Someone called, but they hung up. It (*must + be*) _____ a wrong number.

   b. There (*may + be*) _____ life on Mars long ago.

PRACTICE 13 ▸ Stative (non-progressive) passive. (Chart 11-5)

Complete the sentences in Column A with a verb from Column B.

Column A

1. Uh-oh. I forgot my key, and the door is _____.

2. The museum isn't open today. It's _____.

3. Finally! The report I've been writing for a week is _____.

4. The TV doesn't work. It's _____.

5. Do you know where we are? I think we're _____.

6. Let's go to another restaurant. This one is too _____.

7. What happened to the cookies? They're all _____.

8. It's freezing in this room! I guess the heat isn't _____.

Column B

a. finished

b. lost

c. crowded

d. turned on

e. closed

f. gone

g. locked

h. broken

PRACTICE 14 ▸ Stative (non-progressive passive). (Charts 11-5 and 11-6)

Complete the sentences with the verbs in the box. Use the present tense, active or passive. Add a preposition if necessary.

bore	depend	interest	make	prepare
compose	equip	locate	marry	scare

1. Ismael _____ the history of languages. He is studying linguistics.

2. We may have a picnic on Saturday. It _____ the weather.

3. Sam _____ Salma. They have been married for 24 years.

4. Our son _____ the dark, so we keep a night light on in his room.

5. Golf _____ me. There isn't any action, and it is too slow.

6. These jeans _____ cotton. They're 100% organic cotton.

7. Our class is diverse. It _____ people from nine countries.

8. The Hague _____ the Netherlands.

9. The lab _____ the latest technology.

10. I've been studying all weekend. I _____ my exam.

PRACTICE 15 ▸ Common non-progressive (stative) passive verbs + prepositions.
(Chart 11-6)

Choose the correct completions.

1. Professor Wills is deeply involved   by / in   campus politics.

2. Who is qualified   for / in   this job?

3. Are you worried   for / about   your grade in this class?

4. A lot of people are interested   in / about   the astronauts in space.

5. Your last name is Mason? Are you related   with / to   Tony Mason?

6. Ann doesn't travel on planes. She's terrified   from / of   flying.

7. Mrs. Redmond? No, I'm not acquainted   to / with   her.

8. This is a wonderful book. I'll give it to you when I'm finished   with / for   it.

9. I'm bored   in / with   this movie. Can we leave?

10. Are you satisfied   for / with   our service? Let us know by email.

11. We are tired   from / of   paying rent, so we are going to buy an apartment.

12. Do you recycle? Are you committed   to / by   helping the environment?

PRACTICE 16 ▸ Passive vs. active.   (Charts 11-1 → 11-6)
There is one verb error in each sentence. Correct the error.

1. The plane was arrived very late.

2. Four people injured in the accident.

3. Bella is married with José.

4. People are worried with global warming.

5. Astronomers are interesting in several new meteors.

6. We were surprise by Harold's announcement.

7. Spanish spoken by people in Mexico.

8. This road is not the right one. We lost.

9. Pat should try that new medicine. He might helped.

10. Lunch is been served in the cafeteria right now.

11. Something unusual was happened yesterday.

12. Will be fixed the refrigerator today?

PRACTICE 17 ▸ The passive with get.   (Chart 11-7)
Complete the sentences with the words in the box.

| chilly | dressed | hungry | invited | scared |
| crowded | elected | hurt | lost | stopped |

1. At first, we were the only people in the restaurant, but it quickly got _____.

2. We can eat soon if you're getting _____.

3. Stan followed the map closely and didn't get _____.

4. When I heard those strange sounds last night, I got _____.

5. Wake up and get _____! We have to leave in five minutes.

6. Be careful on these old steps. You could fall and get _____.

7. Lola is disappointed because she didn't get _____ to the party.

8. Wear a jacket. You might get _____ tonight.

9. Don't drive so fast! You could get _____ for speeding!

10. Dr. Sousa is going to get _____ to the city government.

PRACTICE 18 ▸ Participial adjectives. (Chart 11-8)
Choose the correct completions.

1. a. When their team scored the winning point, the fans were   exciting / excited.

   b. The football game was very   exciting / excited.

2. a. The news I just heard was   shocking / shocked.

   b. Everyone was   shocking / shocked   by the news.

3. a. Our 40-mile bike ride was   exhausting / exhausted.

   b. I was   exhausting / exhausted   at the end of our bike ride.

4. a. This work is so   boring / bored.

   b. I'm very   boring / bored   with my work.

5. a. I'm really   confusing / confused.

   b. Professor Eng's explanation was   confusing / confused.

6. a. The ruins of the old city are very   interesting / interested.

   b. Archeologists are   interesting / interested   in the ruins of the old city.

7. a. The experience of climbing Mount Kilimanjaro was   thrilling / thrilled.

   b. The climber's family was   thrilling / thrilled   when she returned safely.

PRACTICE 19 ▸ -ed / -ing adjectives. (Chart 11-8)
Complete the sentences with the correct word from each pair.

1. *fascinating / fascinated*

   a. Your lecture was _____.

   b. I was _____ by your lecture.

2. *exhausting / exhausted*

   a. Listening to Mrs. Wilson complain is _____.

   b. I am _____ by Mrs. Wilson's complaints.

3. *disappointing / disappointed*

   a. Your parents are _____ in your behavior.

   b. Your behavior is _____.

PRACTICE 20 ▸ -ed / -ing adjectives. (Chart 11-8)
Choose all the correct sentences in each group.

1. a. I am confused by these instructions.
   b. I am confusing by these instructions.
   c. These instructions are confused me.
   d. These instructions confuse me.

2. a. The history of civilization interests Professor Davis.
   b. The history of civilization is interesting to Professor Davis.
   c. The history of civilization is interested to Professor Davis.
   d. Professor Davis is interesting in the history of civilization.

3. a. I was embarrassing by all the attention.
   b. I was embarrassed by all the attention.
   c. All the attention embarrassed me.
   d. All the attention was embarrassed to me.

4. a. This is shocked news about your family.
   b. This is shocking news about your family.
   c. I was shocking by the news about your family.
   d. I was shocked by the news about your family.

5. a. Fred is boring by spectator sports.
   b. Spectator sports are boring to Fred.
   c. Fred is bored by spectator sports.
   d. Spectator sports are bored to Fred.

PRACTICE 21 ▸ *-ed / -ing.* (Chart 11-8)
Complete each sentence with the present or past participle of the verbs in parentheses.

1. There was an emergency on campus. We were not allowed to leave the buildings. The situation was very (*frustrate*) _____*frustrating*_____ .

2. As a little boy, Tom's jokes were cute, but as a (*grow*) _____ man, his jokes irritate people. Both Tom and his jokes are (*irritate*) _____ .

3. The invention of the (*wash*) _____ machine was a great help to households everywhere.

4. The pencil is a simple (*write*) _____ instrument.

5. We can eat (*freeze*) _____ yogurt after dinner.

6. This weather is (*depress*) _____ . I've been (*depress*) _____ all day.

7. You're going to laugh a lot when you see that movie. The critics say that it is the most (*entertain*) _____ movie of the year.

8. Here's a well-(*know*) _____ saying: "Don't cry over (*spill*) _____ milk." It means that you shouldn't worry about your past mistakes.

9. Here's a (*comfort*) _____ saying: "(*Bark*) _____ dogs seldom bite." It means that some things may seem dangerous, but they often turn out not to be dangerous.

10. Here's an (*inspire*) _____ saying: "(*Unite*) _____ we stand, (*divide*) _____ we fall." It means that we must stand together against an enemy in order to survive.

PRACTICE 22 ▸ Chapter review.
Choose the correct completions.

Termites are small wood-eating insects. Termites
usually consider / **are usually considered** pests because they
can do serious damage to unprotecting / **unprotected**
buildings and other structures made about / **of** wood.
In Zimbabwe termites build / **are built** enormous mounds.
The termites grow a fungus inside the giant mounds. The
fungus is the termites' primary food source. The fungus
must be keeping / **must be kept** at exactly 87 degrees Fahrenheit,
but temperatures in Zimbabwe **can range** / can be ranged from
35 to 104 degrees Fahrenheit. The termites build heating and
cooling vents on their mounds. The temperature inside the
mound regulates / **is regulated** as the termites constantly open and close the vents. In this way, the
termites maintain / **are maintained** a constant temperature inside their mounds.

The Eastgate Centre in Harare, Zimbabwe is the country's largest
shopping and office complex. Its architecture inspired / **was inspired**
by termite mounds. The building has no air-conditioning system.
Instead, it uses a ventilation system similar to the termite mounds.
Air is drew / **drawn** into the building through the vents. The
air warms or cools / **is warmed or cooled** by the mass of the
concrete building.

The imitation of nature to solve complex human problems
calls / **is called** biomimetics. The Eastgate Centre is an
amazing / amazed example of biomimetics.

CHAPTER 12

Noun Clauses

PRACTICE 1 ▶ Preview.
Read the passage. Underline the five noun clauses.

Patrick's Retirement

The fact that Patrick is retiring soon is not a secret. He has been teaching English at the community college for 35 years. He'll miss his students, but he's excited about his retirement. He's especially excited that he'll be able to travel more often. He told me that he's going to Greece this summer. I wonder what other countries he'll visit. I think that his wife is retiring soon too. We're having a retirement dinner for Patrick at his favorite restaurant next month. Everyone is invited to the dinner.

PRACTICE 2 ▶ Introduction. (Chart 12-1)
Underline the noun clauses. Some sentences don't have one.

1. I couldn't hear what he said.

2. What did he say?

3. I don't know what happened.

4. Why are you calling me?

5. I wonder why Dora is calling me.

6. Do you know who that man is?

7. Do you know where Hank lives?

8. What are they doing?

9. What they are doing is wrong.

10. What should I say?

11. I don't know what I should say.

12. Where will she live?

PRACTICE 3 ▶ Questions and noun clauses beginning with a question word. (Chart 12-2)
Complete the sentences with the given words.

1. they \ do \ want

    What _____*do they want*_____?

2. want \ they \ what

    I don't know _____.

3. Stacy \ live \ does

Where _____?

4. lives \ where \ Stacy

Can you tell me _____?

5. what \ Carl \ likes

Do you know _____?

6. Carl \ does \ like

What _____?

7. is \ Lina \ going

Where _____?

8. is \ where \ going \ Lina

I wonder _____.

PRACTICE 4 ▸ Questions and noun clauses beginning with a question word. (Chart 12-2)
Add punctuation and capitalization. Underline the noun clause if there is one.

1. Where does Lee live does he live downtown

   Where does Lee live? Does he live downtown?

2. I don't know where he lives

   I don't know <u>where he lives</u>.

3. What does Sandra want do you know

4. Do you know what Sandra wants

5. What Yoko knows is important to us

6. We talked about what Yoko knows

7. What do you think did you tell your professor what you think

8. My professor knows what I think

9. Where is the bus stop do you know where the bus stop is

10. What did he report what he reported is important

PRACTICE 5 ▸ Noun clauses beginning with a question word. (Chart 12-2)
Change each question in parentheses to a noun clause.

1. (*How far is it?*) I don't know ____*how far it is*_____.

2. (*What is that on the table?*) I don't know _____.

3. (*How much did it cost?*) Ask her _____.

4. (*What did he say?*) _____ is very interesting.

5. (*When are they leaving?*) Do you know _____?

6. (*Which road should we take?*) Can you tell us _____?

7. (*Who called?*) Please tell me _____.

8. (*What's happening?*) Do you know _____?

9. (*Why do they work at night?*) Nobody knows _____.

10. (*What are they trying to do?*) _____ is difficult.

11. (*What kind of insects are these?*) I don't know _____.

12. (*Whose keys are these?*) I wonder _____.

PRACTICE 6 ▶ Questions and noun clauses beginning with a question word. (Chart 12-2)

Make questions with the given sentences. The words in parentheses are the answer to the question you make. Then change the question to a noun clause.

1. That man is (*Mr. Robertson*).

   QUESTION: _____*Who is that man?*_____

   NOUN CLAUSE: I want to know _____*who that man is.*_____

2. George lives (*in Los Angeles*).

   QUESTION: _____

   NOUN CLAUSE: I want to know _____

3. Ann bought (*a new dictionary*).

   QUESTION: _____

   NOUN CLAUSE: Do you know _____

4. It is (*350 miles*) to Denver from here.

   QUESTION: _____

   NOUN CLAUSE: I need to know _____

5. Jack was late for class (*because he missed the bus*).

   QUESTION: _____

   NOUN CLAUSE: The teacher wants to know _____

6. That is (*Tanya's*) phone.

   QUESTION: _____

   NOUN CLAUSE: Tom wants to know _____

7. Alex saw (*Ms. Frost*) at the meeting.

   QUESTION: _____

   NOUN CLAUSE: I don't know _____

8. (*Jack*) saw Ms. Frost at the meeting.

   QUESTION: _____

   NOUN CLAUSE: Do you know _____

9. Alice likes (*this*) book best, (*not that one*).

   QUESTION: _____

   Noun clause: I want to know _____

10. The plane is supposed to land (*at 7:14 P.M.*).

    QUESTION: _____

    NOUN CLAUSE: Could you tell me _____

PRACTICE 7 ▶ Noun clauses beginning with a question word. (Chart 12-2)
Complete each conversation with the correct phrase from the list. Write the letter.

a. what did he say
b. what he said
c. where are you going
d. where you are going
e. which bus should we take to the stadium
f. which bus we should take to the stadium
g. why did she do that
h. why she did that

1. A: What did the professor just say?

   B: I don't know _____. I couldn't understand anything.

2. A: Hey, Kim, _____?

   B: Downtown. We're going to the new show at the art museum.

3. A: Hello, there! You look lost. Can I help you?

   B: Yes, _____? We want to go to the football stadium in Fairfield.

4. A: Turn the TV up, please. I can't hear the weather reporter. Linda, _____?

   B: He said that there will be a lot of rain tomorrow.

5. A: Hello! Can you please tell us _____?

   B: Sorry, I don't know. I'm a stranger here myself.

6. A: I told you that we are going to Bermuda for a vacation, didn't I?

   B: Well, you told us about the vacation, but you didn't say _____.

7. A: Ms. Holsum just quit her job at the university.

   B: Oh, _____? That was such a good job!

   A: Nobody knows _____. It's a mystery.

PRACTICE 8 ▶ Noun clauses beginning with *whether* or *if*. (Chart 12-3)
Choose the correct completions.

1. We don't know _____.
   a. whether it will snow
   b. whether or not it will snow
   c. whether it will snow or not
   d. if it will snow
   e. if or not it will snow
   f. if it will snow or not

2. _____ doesn't matter to me.
   a. Whether or not it snows
   b. Whether it snows or not
   c. Whether does it snow or not
   d. If or not it snows
   e. If snows or not
   f. If does it snow

3. I wonder _____.
   a. whether or not does she know
   b. whether she knows or not
   c. whether does she know
   d. if docs shc know
   e. if she knows or not
   f. if or not she does know

PRACTICE 9 ▸ Review. (Charts 12-2 and 12-3)
Complete the questions using **Do you know**.

1. How much does this book cost? _____Do you know how much this book costs?_____

2. When is Flight 62 expected? _____

3. Where is the nearest restroom? _____

4. Is this word spelled correctly? _____

5. What time is it? _____

6. Is this information correct? _____

7. How much does it cost to fly from Toronto to London? _____

8. Where is the bus station? _____

9. Whose glasses are these? _____

10. Does this bus go downtown? _____

PRACTICE 10 ▸ Question words followed by infinitives. (Chart 12-4)
Complete each sentence in Column A with a phrase from Column B.

Column A	Column B
1. Where can I find fresh fish? I don't know __d__ .	a. who to vote for
2. Which person will be a better president?	b. whether to look for one
I don't know_____ .	
3. Who can I get to repair the TV?	c. how to fix it
I don't know _____ .	
4. Should I get another job?	✓ d. where to buy it
I don't know _____ .	
5. What's good to eat here?	e. what to order
I don't know _____ .	
6. Is the airport nearby?	f. how many to prepare
I don't know _____ .	
7. What should it cost?	g. how far it is from here
I don't know _____ .	
8. Do we need a lot of sandwiches for the party?	h. how much to spend
I don't know _____ .	

PRACTICE 11 ▸ Noun clauses beginning with _that_. (Chart 12-5)
Complete the sentences with the words in the box. More than one answer may be correct.

angry	confident	lucky	relieved
aware	disappointed	proud	worried

1. We are _____ that our son graduated with honors.

2. I am _____ that the store owner cheated me. That was awful!

3. Our teacher is _____ that all the students did poorly on the test. However, she is encouraging them to do well on the next test.

4. I was not _____ that our boss hired a new assistant. When did this happen?

5. It was _____ that we got off the elevator when we did. Just after we got off, it got stuck between floors, and the other passengers were inside for three hours!

6. Lee always wins the table tennis tournaments at our community center. He is _____ that he will win the one next weekend.

7. We were very _____ that the hurricane was coming our way. But it changed course and went out to sea instead. Now we are _____ that the hurricane didn't hit us.

PRACTICE 12 ▶ Noun clauses beginning with *that*. (Chart 12-5)
Rewrite the sentences in italics in two ways. Use the words from the original sentence.

1. *Nobody stopped to help Sam on the road.* That is surprising.
   a. It _____*is surprising*_____ that nobody stopped to help Sam on the road.
   b. The fact that ____*nobody stopped to help Sam*____ on the road ____*is suprising.*____ .

2. *People in modern cities are distrustful of each other.* That is unfortunate.
   a. It _____ people in modern cities are distrustful of each other.
   b. That _____

3. *People in my hometown always help each other.* That is still true.
   a. It _____
   b. That _____

4. *People need each other and need to help each other.* That is undeniably true.
   a. It _____ people need each other and need to help each other.
   b. That _____ and need to help each other.

5. *People in cities often don't know their neighbors.* That seems strange to me.
   a. It _____ me _____ people in cities often don't know their neighbors.
   b. The fact that _____

PRACTICE 13 ▶ Quoted speech. (Chart 12-6)
Add punctuation and capitalization.

1. Millie said there's an important meeting at three o'clock

2. There's an important meeting at three o'clock she said

3. There is said Millie an important meeting at three o'clock

4. There is an important meeting today it's about the new rules said Millie

5. Where is the meeting Carl asked

6. Robert replied it's in the conference room

7. How long will it last asked Ali

8. I don't know how long it will last replied Millie

9. I'll be a little late said Robert I have another meeting until 3:00 P.M. today

10. Who is speaking at the meeting asked Robert

11. I am not sure who is speaking said Millie but you'd better be there everybody is supposed to be there

PRACTICE 14 ▶ Reported speech. (Chart 12-7)
Complete the sentences with the correct form of the verbs.

1. Tom said, "I am busy." Tom said that he _____was_____ busy.

2. Tom said, "I need some help." Tom said that he _____ some help.

3. Tom said, "I am having a good time." Tom said that he _____ a good time.

4. Tom said, "I have finished my work." Tom said that he _____ his work.

5. Tom said, "I finished it." Tom said that he _____ it.

6. Tom said, "Stay here." Tom told me _____ here.

PRACTICE 15 ▶ Reported speech. (Chart 12-7)
Change the quoted speech to reported speech. Pay attention to whether the reporting verb is past or present.

1. I asked Morgan, "Are you planning to enter law school?"

   I asked Morgan ____if / whether she was planning_____ to enter law school.

2. Liam just asked me, "What time does the movie begin?"

   Liam wants to know _____.

3. Frank asked Carla, "Where have you been all afternoon?"

   Frank asked Carla _____ all afternoon.

4. Jaime just asked, "What is Kim's native language?"

   Jaime wants to know _____.

5. I asked myself, "Am I doing the right thing?"

   I wondered _____ the right thing.

6. Nancy asked, "Why didn't you call me?"

   Nancy wanted to know _____ her.

7. The teacher asked, "Have you been studying for the test?"

   The teacher asked us _____.

8. Rhonda asked Caroline, "Did you find your phone?"

   Rhonda asked Caroline _____.

PRACTICE 16 ▶ Reported speech with modal verbs. (Chart 12-8)
Complete the sentences with the correct form of the verbs.

1. Emily said, "I will arrive at noon." Emily said that she _____ at noon.

2. Emily said, "I am going to be there." Emily said that she _____ there.

3. Emily said, "I can solve that problem." Emily said that she _____

that problem.

4. Emily said, "I may come early." Emily said that she _____ early.

5. Emily said, "I might come early." Emily said that she _____ early.

6. Emily said, "I must leave at eight." Emily said that she _____ at eight.

7. Emily said, "I have to leave at eight." Emily said that she _____ at eight.

8. Emily said, "I should go to the library." Emily said that she _____ to

the library.

PRACTICE 17 ▶ Reported speech with modal verbs. (Chart 12-8)

Change the quoted speech to reported speech. Pay attention to whether the reporting verb is past or present.

1. Jacob asked, "Can we still get tickets for the concert?"

Jacob asked ___*if we could still get*_____ tickets for the concert.

2. Thomas said to us, "How can I help you?"

Thomas wanted to know _____ us.

3. Eva asked, "Can you help me, Mario?"

Eva asked Mario _____ her.

4. Charles said, "When will the final decision be made?"

Charles wanted to know _____ .

5. George asked me, "What time do I have to be at the lab in the morning?"

George asked me _____ to be at the lab in the morning.

6. Yuki asked, "Who should I give this message to?"

Yuki asked me _____ to.

7. The new student asked, "Where might I find an ATM?"

The new student asked me _____ an ATM.

8. The impatient customer asked, "How long must I wait in line?"

The impatient customer wanted to know _____ in line.

9. My son asked, "When are we going to get there?"

My son asked me _____ there.

PRACTICE 18 ▶ Reported speech. (Charts 12-7 and 12-8)

Complete the sentences using the information in the conversation. Use past verb forms in the noun clauses if appropriate and possible.

CONVERSATION 1

"Where are you going, Ann?" I asked.

"I'm on my way to the farmers' market," she replied. "Do you want to come with me?"

"I'd like to, but I have to stay home. I have a lot of work to do."

"OK," Ann said. "Is there anything I can pick up for you?"

"How about a few bananas? And some apples if they're fresh?"

"Sure. I'd be happy to."

When I asked Ann where she _____, she said she _____
on her way to the farmer's market and _____ me to come with her. I said I
_____ to, but that I _____ to stay home because I _____
a lot of work to do. Ann kindly asked me if there _____ anything she _____
pick up for me at the market. I asked her to pick up a few bananas and some apples if they
_____ fresh. She said she'd be happy to.

CONVERSATION 2

"Where are you from?" asked the passenger sitting next to me on the plane.

"Chicago," I said.

"That's nice. I'm from Mapleton. It's a small town in northern Michigan. Have you heard of it?"

"Oh yes, I have," I said. "Michigan is a beautiful state. I've been there on vacation many times."

"Were you in Michigan on vacation this year?"

"No. I went far away from home this year. I went to India," I replied.

"Oh, that's nice. Is it a long drive from Chicago to India?" she asked me. My mouth fell open.
I didn't know how to respond. Some people certainly need to study geography.

The passenger sitting next to me on the plane _____ me where I _____ from.
I _____ her I _____ from Chicago. She _____ that she _____
from Mapleton, a small town in northern Michigan. She wondered if I _____ of
it, and I told her that I _____. I went on to say that I thought Michigan _____
a beautiful state and explained that I _____ there on vacation many times. She
_____ me if I _____ in Michigan on vacation this year. I replied
that I _____ and _____ her that I _____ far away, to
India. Then she asked me if it _____ a long drive from Chicago to India! My mouth fell
open. I didn't know how to respond. Some people certainly need to study geography.

PRACTICE 19 ▸ The subjunctive in noun clauses. (Chart 12-9)
Complete the sentences with the subjunctive form of the verbs in parentheses.

SITUATION: Jenny is taking her driving test next week.

1. It is imperative that she (*arrive*) _____ at the test site on time.

2. It is necessary that she (*provide*) _____ proof of insurance for her vehicle before
   the test begins.

3. The Department of Motor Vehicles recommends that drivers (*get*) _____ plenty
   of practice before they take the driving test.

SITUATION: Joe is bored with his job.

4. He has requested that he (*be*) _____ transferred to another department in his
   company.

5. His boss suggested that he (*apply*) _____ for a promotion.

6. His friend advised that he (*look*) _____ for a job with another company.

PRACTICE 20 ▸ Chapter review.
Part I. Choose the correct completions.

Fitness Trackers

Sherri has been exercising for a year, but she hasn't achieved
the results she had hoped for. Her personal trainer at the
gym suggested that she   gets / get   a fitness tracker. Fitness
trackers have become very popular in recent years. These
gadgets are usually worn as wristbands. A fitness tracker
will count how many   steps Sherri takes / steps does Sherri
take   in a day. Most fitness trackers will also measure how

much sleep   she gets / does she get.   Some are able to calculate body weight and body mass. They
can also show her what   is her heart rate / her heart rate is.   What makes fitness trackers popular
is   whether / what   they help people keep track of their exercise routine. When people set fitness
goals, it is often hard for them to know   if or not / whether or not   they have achieved it. A fitness
tracker keeps a clear record.

Part II. Sherri is talking to Mark, a salesperson at a sporting goods store, about fitness trackers. Add
punctuation to the conversation.

Can you help me find a fitness tracker Sherri asked

Mark replied Absolutely! What features are you looking for

I'm not sure Sherri said Can you tell me what is available

Sure he answered The basic trackers count your steps and monitor your sleep We also have more
sophisticated models if you're looking for a heart rate monitor

I can't decide I think I need to take a look at them she said

Come this way, and I'll show you what we have

CHAPTER 13

Adjective Clauses

PRACTICE 1 ▶ Preview.
Read the passage. <u>Underline</u> the nine adjective clauses.

> **Advisors and Counselors**
>
> When students begin their university studies, they often feel overwhelmed. Most college campuses have several places where students can seek help. The first place that a new student should look for is the advising office. An academic advisor is someone who answers questions that are related to course selection, degree plans, and academic progress. Students usually meet with the same advisor over the course of their university education. The student and advisor develop a relationship in which the advisor serves as a mentor or guide. Another helpful place that students can turn to is the counseling office. A counselor is someone who helps students with personal issues that may or may not be related to the student's academic life. Counselors help students who have trouble with time management, test anxiety, career selection, or similar issues. Both advisors and counselors play an important role in student success.

PRACTICE 2 ▶ Adjective clause pronouns used as the subject. (Chart 13-1)
<u>Underline</u> the adjective clause in each sentence. Draw an arrow to the word it modifies.

1. We are looking for a person <u>who fixes computers</u>.

2. I know a man who lives on a boat.

3. In our office, there is a woman who speaks four languages.

4. There are several people who are bilingual in the office.

5. I work in an office that is in an old building.

6. The other buildings that are in the neighborhood are not as old.

7. Two trees that were over 200 years old were struck by lightning last night.

8. Two other trees which were nearby were not harmed.

9. The traffic jam was caused by one truck that had broken down.

10. The truck which caused the problem was in the middle of the highway.

PRACTICE 3 ▶ Adjective clause pronouns used as the subject. (Chart 13-1)
Choose the correct completions.

1. I thanked the woman _____ brought back our lost cat.
   a. who   b. that   c. which   d. she

2. The aquarium is looking for new employees _____ know a lot about dolphins.
   a. who   b. that   c. which   d. they

3. What is the TV channel _____ has stories about animals?
   a. who   b. it   c. which   d. that

4. On my flight, there was a weight-lifter _____ didn't fit into the airplane seat.
   a. who   b. that   c. he   d. which

5. None of the houses _____ have protective shutters were damaged in the typhoon.
   a. who   b. that   c. which   d. they

6. I'm transferring to a school _____ has a well-known program in cinematography.
   a. who   b. that   c. which   d. it

PRACTICE 4 ▸ Adjective clause pronouns as the object of a verb. (Chart 13-2)
Underline the adjective clause in each sentence. Draw an arrow to the word it modifies.

1. There's the man that I met last night.

2. There's the woman that Sandro is going to marry.

3. All the people whom we invited have accepted the invitation.

4. The book which I just read is going to be made into a movie.

5. I can't figure out how to use the software program that Jason installed.

6. We are still living in the house we built in 1987.

7. What happened to the cake I left on the table?

8. I bought the book my professor wrote.

PRACTICE 5 ▸ Adjective clause pronouns as the object of a verb. (Chart 13-2)
Choose the correct completions.

1. That's the woman _____ the people elected.
   a. who   b. whom   c. that   d. which   e. she   f. Ø

2. The man _____ the police arrested was not the thief.
   a. whom   b. he   c. that   d. which   e. who   f. Ø

3. I'd already seen the movie _____ we watched last night
   a. who   b. it   c. Ø   d. which   e. that   f. whom

4. Ms. McCarthy is a teacher _____ everyone loves.
   a. who   b. whom   c. Ø   d. which   e. that   f. her

5. Many of the people _____ we met on our vacation were very friendly.
   a. who   b. which   c. that   d. whom   e. Ø   f. they

6. A man _____ I know is going to be interviewed on a morning TV program.
   a. who   b. that   c. whom   d. which   e. him   f. Ø

PRACTICE 6 ▸ Adjective clause pronouns used as the subject or object of the verb.
         (Charts 13-1 and 13-2)
Complete the sentences with the correct adjective clause.

1. The book was good. I read it.

   The book that ____I read was good____.

2. The movie was very sad. I saw it.

   The movie that _____.

3. Elephants are animals. They can live a long time.

   Elephants are animals that _____.

4. At the zoo, there were two fifty-year-old elephants. We photographed them.

   At the zoo, there were two fifty-year-old elephants which _____.

5. Sarah is a person. She does many things at the same time.

   Sarah is a person who _____.

6. Bill is a person. You can trust him.

   Bill is a person you _____.

7. The painting was valuable. The thieves stole it.

   The painting _____.

PRACTICE 7 ▸ Adjective clause pronouns used as the object of a preposition. (Chart 13-3)

Choose all possible completions.

1. The person _____ was Bob Jones in the customer service department.
   a. which I spoke to
   b. to which I spoke
   c. whom I spoke to
   d. to whom I spoke
   e. who I spoke to him
   f. to who I spoke
   g. that I spoke to
   h. to that I spoke
   i. I spoke to
   j. I spoke to him

2. This is the explanation _____.
   a. which I was referring to
   b. to which I was referring
   c. whom I was referring to
   d. to whom I was referring
   e. which I was referring to it
   f. that I was referring to
   g. to that I was referring
   h. I was referring to
   i. I was referring to it

PRACTICE 8 ▸ Adjective clauses. (Charts 13-1 → 13-3)

Write all the possible completions.

1. Mr. Green is the man
   | that |
   | who |
   | whom |
   | Ø |
   I was talking about.

2. She is the woman [   ] sits next to me in class.

3. The hat [   ] Tom is wearing is unusual.

4. Hunger and poverty are worldwide problems to [   ] solutions must be found.

5. I enjoyed talking with the man [ ] I sat next to on the plane.

6. People [ ] fear flying avoid traveling by plane.

7. The people about [ ] the novelist wrote were factory workers and their families.

8. A barrel is a large container [ ] is made of wood or metal.

PRACTICE 9 ▸ Adjective clauses. (Charts 13-1 → 13-3)
Correct the errors in the adjective clauses. Do not change any punctuation.

1. That's a subject I don't want to talk about it.

2. A person who he writes with his left hand is called a lefty.

3. Our family brought home a new kitten that we found it at the animal shelter.

4. What is the name of the podcast to that we listened last night?

5. The candidate for who you vote should be honest.

6. Here's a picture of Nancy who I took with my phone.

7. People have high cholesterol should watch their diets.

8. Suzie is going to marry the man she has always loved him.

9. There's an article in today's newspaper about a woman that she is 7 feet tall.

10. Passengers which have children may board the plane first.

PRACTICE 10 ▸ Whose vs. Who's. (Chart 13-4)
Choose the correct completions.

1. a. This class is for students _____ English needs improvement.
   a. who's   b. whose

   b. Belinda is a student _____ good in both math and languages.
   a. who's   b. whose

   c. Will the student _____ cell phone is ringing please turn it off?
   a. who's   b. whose

2. a. A customer _____ dissatisfied is not good for a business.
   a. who's   b. whose

   b. The customer _____ young son was crying tried to comfort him.
   a. who's   b. whose

3. a. Life is sometimes difficult for a child _____ parents are divorced.
    a. who's   b. whose

   b. I know a child _____ a chess prodigy.
    a. who's   b. whose

4. a. You should look for a doctor _____ right for you.
    a. who's   b. whose

   b. Do you know a doctor _____ office is close to campus?
    a. who's   b. whose

PRACTICE 11 ▸ Using *whose*. (Chart 13-4)
Combine the sentences into one using ***whose***.

1. Do you know the man? His car is parked over there.

   _____

2. I know a skin doctor. His name is Dr. Skinner.

   _____

3. The people were very hospitable. We visited their home.

   _____

4. Mrs. Lake is the teacher. I enjoy her class the most.

   _____

5. The teacher asked the parents to confer with her. Their children were failing.

   _____

PRACTICE 12 ▸ Understanding adjective clauses. (Charts 13-1 and 13-4)
Check (✓) all the correct meanings for each sentence.

1. The secretary that trained my office assistant was arrested for ID theft.

   a. _____ My office assistant was arrested for ID theft.

   b. _✓_ A secretary trained my office assistant.

   c. _✓_ A secretary was arrested for ID theft.

2. The nurse who gave the patient her medication was unusually talkative.

   a. _____ The nurse was unusually talkative.

   b. _____ The patient was unusually talkative.

   c. _____ The patient received medication.

3. The taxi driver who turned in a lost wallet to the police received a large reward.

   a. _____ The taxi driver lost a wallet.

   b. _____ The police received a reward.

   c. _____ The taxi driver received a reward.

4. The math teacher whose methods include memorization and a focus on basic skills is very popular with parents.

   a. _____ The parents like the math teacher.

   b. _____ The parents focus on basic skills.

   c. _____ The math teacher requires memorization.

5. The computer that couldn't read your files had a virus.

   a. _____ The computer couldn't read your files.

   b. _____ The computer had a virus.

   c. _____ Your files had a virus.

6. A friend of mine whose husband is a firefighter accidentally started a fire in their kitchen.

   a. _____ My friend is a firefighter.

   b. _____ My friend started a fire.

   c. _____ The firefighter started a fire.

7. The surgeon who operated on my mother is undergoing surgery today.

   a. _____ The surgeon is having surgery today.

   b. _____ My mother is having surgery today.

   c. _____ My mother already had surgery.

PRACTICE 13 ▶ Using *where* in adjective clauses. (Chart 13-5)
Complete the sentences in two different ways with the given words.

1. grew up / in / I / which / where

   a. The town _____ has changed.

   b. The town _____ has changed.

2. I / which / lived / in / where

   a. The house _____ isn't there anymore.

   b. The house _____ isn't there anymore.

3. on / lived / which / where / I

   a. The street _____ is now a parking lot.

   b. The street _____ is now a parking lot.

4. where / which / I / played / in

   a. The park _____ is now a mall.

   b. The park _____ is now a mall.

PRACTICE 14 ▶ Using *when* in adjective clauses. (Chart 13-6)
Complete the sentences in three different ways with the given words.

1. on / which / when / I / go / that

   a. Saturday is the day _____ to the movies with my grandmother.

   b. Saturday is the day _____ to the movies with my grandmother.

   c. Saturday is the day _____ to the movies with my grandmother.

2. when / that / which / on / I play tennis

   a. Sunday is the day _____ with my friend.

   b. Sunday is the day _____ with my friend.

   c. Sunday is the day _____ with my friend.

PRACTICE 15 ▸ Using *where* and *when* in adjective clauses. (Charts 13-5 and 13-6)
Complete each conversation with the correct clause from the list. Write the letter.

a. that George Washington slept in
b. when I spend time with my family
c. when they were really in love
d. where I was born

e. where we can sit and talk
f. which I start my new job
g. which people here celebrate their independence
h. which you can do all the things you never could before

1. A: Where do you want to go after the movie?

   B: Let's go to a place _____ .

2. A: Sal and Lil broke up? That's impossible!

   B: There was a time _____ , but not anymore.

3. A: See you Monday!

   B: No. Don't you remember? Monday is the day on _____ .

4. A: Are you new in town?

   B: New? Are you kidding? This is the place _____ .

5. A: Is there something special about that house? It looks historic.

   B: Yes. They say it's a house _____ when he was on his way to Philadelphia.

6. A: Grandma is never home. Since she's retired, she's always doing something.

   B: Right. She says that retirement is the time in _____ .

7. A: What's the celebration here? Is it a holiday?

   B: Yes. It's the day on _____ .

8. A: Would you like to go out this weekend?

   B: No, thanks. Saturdays and Sundays are the days _____ .

PRACTICE 16 ▸ Adjective clauses. (Charts 13-1 → 13-6)
Choose all possible completions for each sentence.

1. Yoko told me about a student _____ has taken the entrance exam 13 times.
   a. who   b. whom   c. which   d. that

2. Is this the room _____ the meeting is going to be?
   a. which   b. where   c. that   d. Ø

3. Judge Savitt is a judge _____ people respect.
   a. whose   b. which   c. whom   d. Ø

4. I'll never forget the day _____ I met Bobbi.
   a. Ø   b. that   c. when   d. which

5. We're looking for a teacher _____ specialty is teaching dyslexic students.
   a. who   b. his   c. that   d. whose

6. I'm looking for an electric can opener _____ can also sharpen knives.
   a. who   b. which   c. that   d. Ø

7. The problems _____ Tony has seem insurmountable.
   a. what   b. whom   c. that   d. Ø

8. People _____ live in glass houses shouldn't throw stones.
   a. who   b. whom   c. which   d. Ø

PRACTICE 17 ▸ Using adjective clauses to modify pronouns. (Chart 13-7)

Complete the sentences in Column A with a clause from Column B.

Column A

1. May I ask you a question? There is something _____ .

2. I don't have any more money. This is all _____ .

3. Do you get the calculus homework?

   Anyone _____ must be a genius.

4. He's a spoiled child. His parents give him everything _____ .

5. I'm sorry I can't help you. There's nothing _____ .

Column B

a. who understands it

b. I can do

c. he wants

d. I want to know

e. that I have

PRACTICE 18 ▸ Punctuating adjective clauses. (Chart 13-8)

Add a comma to the adjective clauses that need one. Some adjectives clauses do not require commas.

1. I made an appointment with a doctor who is an expert on eye disorders.

2. I made an appointment with Dr. Raven who is an expert on eye disorders.

3. Bogotá which is the capital of Colombia is a cosmopolitan city.

4. The city that is the capital of Colombia is a large, cosmopolitan city.

5. South Beach which is clean, pleasant, and fun is known as a party town.

6. The person who writes the best essay will win a prize.

7. The first prize was given to Miranda Jones who wrote a touching essay about being an adopted child.

8. On our trip to Africa we visited Nairobi which is near several fascinating game reserves and then traveled to Egypt to see the pyramids.

9. To see wild animals, you have to fly to a city that is near a game reserve and then take a small plane to the reserve itself.

10. Someone who understands physics better than I do is going to have to help you.

11. Violent tropical storms that occur in western Asia are called typhoons.

12. Similar storms that occur on the Atlantic side of the Americas are called hurricanes rather than typhoons.

13. A typhoon which is a violent tropical storm can cause great destruction.

14. According to the news report, the typhoon that threatened to strike the Indonesian coast has moved away from land and toward open water.

15. Typhoon Haiyan which destroyed parts of Southeast Asia occurred in 2013.

PRACTICE 19 ▸ Punctuating adjective clauses. (Chart 13-8)

Choose the correct meaning for each sentence.

1. The students, who attend class five hours per day, have become quite proficient in their new language.
   a. All of the students attend class five hours per day.
   b. Some of the students attend class five hours per day.

2. The students who attend class five hours per day have become quite proficient in their new language.
   a. All of the students attend class five hours per day.
   b. Some of the students attend class five hours per day.

3. The orchestra conductor signaled the violinists, who were to begin playing.
   a. All of the violinists were to begin playing.
   b. Some of the violinists were to begin playing.

4. The orchestra conductor signaled the violinists who were to begin playing.
   a. All of the violinists were to begin playing.
   b. Some of the violinists were to begin playing.

5. I put the vase on the bookshelf, which is in the living room.
   a. I have more than one bookshelf.
   b. I have only one bookshelf.

6. I put the vase on the bookshelf that is in the living room.
   a. I have more than one bookshelf.
   b. I have only one bookshelf.

7. Trees which lose their leaves in winter are called deciduous trees.
   a. All trees lose their leaves in winter.
   b. Some trees lose their leaves in winter.

8. Pine trees, which are evergreen, grow well in a cold climate.
   a. All pine trees are evergreen.
   b. Some pine trees are evergreen.

PRACTICE 20 ▸ Using expressions of quantity in adjective clauses. (Chart 13-9)

Combine the sentences. Use the second sentence as an adjective clause. Add commas as necessary.

1. I received two job offers. I accepted neither of them.

   I received two job offers, neither of which I accepted.

2. I have three brothers. Two of them are professional athletes.

   _____

3. Jerry is engaged in several business ventures. Only one of them is profitable.

   _____

4. The two women have almost completed law school. Both of them began their studies at age 40.

   _____

5. Eric is proud of his success. Much of it has been due to hard work, but some of it has been due to good luck.

   _____

6. We ordered an extra-large pizza. Half of it contained meat and half of it didn't.

   _____

7. The scientist won the Nobel Prize for his groundbreaking work. Most of his work was on genomes.

   _____

8. The audience gave a tremendous ovation to the Nobel Prize winners. Most of them were scientists.

   _____

PRACTICE 21 ▸ Using *which* to modify a whole sentence. (Chart 13-10)

Combine the sentences. Include an adjective clause that begins with *which* in the new sentence.

1. Mike was accepted at the state university. This is surprising.

   _____

2. Mike did not do well in high school. This is unfortunate.

   _____

3. The university accepts a few students each year with a low grade-point average. This is lucky for Mike.

   _____

4. The university hopes to motivate these low-performing students. This is a fine idea.

   _____

5. Mike might actually be a college graduate one day. This would be a wonderful!

   _____

PRACTICE 22 ▸ Reducing adjective clauses to adjective phrases. (Chart 13-11)

Change the adjective clauses to adjective phrases. Cross out the adjective clause and write the adjective phrase above it.

1. Do you see that man ~~who is wearing a green hat~~? *wearing a green hat*

2. The person who is in charge of this department is out to lunch.

3. The picture which was painted by Picasso is extremely valuable.

4. The professors who are doing research will not teach classes next year.

5. The students' research projects which are in progress must be finished by the end of the year.

6. The students' research projects which are scheduled to begin in September will have to be completed by the middle of next year.

7. Toronto, which is the largest city in Canada, is not the capital.

8. In our solar system, there are eight planets that orbit the sun.

9. Pluto, which was formerly known as a planet, was reclassified as a dwarf planet in 2006.

10. Now there is a slang verb, *to pluto*, which means "to devalue someone or something."

PRACTICE 23 ▸ Reducing adjective clauses to adjective phrases. (Chart 13-11)

Combine the sentences. Use the second sentence as an adjective phrase. Add commas as necessary.

1. Brasilia is the capital of Brazil. It was officially inaugurated in 1960.

   Brasilia, officially inaugurated in 1960, is the capital of Brazil.

2. Rio de Janeiro used to be its capital. It is the second largest city in Brazil.

   _____

3. Two languages, Finnish and Swedish, are spoken in Helsinki. It is the capital of Finland.

   _____

4. In Canada, you see signs. They are written in both English and French.

   _____

5. Libya is a leading producer of oil. It is a country in North Africa.

_____

6. Simon Bolivar led the fight for independence early in the nineteenth century. He was a great South American general.

_____

7. Five South American countries are Venezuela, Colombia, Ecuador, Panama, and Peru. They were liberated by Bolivar.

_____

8. We need someone to design this project. He or she holds a degree in electrical engineering.

_____

9. The project will be finished next year. It is being built in Beijing.

_____

10. A lot of new buildings were constructed in Beijing in 2008. Beijing was the site of the summer Olympics that year.

_____

PRACTICE 24 ▸ Chapter review.

All of the following sentences contain one or two errors in adjective clauses, adjective phrases, or punctuation. Correct the errors using a correct adjective clause or adjective phrase, and the correct punctuation.

1. When we walked past the theater, we saw a lot of people waited in a long line outside the box office.
2. Students who living on campus are close to their classrooms and the library.
3. If you need any information, see the librarian sits at the central desk on the main floor.
4. My best friend is Anna who her birthday is the same day as mine.
5. Hiroko was born in Sapporo that is a city in Japan.
6. Patrick who is my oldest brother. He is married and has one child.
7. The person sits next to me is someone I've never met him.
8. My favorite place in the world is a small city is located on the southern coast of Thailand.
9. Dr. Darnell was the only person to that I wanted to speak.
10. Yermek whom is from Kazakhstan teaches Russian classes at the college.
11. The people who we met them on our trip last May are going to visit us in October.
12. Dianne Baxter that used to teach Spanish has organized a tour of Central America for senior citizens.
13. I've met many people since I came here who some of them are from my country.
14. People can speak English can be understood in many countries.
15. Grandpa is getting married again. This is a big surprise.

CHAPTER 14

Gerunds and Infinitives, Part 1

PRACTICE 1 ▸ Introduction. (Chart 14-1)

Read the passage. <u>Underline</u> the six gerunds. Circle the eight infinitives.

Geochaching

Geocaching has become a popular outdoor activity in recent years. A geocache is a small container that someone has hidden outside. Participants use a GPS or a mobile device to find or hide geocaches. There are millions of geocaches around the world.

Ray and Isabel are looking for a geocache that someone has hidden. GPS coordinates have been posted on a website. Websites suggest leaving clues in addition to the coordinates, so Ray and Isabel are also using clues.

The geocache contains a logbook for signing and dating. Some participants like to place a small trinket or toy in the geocache. After Ray and Isabel find the geocache, they will sign the logbook. Then they need to place the geocache back exactly where they found it.

Ray and Isabel enjoy finding these hidden surprises, but they aren't having much luck today. They have been looking for over an hour, but they can't seem to find it. Ray wants to quit. He's tired and hungry. Isabel prefers to continue searching. She doesn't like to give up!

PRACTICE 2 ▸ Common verbs followed by gerunds. (Chart 14-2)

Complete the sentences with the gerund form of the verbs in the box.

argue	have	play	sell
drive	pay	read	smoke

1. Boris's hobby is chess. He enjoys _____ chess.

2. Leon's asthma is better now. He is breathing easier since he quit _____ a year ago.

3. I don't mind _____ an hour to work every day. I always listen to a good audio book in my car.

4. I put off _____ my taxes for too long; I missed the deadline and had to pay a penalty.

5. You should avoid _____ with your boss. Try to get along better.

6. Would you consider _____ your house at a lower price than you are asking?

7. Our teacher is so great! We really appreciate _____ a teacher like her.

8. When you finish _____ that book, may I borrow it?

Gerunds and Infinitives, Part 1 **129**

PRACTICE 3 ▸ Common verbs followed by infinitives. (Chart 14-3)
Complete the sentences with the infinitive form of the verbs in the box.

arrive	fly	paint	transfer
cook	make	tell	work

1. Let's go to a restaurant. I don't want _____ tonight.

2. Ramzy doesn't go to school here any longer. He decided _____ to another school.

3. Scott has a terrible toothache. He needs _____ an appointment with a dentist.

4. Zach held out his arms and pretended _____ like a bird.

5. Reagan is a talented artist. She has offered _____ a picture of our family.

6. Caroline is graduating from law school this year. She plans _____ in a law firm next year.

7. Where's Jeff? He promised _____ on time today.

8. Jill seems upset. I've asked her what's wrong, but she refuses _____ me.

PRACTICE 4 ▸ Gerund or infinitive. (Charts 14-2 and 14-3)
Choose the correct completions.

1. William wants _____ us for dinner tonight.
   a. to join   b. joining

2. We offered _____ ice cream for all the kids.
   a. to buy   b. buying

3. I enjoy _____ large dishes of Indian food for my friends.
   a. to cook   b. cooking

4. Avoid _____ Highway 98. There's a lot of construction going on.
   a. to take   b. taking

5. Keep on _____! Sooner or later, you'll be able to finish the puzzle.
   a. to try   b. trying

6. Would you mind _____ up the heat? It's freezing in here.
   a. to turn   b. turning

7. I pretended _____ what Irv was saying, but in reality, I didn't understand a thing.
   a. to understand   b. understand

8. Phil seems _____ in a bad mood. Do you know why?
   a. to be   b. being

9. You should consider _____ this course. It's too hard for you.
   a. to drop   b. dropping

10. Because of the stormy weather, everyone was allowed _____ work early.
    a. to leave   b. leaving

11. Students are not permitted _____ their phones in class.
    a. to use   b. using

12. If you quit _____ coffee, you might sleep better.
    a. to drink   b. drinking

PRACTICE 5 ▸ Gerund or infinitive. (Charts 14-2 and 14-3)
Choose the correct completions.

1. John doesn't mind   to live / living   alone.

2. The traffic sign warns drivers   to be / being   careful on the slippery road.

3. Travelers are required   to show / showing   their IDs at the gate.

4. Don't delay   to make / making   your reservations. Book your travel now!

5. We expect the plane   to be / being   on time.

6. I certainly appreciate   to be / being   here! Thank you for inviting me.

7. Please stop   to hum / humming   that song over and over. It bothers me.

8. My doctor suggests   to exercise / exercising   for 30 minutes every day.

9. I was advised   to exercise / exercising   for 30 minutes every day by my doctor.

10. Jessica hopes   to graduate / graduating   next spring.

PRACTICE 6 ▸ Infinitives with objects. (Chart 14-4)
Choose all the possible completions for each sentence.

1. I want _____ that movie.
   a. to see   b. seeing   c. him to see

2. They told _____ them as soon as I got home.
   a. to call   b. calling   c. me to call

3. I expect _____ there early.
   a. to be   b. being   c. you to be

4. The police ordered _____ the building.
   a. not to enter   b. not entering   c. the people not to enter

5. We were asked _____ food and clothing for the hurricane victims.
   a. to contribute   b. contributing   c. them to contribute

6. Lisa expected _____ the lecture.
   a. to attend   b. attending   c. us to attend

PRACTICE 7 ▸ Infinitives with objects. (Chart 14-4)
Complete the sentences with *to work* or *me to work*. Write the correct completion(s). In some cases, both are possible.

1. She hoped ___to work___ .

2. He ordered ___me to work___ .

3. They wanted ___to work / me to work___ .

4. We agreed _____ .

5. She promised _____ .

6. They refused _____ .

7. He pretended _____ .

8. They didn't allow _____ .

9. You told _____ .

10. They would like _____ .

11. They expected _____ .

12. She decided _____ .

13. They needed _____ .

14. They required _____ .

PRACTICE 8 ▸ Gerund or infinitive. (Charts 14-2 → 14-4)

Complete the sentences with the gerund or infinitive form of the *italicized* verbs. Use *him* if an object is required.

Part I. Complete the sentences with *stay*.

1. I expect _____.
2. I want _____.
3. I forced _____.
4. I invited _____.
5. I considered _____.

6. I told _____.
7. I was told _____.
8. I refused _____.
9. I encouraged _____.
10. I would like _____.

Part II. Complete the sentences with *travel*.

1. He doesn't mind _____.
2. He enjoys _____.
3. He needed _____.
4. He quit _____.
5. He is allowed _____.

6. He put off _____.
7. He recommends _____.
8. He can't stand _____.
9. He finished _____.
10. He mentioned _____.

Part III. Complete the sentences with *work*.

1. They discussed _____.
2. They intend _____.
3. They were ordered _____.
4. They decided _____.
5. They offered _____.

6. They delayed _____.
7. They required _____.
8. They hope _____.
9. They plan _____.
10. They avoided _____.

PRACTICE 9 ▸ Common verbs followed by either gerunds or infinitives. (Chart 14-5)

Complete the sentences with the gerund or infinitive form of the verbs in parentheses.

1. a. Don't forget (*turn*) _____ off your computers before you leave the office.

   b. I'll never forget (*meet*) _____ the president when I was a child.

2. a. I'll remember (*stop*) _____ at the grocery store if I write myself a note and

   stick it in the window of my car.

   b. Do you remember (*see*) _____ a man running out of the bank with a large

   bag in his hand?

3. a. Don't give me any more advice. Please stop (*tell*) _____ me what to do.

   b. At the mall, I met my old English teacher. We stopped (*talk*) _____ for a

   while. That was very pleasant.

   c. I had a bad argument with my friend David two years ago. We stopped

   (*speak*) _____ then and haven't spoken since.

4. a. We regret (*buy*) _____ this house. It needs too many repairs.

   b. The letter said, "I regret (*tell*) _____ you that your application

   has been denied."

5. a. Mazzen tried very hard (*learn*) _____ Chinese, but he couldn't do it. He's just not good at languages.

   b. We don't know how to communicate with that man. We've tried (*talk*) _____ to him in Spanish, we've tried in Greek, we've tried in German, and we've tried in French. So far nothing's worked.

PRACTICE 10 ▸ Common verbs followed by either gerunds or infinitives. (Chart 14-5)
Choose the sentence that has the same meaning as the given sentence.

1. Jean and her husband stopped drinking coffee.
   a. They had a cup of coffee together.
   b. They don't drink coffee anymore.

2. I regret to inform you that your application has been denied.
   a. I am sorry to tell you that your application was not accepted.
   b. I am sorry I told you the news about your application.

3. Rita remembers locking the door this morning.
   a. Rita never forgets to lock the door in the morning.
   b. Rita remembers that she locked the door this morning.

4. I forgot to call my grandmother.
   a. I didn't call my grandmother.
   b. I don't remember whether I called my grandmother or not.

5. My back was sore from being at the computer all morning. I stopped to rest.
   a. I kept working.
   b. I took a break.

PRACTICE 11 ▸ Common verbs followed by either gerunds or infinitives. (Chart 14-5)
Choose the correct completions. In some sentences, both are correct.

1. It was raining hard, but we continued _____.
   a. to drive   b. driving

2. The veterinarian tried _____ the horse's life, but he failed.
   a. to save   b. saving

3. As soon as the play ended, the audience began _____ wildly.
   a. to applaud   b. applauding

4. I prefer _____ a movie rather than see one in a theater.
   a. to rent   b. renting

5. I prefer _____ movies at home.
   a. to see   b. seeing

6. I hate _____ in the house when the weather is beautiful.
   a. to stay   b. staying

7. I love _____ on the beach.
   a. to walk   b. walking

8. Most people enjoy _____ to music.
   a. to listen   b. listening

9. When you finish _____, call me and I'll come to pick you up.
   a. to shop   b. shopping

10. Please don't whine. I can't stand _____ you whine.
    a. to listen   b. listening to

PRACTICE 12 ▶ Using gerunds as the objects of prepositions. (Chart 14-6)
Complete the sentences with the gerund form of the verbs in the box.

buy	fly	hear	lower
drink	go	improve	take

1. Thank you for _____ care of my plants while I was in the hospital.

2. The kids are excited about _____ to the circus tomorrow.

3. Students who are interested in _____ their English conversation skills can sign up for special private classes.

4. Psychiatrists say that dreaming about _____ in the sky is quite common.

5. The candidate says he is committed to _____ taxes.

6. We are thinking about not _____ tickets for the opera this year. They have become so expensive.

7. I'm used to _____ tea with my meals. I never drink coffee.

8. We look forward to _____ from you soon.

PRACTICE 13 ▶ Using gerunds as the objects of prepositions. (Chart 14-6)
Choose the correct completions.

1. We are talking _____ opening a vegetarian restaurant in our neighborhood.
   a. to   b. about   c. with

2. Don't worry _____ being on time today. Everybody's going to be late because of the weather.
   a. to   b. about   c. with

3. Aren't you tired _____ studying? Let's take a break.
   a. with   b. about   c. of

4. Beth is a chocoholic. Nothing can stop her _____ eating chocolate whenever she feels like it.
   a. of   b. for   c. from

5. We are looking forward _____ seeing you again.
   a. to   b. of   c. from

6. Let's go dancing instead _____ going to the movies.
   a. with   b. about   c. of

7. Andy is still angry at me. He accused me _____ breaking his phone.
   a. of   b. for   c. in

8. He blames me _____ being too careless.
   a. of   b. about   c. for

9. I apologized _____ losing it, and I offered to replace it.
   a. of   b. in   c. for

10. Believe it or not, Andy is not interested _____ being my friend anymore.
   a. about   b. in   c. of

PRACTICE 14 ▶ Using gerunds as the objects of prepositions. (Chart 14-6)
Write the correct preposition and the correct form of the verbs in parentheses.

1. Henry is excited _____ (leave) _____ for India.

2. I have no excuse _____ (be) _____ late.

3. The rain prevented us _____ (complete) _____ the work.

4. Fred is always complaining _____ (have) _____ a headache.

5. Instead _____ (study) _____, Margaret went to a baseball game with some of her friends.

6. The weather is terrible tonight. I don't blame you _____ (want, not) _____ to go to the meeting.

7. Who is responsible _____ (wash) _____ and (dry) _____ the dishes after dinner?

8. The thief was accused _____ (steal) _____ a woman's purse.

9. I'm going to visit my family during the school vacation. I'm looking forward _____ (eat) _____ my mother's cooking and (sleep) _____ in my own bed.

10. I thanked my friend _____ (lend) _____ me lunch money.

PRACTICE 15 ▶ Using gerunds as the objects of prepositions. (Chart 14-6)
Complete each sentence with a preposition and a verb in the box. Write the verb in its gerund form.

answer	buy	clean	live	✓ take	write
arrive	change	fail	save	waste	

1. I'm thinking ___*about taking*___ a class in digital photography.

2. Are you interested _____ a new computer?

3. Brrr! I don't like this cold weather. I'm used _____ in warmer climates.

4. Please forgive me (not) _____ your email until now. I've been very busy.

5. If you are worried _____ this class, why don't you get a tutor?

6. Everybody talks _____ the situation, but nobody does anything about it.

7. This room is a mess! Isn't anyone responsible _____ it up?

8. Bad weather prevented the plane _____ on time.

9. Thank you _____ a letter of recommendation for me.

10. The environmental group believes _____ energy. They want to stop people _____ electricity.

PRACTICE 16 ▶ Go + gerund. (Chart 14-7)
Look at the pictures of the activities that the Green family and the Evans family enjoy. Use expressions in Chart 14-7 to describe the activities. Write the correct tense of **go** + a gerund.

Part I. The Green family enjoys the outdoors.

1.   2.   3.   4.

1. Every weekend they _____ on the trails near their home.

2. In the summers they _____ on the lake. They like to go out in boats that have no motors.

3. In the winters they _____ in the mountains.

4. Last year they took a trip to Costa Rica, where they saw many
   colorful birds. They _____ .

5. On that trip, they also _____
   on a river.

5.

Part II. The Evans family enjoys different kinds of activities.

6.   7.   8.   9.

6. On Friday nights, they _____ at a social club near their home.

7. Every Monday night, they _____ at an alley at the mall.

8. Next year they are going on a tour of Europe, where they _____
   in five major cities. They'll see famous buildings, museums, and other landmarks.

9. Maybe they won't buy anything, but they _____ to see what's
   in the shops.

PRACTICE 17 ▸ Special expressions followed by *-ing.* (Chart 14-8)
Complete the sentences with the correct form of the verbs in the box.

do	lie	locate	look	play	watch

1. A: How was the picnic?

   B: Great! We had a lot of fun _____ volleyball on the beach.

2. A: What's the matter with Katy?

   B: She's very depressed. She spends all day _____ in bed, and she cries easily.

3. A: Oh, wow! You actually got in touch with Mr. Gordon, our twelfth-grade English teacher.

   B: Yes, I had a hard time _____ him, but I discovered that he was living in a
   retirement home.

4. A: George got fired? Really? Why?

   B: The boss caught him _____ through her private papers in her office.

5. A: Do you ever see Wilma these days?

   B: No. She spends all her time _____ research for her Ph.D.

6. A: Lillian doesn't let her children waste time _____ TV.

   B: Not all TV is bad. There are many good educational programs.

PRACTICE 18 ▸ *It* + infinitive; gerunds and infinitives as subjects. (Chart 14-9)

Choose the correct completions.

1. Is / It's   easy to use a computer.

2. Using a computer   is / it's   easy.

3. To speak another language   is / it's   not easy.

4. Is it / Is   difficult to speak another language?

5. Go / Going   dancing is fun.

6. It's / Is   fun to go dancing.

7. Traveling   is / it's   sometimes tiring.

8. It's dangerous   jump / to jump   out of airplanes in a parachute.

9. See / To see   the Grand Canyon is a thrilling experience.

10. Is / Is it   collecting coins an interesting hobby?

PRACTICE 19 ▸ Chapter review.

Complete the sentences with the correct form of the verbs in the box.

apply	end	operate	run	speak	use
camp	get	read	sleep	turn	watch

1. Our family goes _____ in the summer and fall. We love to cook outdoors and
   sleep in tents under the stars.

2. The doctor was forced _____ immediately to save the patient's life.

3. I have to drive more carefully. I can't risk _____ another speeding ticket.

4. Think about _____ for that new job. You can do it, I know.

5. The sign at the intersection warns drivers not _____ right when the light is red.

6. When Beth entered the room, she found her two cats _____ on her bed.

7. When you get through _____ the newspaper, could you please give me a little
   help in the kitchen?

8. I was furious at Bill's rude behavior. I threatened _____ our friendship.

9. Bill regretted _____ rude language and apologized for
   _____ to me in the way that he did.

10. The customers at the bank just stood _____ helplessly as a masked gunman
    held everyone at gunpoint.

11. But two police officers caught the gunman _____ out of the bank carrying two
    large bags of money.

PRACTICE 20 ▸ Chapter review.

Correct the errors. All the errors are in the use of gerunds and infinitives and the words that go with them.

Exercising the Brain

1. It's important keep your mind active.

2. Watch TV is not good brain exercise.

3. I prefer to spend time to play board games and computer games.

4. There is some evidence that older people can avoid to become senile by exercise their brain.

5. Playing word games it is one good way to stimulate your brain.

6. In addition, is beneficial for everyone to exercise regularly.

7. Physical exercise helps the brain by increase the flow of blood and deliver more oxygen to the brain.

8. Some studies show that to eat any type of fish just once a week increases brain health.

9. Doctors advise older people eating fish two or three times a week.

10. Everyone should try keep a healthy brain.

PRACTICE 21 ▸ Chapter review.

Correct the errors. All the errors are in the use of gerunds and infinitives and the words that go with them.

Studying Abroad

1. Pedro is interested to learn about other cultures.

2. He has always wanted studying abroad.

3. He had difficulty to decide where to study.

4. He has finally decided to living in Japan next year.

5. He's excited about attend a university there.

6. Right now he is struggling learning Japanese.

7. He has a hard time to pronounce the words.

8. He keeps on to study and to practice.

9. At night, he lies in bed to listen to Japanese language-teaching programs.

10. Then he dreams to travel to Japan.

CHAPTER 15

Gerunds and Infinitives, Part 2

PRACTICE 1 ▶ Preview.

Read the passage. Choose the correct completions. In some sentences, both choices are correct.

Life Hacks

Life hack is a term that is used for any trick or shortcut that people use in order   to be / being   more productive and efficient. There are several life hacks related to cleaning. For example, if you have food residue in a microwave that is too difficult   to remove / to be removed,   you can try   to place / placing   a small bowl or cup of water in the microwave and heating it for a couple of minutes. The steam from the water makes the old food   loosen up / to loosen up.   Afterwards, it is easy to wipe the microwave clean. There's a similar trick for blenders and food processors that need   cleaning / to be cleaned.   It takes a lot of time   to scrub / for scrubbing   a blender clean.   Running / To run   the blender with hot soapy water for about a minute beforehand will make it very easy to clean. Life hacks are simple solutions to everyday problems. They help us to manage / manage   our time more efficiently.

PRACTICE 2 ▶ Infinitive of purpose: *in order to.* (Chart 15-1)

Choose the correct completions. In some sentences, both choices are correct.

1. Emily likes _____ ice skating every weekend.
   a. to go   b. in order to go

2. Darcy opened the door _____ some fresh air in.
   a. to let   b. in order to let

3. Beth practices night and day _____ ready for her piano recital next month.
   a. to be   b. in order to be

4. Susie sent me an email _____ me that the meeting had been canceled.
   a. to inform   b. in order to inform

5. We've decided not _____ a vacation this year.
   a. to take   b. in order to take

6. Did you remember _____ Mr. Johnson?
   a. to call   b. in order to call

7. On nice summer nights, we often walk on the beach _____ the sunsets.
   a. to watch   b. in order to watch

8. The boys were so noisy that I had to ring a loud bell _____ their attention.
   a. to get   b. in order to get

9. Airport workers wear ear protectors _____ their ears from jet noise.
   a. to protect   b. in order to protect

10. I need _____ for my grammar test.
    a. to study   b. in order to study

PRACTICE 3 ▶ Infinitive of purpose: *in order to.* (Chart 15-1)
Complete the sentences with *to* or *for.*

David is in Mexico ...

1. visit.

2. a visit.

3. a convention.

4. his cousin's wedding.

5. go sightseeing.

6. learn Spanish.

7. his health.

8. see the Mayan ruins.

9. the cool mountain air.

PRACTICE 4 ▶ Adjectives followed by infinitives. (Chart 15-2)
Complete each conversation with the correct phrase from the list. Write the letter.

    a. to hear that
    b. to bring the paper cups and paper plates
    c. to get into one

    d. to be alive
    e. to introduce our country's president
    f. to lose the next game

1. A: Marta had a bad accident, I heard.

    B: Yes, she did. She's lucky ____.

2. A: Why does Mr. Carlin walk up 12 flights of stairs every day? Is it for the exercise?

    B: No, not at all. He has a phobia about elevators. He's afraid ____.

3. A: Who is going to cook dinner for our next meeting?

    B: I can't cook, but I'm willing ____.

4. A: Our dog died.

    B: Oh, that's a shame. I'm very sorry ____.

5. A: Our three best soccer players are out with injuries.

    B: I know. Without them, you're likely ____.

6. A: Turn the volume up. I want to hear what the senator is saying.

    B: "Ladies and gentlemen, I am proud ____."

PRACTICE 5 ▶ Using infinitives with *too* and *enough.* (Chart 15-3)
Complete the sentences with *too* or *enough.*

1. John dropped his physics course because it was _____ difficult for him.

2. We'd like to go out in our sailboat today, but there isn't _____ wind to sail.

3. I think it's _____ late to get tickets to the concert. I heard they were sold out.

4. Peter has turned 20. Now he's _____ old to take part in the ski races for teenagers.

5. It's _____ hot to take my daily walk. I'm staying inside.

6. It's hot _____ to fry an egg on the sidewalk!

7. Professor Andrews is always interesting, but I'm _____ tired to go to the lecture tonight.

8. I need to work on my essay all weekend. I barely have _____ time to finish it.

9. Ramzy just turned 13 years old. Do you think he's old _____ to take scuba diving lessons?

10. Hannah is _____ young to understand. She'll understand when she's older.

11. I'm _____ sleepy to watch the rest of the TV movie. Let me know how it turns out in the end.

12. These new windows are made of specially treated glass. It's strong _____ to resist the strong winds of hurricanes.

13. It's _____ dark to see in here. Please turn on the lights.

14. There's not _____ light in here. Can you turn on another light?

15. A trip to Europe is _____ expensive for our family this year. We don't have _____ money to travel this year.

16. You're _____ young to drive a car, Emily. You're only 12 years old! There will be time _____ to drive when you're older.

PRACTICE 6 ▸ Using infinitives with *too* and *enough*. (Chart 15-3)
Choose the correct statement for each situation. In some cases, both answers are correct.

1. Karen has been saving up for an electric car. She went to the car dealership today. She has more than enough money to buy a gasoline car, but she needs to save a little more for an electric car.
   a. An electric car is too expensive for Karen to buy.
   b. Karen has enough money to buy an electric car.

2. Ben wants to apply for a position as a web developer at the university. The job requires a bachelor's degree and five years of experience. Ben has a bachelor's degree, but he has only worked as a web developer for two years.
   a. He does not have enough experience for the position.
   b. He is too inexperienced for the position.

3. I went to an excellent presentation last night. The huge auditorium was completely filled with people who were excited to see the popular speaker. I had to sit in the very back, but I was still able to hear every word.
   a. The speaker was too loud.
   b. The speaker was loud enough.

4. Harry wants to run in the Boston Marathon. He has to be able to run a marathon in three hours and forty seconds in order to qualify for the race. Harry can run a marathon in three hours and twenty-five seconds.
   a. He is fast enough to qualify for the race.
   b. He is too slow to qualify for the race.

PRACTICE 7 ▸ Passive infinitives and gerunds: present. (Chart 15-4)
Complete the sentences with the passive form of the verbs in parentheses.

1. I hope (*accepted*) _____ at State College.

2. I would like (*given*) _____ a scholarship.

3. Leo wants (*picked*) _____ for the soccer team.

4. Cats enjoy (*petted*) _____ .

5. Babies need (*held*) _____ .

6. I really appreciate (*asked*) _____ to join this group.

7. Daniel is shy. He avoids (*noticed*) _____ .

8. Annie mentioned (*invited*) _____ to a party at her boss's house.

9. I can't go out tonight. My essay needs (*finished*) _____
   by tomorrow morning.

10. Your essay was supposed (*submitted*) _____ yesterday. You missed the deadline.

PRACTICE 8 ▶ Passive infinitives and gerunds: present. (Chart 15-4)
Choose the correct completions.

1. The mail is supposed _____ before noon.
   a. to deliver   b. to be delivered

2. The mail carrier is supposed _____ the mail before noon.
   a. to deliver   b. to be delivered

3. Janice is going to fill out an application. She wants _____ for the job.
   a. to consider   b. to be considered

4. I expect _____ at the airport by my uncle.
   a. to meet   b. to be met

5. Mr. Steinberg offered _____ us to the train station.
   a. to drive   b. to be driven

6. The kids appear _____ about the trip.
   a. to excite   b. to be excited

7. My co-worker and I agreed _____ the work equally.
   a. to divide   b. to be divided

8. Our boss appears _____ with this arrangement.
   a. to please   b. to be pleased

PRACTICE 9 ▶ Passive infinitives and gerunds: present. (Chart 15-4)
Choose the correct completions.

1. Shhh! Don't ask questions! The professor doesn't appreciate _____ when he's speaking.
   a. interrupting   b. being interrupted

2. Avoid _____ Highway 77. There are a lot of delays because of construction.
   a. taking   b. being taken

3. The mountain climbers are in danger of _____ by an avalanche.
   a. killing   b. being killed

4. Does Dr. Johnson mind _____ at home if his patients need his help?
   a. calling   b. being called

5. I'm interested in _____ my conversational skills.
   a. improving   b. being improved

6. When Alex got home from school, he didn't mention _____ by his teacher.
   a. scolding   b. being scolded

7. Sally's low test scores kept her from _____ to the university.
   a. admitting   b. being admitted

8. Mr. Miller gave no indication of _____ his mind.
   a. changing   b. being changed

PRACTICE 10 ▸ Passive infinitives and gerunds: present. (Chart 15-4)
Complete the sentences with the correct form of the verbs in parentheses.

1. We turn off the phone during dinner. We don't want (*call*) _____ at that time.

2. Not many people enjoy (*call*) _____ by salespeople.

3. I need (*call*) _____ the credit card company. I think there's a mistake on my bill.

4. Each candidate hopes (*elect*) _____ by a large majority of the people.

5. It's not easy (*elect*) _____ .

6. Our mayor has an excellent chance of (*re-elect*) _____ .

7. Some people want (*elect*) _____ a new mayor.

8. Sometimes teenagers complain about not (*understand*) _____ by their parents.

9. Many parents try (*understand*) _____ their teenage children.

10. Some parents get tired of (*try*) _____ to understand their teenagers.

11. Sometimes teenagers would like just (*leave*) _____ alone.

PRACTICE 11 ▸ Past forms of infinitives and gerunds. (Chart 15-5)
Choose the correct completions. More than one answer may be correct.

1. Scott didn't finish his reading homework. When he got to class, he pretended _____ the assignment.
   a. to have read
   b. reading
   c. having read
   d. having been read

2. I would like _____ the Statue of Liberty when I was in New York, but I didn't have time.
   a. to visit
   b. visiting
   c. to have visited
   d. having been visited

3. Lily is worried about _____ her driver's license. She doesn't want to be a victim of identity theft.
   a. to lose
   b. losing
   c. having lost
   d. to have lost

4. I'm honored _____ as a candidate.
   a. to have chosen
   b. to be chosen
   c. to have been chosen
   d. being chosen

5. Rhonda regrets _____ to a small town. She misses all the conveniences of the city.
   a. to move
   b. having moved
   c. to have moved
   d. moving

6. Carlos was an outstanding student. Dr. Clement was happy _____ a letter of recommendation for him.
   a. writing
   b. being written
   c. to have written
   d. to write

7. You mentioned _____ to Nepal. Did you enjoy your trip?
   a. traveling
   b. having traveled
   c. to have traveled
   d. to travel

8. Maya was very disappointed. She was expecting _____ a scholarship.
   a. to receive
   b. to be received
   c. to have received
   d. to have been received

9. Is Gavin OK? He appeared _____ very sick yesterday.
   a. having been
   b. being
   c. to be
   d. to have been

PRACTICE 12 ▶ Using gerunds or passive infinitives following *need*. (Chart 15-6)
Choose all of the sentences that can follow the given sentence.

1. A lot of things in our house don't work.
   a. We need to repair them.
   b. They need to repair.
   c. They need to be repaired.
   d. They need repairing.

2. The refrigerator is so old that it hardly works anymore.
   a. We need to replace the refrigerator.
   b. It needs to replace.
   c. It needs to be replaced.
   d. It needs replacing.

3. The sink has been leaking for a month.
   a. A plumber needs to fix the sink.
   b. The sink needs fixing.
   c. The sink needs to be fixed.
   d. The sink needs to fix.

4. The color of the walls has faded.
   a. We need to paint the walls.
   b. The walls need to be painted.
   c. The walls need to paint.
   d. The walls need painting.

5. We don't have a good repair person.
   a. We need to find a good repair person.
   b. A good repair person needs to find.
   c. A good repair person needs to be found.
   d. We need a repair person to find.

6. Please tell your repair person to call me.
   a. I need to call your repair person.
   b. I need to be called by your repair person.
   c. Your repair person needs to call me.
   d. Your repair person needs calling.

PRACTICE 13 ▸ Using verbs of perception. (Chart 15-7)

Complete the sentences with a verb in the box. Use each word only once. Use the simple form or the *-ing* form, whichever seems better to you. Sometimes both are OK.

arrive	do	pass	reach	talk
cry	leave	practice	rock	win

1. Whenever I can, I like to watch the basketball team _____ for the upcoming game.

2. It's interesting to sit in the airport and watch all the people _____ by.

3. I heard an upset baby _____.

4. Did you see Charles _____ the office? He ran out in a really big hurry.

5. It was a thrill to see my brother _____ the chess tournament last year.

6. I was amazed to see the police _____ so soon after my call.

7. I can't stand to be on a boat. When I feel the boat _____, I get seasick.

8. When I watch my yoga instructor _____ the exercises, it seems easy, but when I try them, it is hard.

9. We listened to the newscaster _____ about rising prices.

10. A security guard at the bank observed a suspicious-looking man _____ into his pocket for something. The guard thought it was a gun, but it turned out to be the man's asthma inhaler.

PRACTICE 14 ▸ Using the simple form after *let* and *help*. (Chart 15-8)

Choose the correct completions. More than one completion may be correct.

1. The school guard stopped all the traffic to let the children _____ the street.
   a. cross   b. to cross   c. crossing

2. My friend Ole is very relaxed. He never lets anything _____ him.
   a. to bother   b. bother   c. bothering

3. My daughter helped me _____ an application online.
   a. filling out   b. filled out   c. fill out

4. Will you please help me _____ the kitchen? Otherwise, I'll be here all night!
   a. clean up   b. to clean up   c. cleaning up

5. Elsa used to have very short hair, but now it is longer. She is letting it _____.
   a. growing   b. to grow   c. grow

6. We don't let our dog _____ around outside. We always take him for walks on a leash.
   a. run   b. to run   c. running

7. Is it true that if you eat fish every day, it will help you _____ smarter?
   a. to become   b. becoming   c. become

8. Did someone help you _____ this research paper?
   a. write   b. wrote   c. writing

PRACTICE 15 ▶ Using causative verbs: *make, have, get*. (Chart 15-9)
Complete the sentences with the correct form of the verbs in parentheses.

1. The general made the soldiers (*stand*) _____ at attention.

2. Don't get rid of those shoes just because they are old. Have them (*fix*) _____ at the shoe repair shop.

3. Exercise makes your heart (*beat*) _____ faster.

4. What can we do to get Marissa (*stop*) _____ smoking?

5. Jean finally got her son (*clean*) _____ his room.

6. Paula's new haircut makes her (*look*) _____ ten years younger.

7. I'm sorry, sir. Your prescription has expired. Have your physician (*call*) _____ us here at the pharmacy, and then we can refill it for you.

8. Please take this document to the copy store and have 15 copies (*make*) _____. There are 150 pages, so you'd better have spiral bindings (*put*) _____ on too.

PRACTICE 16 ▶ Using causative verbs: *make, have, get*. (Chart 15-9)
Choose the correct completions. More than one completion may be correct.

1. You can _____ the company credit your account when you return the shoes.
   a. make   b. have   c. get

2. If you're nice to James, maybe you can _____ him to drive you to the airport.
   a. make   b. have   c. get

3. I'll _____ the taxi driver take me to the airport.
   a. make   b. have   c. get

4. The comedian is so funny. I can't help laughing even though I'm sad. That comedian can _____ anyone laugh.
   a. make   b. have   c. get

5. The students tried to _____ the professor to postpone the exam, but he didn't.
   a. make   b. have   c. get

6. I'm going to _____ my car washed on Saturday.
   a. make   b. have   c. get

7. Ms. Andrews isn't there? _____ her call me, please.
   a. Make   b. Have   c. Get

8. You don't have to go to the party. No one can _____ you go.
   a. make   b. have   c. get

PRACTICE 17 ▶ Using a possessive to modify a gerund. (Chart 15-10)
Complete the sentences with the correct form of the *italicized* pronouns.

1. *you* a. FORMAL: I appreciate _____ taking time to meet with me today.

     b. INFORMAL: I appreciate _____ taking time to meet with me today.

2. *he* a. FORMAL: Every morning, Charlie takes a long shower and sings at the top of his lungs.

     I can't stand _____ singing in the shower.

     b. INFORMAL: I can't stand _____ singing in the shower.

3. *she* a. FORMAL: Joy shouldn't be driving. I'm worried about _____ driving so soon after her eye surgery.

b. INFORMAL: I'm worried about _____ driving so soon after her eye surgery.

4. *they* a. FORMAL: Some students were trying to check their messages during class. The teacher insisted on _____ putting away all electronic devices.

b. INFORMAL: The teacher insisted on _____ putting away all electronic devices.

5. *I* a. FORMAL: My brother was annoyed by _____ borrowing his jacket without asking him first.

b. INFORMAL: My brother was annoyed by _____ borrowing his jacket without asking him first.

6. *we* a. FORMAL: I hope you don't mind _____ having to leave the party a little early.

b. INFORMAL: I hope you don't mind _____ having to leave the party a little early.

PRACTICE 18 ▶ Verb form review. (Chapters 14 and 15)
Choose the correct completions.

1. I enjoy _____ to the park on summer evenings.
   a. to go   b. going   c. being gone   d. go

2. Don't forget _____ as soon as you arrive home.
   a. to call   b. calling   c. call   d. to be called

3. When we kept getting unwanted calls, I called the phone company and had my phone number _____.
   a. change   b. changed   c. to change   d. changing

4. Julie should seriously consider _____ an actress. She's a very talented performer.
   a. to become   b. become   c. becoming   d. will become

5. _____ TV is not recommended for young children.
   a. Watch   b. Being watched   c. Watching   d. To be watched

6. After their children had grown up, Mr. and Mrs. Sills decided _____ to a condominium in the city.
   a. moved   b. moving   c. move   d. to move

7. Are you interested in _____ the movie at University Theater?
   a. see   b. to see   c. being seen   d. seeing

8. The store manager caught the cashier _____ money from the cash register and promptly called the police. They discovered that it had been going on for a long time.
   a. to steal   b. stealing   c. stole   d. being stolen

9. The city authorities advised us _____ all drinking water during the emergency.
   a. to boil   b. to be boiled   c. boiling   d. boil

10. If we leave now for our trip, we can drive half the distance before we stop _____ lunch.
    a. having   b. to have   c. have   d. for having

11. It was difficult _____ the dialogue in the movie. The acoustics in the theater were very bad.
    a. to hear   b. hearing   c. heard   d. to heard

12. Our school basketball team won the championship game by _____ two points in the last five seconds. It was the most exciting game I have ever attended.
    a. being scored   b. to score   c. scoring   d. score

13. The flight attendants made all the passengers _____ their seat belts during the turbulence.
    a. to buckle   b. buckling   c. to buckled   d. buckle

14. At our class reunion, we had a lot of fun _____ at pictures of ourselves from 20 years ago.
    a. looking   b. look   c. looked   d. to look

15. It has become necessary _____ water in the metropolitan area because of the severe drought.
    a. rationing   b. ration   c. have rationed   d. to ration

16. Ethan got a bad grade on his first essay, but he seems _____ his lesson. He edits his work very carefully now.
    a. to have learned   b. having learned   c. learning   d. to have been learned

17. Scott is very upset about _____ his cell phone. It had hundreds of his family photos stored in it.
    a. having been lost   b. having lost   c. to have lost   d. to have been lost

18. I passed a terrible car accident on my way home. Several people appeared _____ .
    a. to have injured   b. being injured   c. to injure   d. to have been injured

PRACTICE 19 ▸ Verb form review. (Chapters 14 and 15)
Complete the sentences with the correct form of the verbs in parentheses. Some sentences are passive.

1. Bill decided (*buy*) _____ a new car rather than a used one.

2. We delayed (*open*) _____ the doors of the testing center until exactly 9:00.

3. I really dislike (*ask*) _____ to answer questions in class when I haven't prepared my homework.

4. I certainly didn't anticipate (*have*) _____ to wait in line for three hours for tickets to the baseball game!

5. When I was younger, I used (*wear*) _____ mini-skirts and bright colors. Now I am accustomed to (*dress*) _____ more conservatively.

6. Skydivers must have nerves of steel. I can't imagine (*jump*) _____ out of a plane and (*fall*) _____ to the earth. What if the parachute doesn't open?

7. We are looking forward to (*take*) _____ on a tour of Athens by our Greek friends.

8. I told the mail carrier that we would be away for two weeks on vacation. I asked her
   (*stop*) _____ (*deliver*) _____ our mail until the 21st. She told me
   (*fill*) _____ out a form at the post office so that the post office would hold our mail
   until we returned.

9. The elderly man next door is just sitting in his rocking chair (*gaze*) _____ out the window. I wish there were something I could do (*cheer*) _____ him up.

10. I resent (*have*) _____ to work on this project with Fred. I know I'll end up with most of the work falling on my shoulders.

PRACTICE 20 ▸ Verb form review. (Chapters 14 and 15)

Choose the correct completions.

1. Alice didn't expect _____ to Bill's party.
   a. to ask   b. to be asked   c. asking

2. Matthew left the office without _____ anyone.
   a. tell   b. telling   c. told

3. It's useless. Give up. Enough's enough. Don't keep _____ your head against a brick wall.
   a. beat   b. beating   c. to beat

4. I hope _____ a scholarship for the coming semester.
   a. to award   b. to be awarded   c. being awarded

5. We are very pleased _____ your invitation.
   a. to accept   b. to be accepted   c. accept

6. It was exciting _____ to faraway places last year.
   a. travel   b. to travel   c. to traveled

7. Conscientious parents don't let their children _____ too much screen time.
   a. have   b. to have   c. having

8. Did you see that deer _____ across the road?
   a. run   b. ran   c. to run

9. Mr. Carson was very lucky _____ to represent the company in Paris.
   a. to be chosen   b. choosing   c. to chose

10. Last Saturday, we went _____.
    a. to shop   b. shopping   c. to shopping

11. _____ in the mountains is Tom's favorite activity.
    a. Hike   b. Hiking   c. Go to hike

12. The physical activity makes him _____ good.
    a. feel   b. to feel   c. feeling

13. Martha opened the window _____ in some fresh air.
    a. let   b. letting   c. to let

14. Scott wastes a lot of time _____ out with his friends at the mall.
    a. hanging   b. to hang   c. hang

15. Did you remember _____ the front door?
    a. lock   b. to lock   c. locking

16. I don't remember ever _____ that story before.
    a. hearing   b. heard   c. to hear

17. You should stop _____ if you get sleepy.
    a. drive   b. driving   c. to drive

18. I have trouble _____ asleep at night.
    a. fall   b. to fall   c. falling

19. After driving for three hours, we stopped _____ something to eat.
    a. to get   b. getting   c. got

20. The refrigerator needs _____ again.
    a. to be fixed   b. to fix   c. fixed

21. That pan is really hot. It's too hot _____ up without an oven mitt.
    a. pick   b. picking   c. to pick

22. Braden was annoyed _____ his driving test by only one question.
    a. to be failed   b. to failed   c. to have failed

23. Alyssa parked her car in a fire zone. Now her car is gone. It appears _____ .
    a. to have towed   b. to have been towed   c. having towed

24. Thank you for _____ honest.
    a. being   b. been   c. to be

25. I appreciate _____ the truth.
    a. to be told   b. to have told   c. having been told

PRACTICE 21 ▶ Verb form review. (Chapters 14 and 15)
Correct the errors.

1. You shouldn't let children playing with matches.

2. Maddie was lying in bed to cry.

3. You can get there more quickly by take River Road instead of the interstate highway.

4. Nathan expected being admitted to the university, but he wasn't.

5. Our lawyer advised us not signing the contract until she had a chance to study it very carefully.

6. John was responsible for to notify everyone about the meeting.

7. Apparently, he failed to calling several people.

8. I couldn't understand what the reading said, so I asked my friend translated it for me.

9. You can find out the meaning of the word by look it up in a dictionary.

10. No, that's not what I meant to say. How can I make you understanding?

11. Serena wore a large hat for protect her face from the sun.

12. We like to go to fish on weekends.

13. Maybe you can get Charlie taking you to the airport.

14. My doctor advised me not eating food with a high fat content.

15. Doctors always advise eat less and exercising more.

16. Allen smelled something to burn. When he ran into the kitchen, he saw fire coming out of the oven.

17. The player appeared to have been injure during the basketball game.

18. David mentioned having been traveled to China last year.

Coordinating Conjunctions

PRACTICE 1 ▸ Preview.
Read the passage. Complete the sentences.

Community Gardening

Gardening is a popular hobby. Some people have herb gardens with plants such as thyme, basil, mint, and oregano. These herbs are useful for seasoning food, brewing in tea, or making medicinal remedies. Other people grow vegetable gardens for food. Some people prefer to grow flower gardens. They enjoy the beauty and fragrance of their plants.

It is not easy for people who live in large cities to grow a garden. Not only do most city dwellers lack the space for a garden, many also lack the knowledge to plan and maintain a garden. One solution to this problem is a community garden. A community garden is a large piece of land that is gardened by several people. In some cases, everyone works together in one large garden. In other cases, each person has his or her own small garden plot.

There are several benefits to community gardens. These gardens give people who live in cities an opportunity to grow their own fresh vegetables and herbs; they offer people the chance to participate in a fun hobby; and they provide people with a sense of community and a connection to the environment.

1. Four examples of herbs are _____, _____, _____, and

   _____ .

2. Three common uses for herbs are _____ food, _____ in tea,

   and _____ medicinal remedies.

3. Three types of gardens are _____, _____, and _____

   gardens.

4. It might be difficult for people who live in large cities to grow a garden because they lack the

   _____ and _____ needed to grow a garden.

5. Four benefits of community gardens include having fresh _____ and

   _____, a fun _____, a sense of _____,

   and a _____ to the environment.

PRACTICE 2 ▸ Parallel structure. (Chart 16-1)

Choose the correct completions.

1. In the winter, Iceland is cold and _____ .
   a. ice　　　　　　　　b. dark　　　　　　　　c. a country

2. Dan opened the door and _____ the room.
   a. enter　　　　　　　b. entering　　　　　　c. entered

3. This dish is made of meat, potatoes, and _____ .
   a. spicy　　　　　　　b. salty　　　　　　　　c. vegetables

4. Lindsey was listening to music and _____ homework at the same time.
   a. does　　　　　　　b. doing　　　　　　　　c. did

5. Mimi learned how to sing and _____ at the Academy of the Arts.
   a. danced　　　　　　b. dancing　　　　　　　c. dance

6. I have written and _____ her, but I have received no response.
   a. call　　　　　　　b. calling　　　　　　　c. called

7. Somebody called and _____ up.
   a. hung　　　　　　　b. hang　　　　　　　　c. hanging

8. Don't call and _____ up. Leave a short message.
   a. hung　　　　　　　b. hang　　　　　　　　c. hanging

PRACTICE 3 ▸ Parallel structure. (Chart 16-1)

Circle the conjunction that joins the parallel words. Then <u>underline</u> the words that are parallel and choose the part of speech that describes them.

1. These apples are <u>fresh</u> (and) <u>sweet</u>.
   a. adjective　　　　　d. adverb
   b. noun　　　　　　　e. gerund
   c. verb　　　　　　　f. infinitive

2. These apples and pears are fresh.
   a. adjective　　　　　d. adverb
   b. noun　　　　　　　e. gerund
   c. verb　　　　　　　f. infinitive

3. I washed and dried the apples.
   a. adjective　　　　　d. adverb
   b. noun　　　　　　　e. gerund
   c. verb　　　　　　　f. infinitive

4. I am washing and drying the apples.
   a. adjective　　　　　d. adverb
   b. noun　　　　　　　e. gerund
   c. verb　　　　　　　f. infinitive

5. We ate the fruit happily and quickly.
   a. adjective　　　　　d. adverb
   b. noun　　　　　　　e. gerund
   c. verb　　　　　　　f. infinitive

6. Those organic apples are delicious but expensive.
   a. adjective　　　　　d. adverb
   b. noun　　　　　　　e. gerund
   c. verb　　　　　　　f. infinitive

7. Apples, pears, and bananas are kinds of fruit.
   a. adjective   d. adverb
   b. noun   e. gerund
   c. verb   f. infinitive

8. I like an apple or a banana with my cereal.
   a. adjective   d. adverb
   b. noun   e. gerund
   c. verb   f. infinitive

9. Those apples are red, ripe, and juicy.
   a. adjective   d. adverb
   b. noun   e. gerund
   c. verb   f. infinitive

PRACTICE 4 ▶ Parallel structure. (Chart 16-1)

Complete each conversation with the correct word or phrase from the list. Write the letter.

a. carefully   e. reliable health care
b. excellence in   f. responsible
c. in agriculture   g. seeking practical solutions
d. provide quality education   h. finds a way to get the important jobs done

1. Mr. Li has had a wide range of experience. He has worked in business, in the news media, and _____.

2. People want safe homes, good schools, and _____.

3. As a taxpayer, I want my money used wisely and _____.

4. Ms. Adams is respected for researching issues and _____.

5. Ms. Hunter has established a record of effective and _____ leadership in government.

6. She has worked hard to control excess government spending, protect our environment, and _____.

7. Carol is a hard-working personnel manager who welcomes challenges and _____.

8. I will continue to fight for adequate funding of and _____ education.

PRACTICE 5 ▶ Parallel structure: using commas. (Chart 16-2)

Add commas as necessary.

1. Jack was calm and quiet.

2. Jack was calm quiet and serene.

3. The soccer players practiced kicking and passing the ball and they ran laps.

4. The soccer players practiced kicking passing and running.

5. The kids collected rocks and insects had a picnic and flew kites.

6. The teacher told the students to put their phones away open their reading books and review their notes.

7. The teacher told the students to put their phones away and open their reading books.

8. Did you know that the pupil of your eye expands and contracts slightly with each heartbeat?

— pupil

9. Our server carried two cups of coffee three glasses of water one glass of orange juice and three orders of eggs on her tray.

10. My parents were strict but fair with their children.

PRACTICE 6 ▸ Parallel structure. (Charts 16-1 and 16-2)

Underline the words that are supposed to be parallel. Write "C" if the parallel structure is correct. Write "I" if the parallel structure is incorrect, and make any necessary corrections.

1. __I__ I admire my brother for his intelligence, cheerful disposition, and ~~he is honest~~. *honesty*

2. __C__ Abraham Lincoln was a lawyer and a politician.

3. _____ The boat sailed across the lake smoothly and quiet.

4. _____ Barbara studies each problem carefully and works out a solution.

5. _____ Aluminum is plentiful and relatively inexpensive.

6. _____ Many visitors to Los Angeles enjoy visiting Disneyland and to tour movie studios.

7. _____ Children are usually interested in but a little frightened by snakes.

8. _____ So far this term, the students in the writing class have learned how to write thesis statements, organize their material, and summarizing their conclusions.

9. _____ When I looked more closely, I saw that it was not coffee but chocolate on my necktie.

10. _____ Physics explains why water freezes and how the sun produces heat.

11. _____ All plants need light, a suitable climate, and they require an ample supply of water and minerals from the soil.

12. _____ With their keen sight, fine hearing, and refined sense of smell, wolves hunt day or night in quest of elk, deer, moose, or caribou.

PRACTICE 7 ▸ Separating independent clauses with periods; connecting them with *and* and *but*. (Chart 16-3)

Punctuate the sentences by adding commas or periods. Do not add any words. Add capitalization as necessary.

1. The rain stopped the winds died down.

2. The rain stopped and the winds died down.

3. The rain stopped the winds died down and the clouds disappeared.

4. A young boy ran out on the street his mother ran after him.

5. A young boy ran out on the street and his mother ran after him.

6. A young boy ran out on the street his mother ran after him and caught him by his shirt collar.

7. The café serves delicious pastries and coffee and it is always crowded.

8. The café serves delicious pastries and coffee it is always crowded.

9. The café serves delicious pastries, coffee, and ice cream but it is never crowded.

PRACTICE 8 ▸ Connecting independent clauses with *and* and *but*. (Chart 16-3)

Combine each pair of sentences with the conjunction in parentheses.

1. (*and*) Sherri's graduation was last week. Now she's looking for a job.

   _____

2. (*and*) She completed her degree in nursing. She also has a certificate in radiology.

   _____

3. (*but*) Sherri doesn't have any full-time work experience. She completed a one-year internship at the hospital.

_____

4. (*but*) There is a job opening at Lakeside Hospital. It requires five years of nursing experience.

_____

PRACTICE 9 ▸ Separating independent clauses with periods; connecting them with *and* and *but*. (Chart 16-3)

Correct the errors in punctuation and capitalization.

1. My brother is visiting me for a couple of days we spent yesterday together in the city and we had a really good time.

2. first I took him to the waterfront we went to the aquarium we saw fearsome sharks some wonderfully funny marine mammals and all kinds of tropical fish after the aquarium, we went downtown to the mall and went shopping.

3. I had trouble thinking of a place to take him for lunch because he's a strict vegetarian but I remembered a restaurant that has vegan food we went there and we had a wonderful lunch of fresh vegetables and whole grains I'm not a vegetarian but I must say that I really enjoyed the meal.

4. In the afternoon it started raining we decided to go to a movie it was pretty good but had too much violence for me I felt tense when we left the theater I prefer comedies or dramas my brother loved the movie.

5. We ended the day with a delicious home-cooked meal and some good conversation in my living room it was an excellent day I like spending time with my brother.

PRACTICE 10 ▸ Paired conjunctions: *both ... and; not only ... but also; either ... or; neither ... nor.* (Chart 16-4)

Complete the sentences with the correct present tense form of the verbs in parentheses.

1. Neither the students nor the teacher (*know*) _____*knows*_____ the answer.

2. Neither the teacher nor the students (*know*) _____*know*_____ the answer.

3. Not only the students but also the teacher (*know*) _____ the answer.

4. Not only the teacher but also the students (*know*) _____ the answer.

5. Both the teacher and the students (*know*) _____ the answer.

6. Neither Alan nor Carol (*want*) _____ to go skiing this weekend.

7. Both John and Ted (*like*) _____ to go cross-country skiing.

8. Either Jack or Alice (*have*) _____ the information you need.

9. Neither my parents nor my brother (*agree*) _____ with my decision.

10. Both intelligence and skill (*be*) _____ essential to good teaching.

11. Neither my classmates nor my teacher (*realize*) _____ that I have no idea what's going on in class.

12. Not only my husband but also my children (*be*) _____ in favor of my decision to return to school and finish my graduate degree.

PRACTICE 11 ▸ Paired conjunctions: *both ... and; not only ... but also; either ... or; neither ... nor.* (Chart 16-4)

Write sentences with the given words and the paired conjunctions. Use capital letters and punctuation as necessary.

1. Mary drinks coffee. Her parents drink coffee.

   a. both ... and _____ .

   b. neither ... nor _____ .

2. John will do the work. Henry will do the work.

   a. either ... or _____ .

   b. neither ... nor _____ .

3. Our school recycles trash. Our school recycles old electronics.

   a. not only ... but also _____ .

   b. both ... and _____ .

PRACTICE 12 ▸ Paired conjunctions: *both ... and; not only ... but also; either ... or; neither ... nor.* (Chart 16-4)

Complete the sentences.

Part I. Use *both ... and*.

1. You know her mother. Do you know her father too?

   Yes, _____*I know both her mother and her father.*_____

2. The nurses usually arrive early. Does the doctor arrive early too?

   Yes, _____ early.

3. Bananas originated in Asia. Did mangos originate in Asia too?

   Yes, _____ in Asia.

4. Whales are mammals. Are dolphins mammals too?

   Yes, _____ mammals.

Part II. Use *not only ... but also*.

5. Ethiopia exports coffee. Does it export oil too?

   Ethiopia _____ .

6. Air Greenland flies to Greenland. What about Icelandair?

   _____ to Greenland.

7. You bought a lime-green jacket. What about pants? Did you buy lime-green pants too?

   Yes, I bought _____ to go

   with it.

8. Al attended Harvard University. Did he attend Harvard Law School too?

   Yes, Al _____ .

Part III. Use *either ... or*.

9. Someone knows the answer. Is it Ricky? Paula? One of them knows.

   _____ the answer.

10. You're going to Mexico on your vacation. Are you going to Costa Rica too?

    We're going _____, not

    to both.

11. Who will take Taka to the airport: Jim or Taka's parents?

    _____ to the airport.

12. Helen's buying salmon. Is she buying tuna too?

    No. She's buying _____,

    whichever looks fresher.

Part IV. Use *neither ... nor*.

13. Fred doesn't eat red meat. Do his children eat red meat?

    No, _____ eat red meat.

14. She doesn't have health insurance. Do her children have health insurance?

    No, _____ health insurance.

15. Luis doesn't have a family. Does he have friends?

    No, _____.

16. How's the weather there? Is it hot? Is it cold?

    It's perfect! It's _____.

PRACTICE 13 ▸ Chapter review.
Correct the errors. Add the necessary punctuation.

1. Either John will call Mary or Bob.

2. Not only Sue saw the mouse but also the cat.

3. Both my mother talked to the teacher and my father.

4. Either Mr. Anderson or Ms. Wiggins are going to teach our class today.

5. I enjoy not only reading novels but also magazines I enjoy.

6. Smallpox is a dangerous disease. Malaria too. Both are dangerous.

7. She wants to buy a compact car, she is saving her money.

8. According to the news report, it will snow tonight the roads may be dangerous in the morning.

9. While we were in New York, we attended an opera, while we were in New York, we ate at marvelous

   restaurants, we visited some old friends.

PRACTICE 14 ▶ Chapter review.
Complete the crossword puzzle. Use the clues under the puzzle. All the words come from Chapter 16.

Across

3. I drink tea, _____ I don't drink coffee.

4. Carl is not _____ a chemist but also a biologist.

6. Thankfully, _____ Mary or Joe will help us.

7. He has neither friends _____ money.

Down

1. _____ Jane nor Al speaks Spanish.

2. _____ Sue and Sam are doctors.

5. Salt _____ pepper are on the table.

Adverb Clauses

PRACTICE 1 ▶ Preview.

Read the passage. Answer the questions.

Staying Connected

Before social media sites existed, it was often difficult to stay connected with friends and family or find old friends. Now that we have access to a multitude of social media sites, it's easy to be in touch with people. While most people agree that this is true, some are worried that social media does exactly the opposite. Even though we can stay in touch with a large number of people through social media, those connections are not always very deep. As more and more people rely on social media for communication, they are spending less time having real conversations. Whenever we  have an important announcement to make to our friends, we might write a couple of sentences on a social media site for everyone to see because it is more efficient than making several phone calls. In some extreme cases, people report communicating with their friends mostly through social media sites even if they live in the same house as those friends. Whether or not we like it, social media sites are probably here to stay. They can be beneficial as long as we remember that it's also important to connect with our friends individually through phone calls or face-to-face meetings.

---

1. Which words express a time relationship?

   _____

2. Which words express a cause-and-effect relationship?

   _____

3. Which words express contrast?

   _____

4. Which words express condition?

   _____

PRACTICE 2 ▶ Adverb clauses. (Chart 17-1)

<u>Underline</u> the adverb clause in each sentence.

1. Sanae dropped a carton of eggs as she was leaving the store.

2. Tomorrow, we'll all go for a run in the park before we have breakfast.

3. Since Douglas fell off his bike last week, he has had to use crutches to walk.

4. Because I already had my boarding pass, I didn't have to stand in line at the airline counter.

5. Productivity in a factory increases if the workplace is made pleasant.

6. After Ceylon had been independent for 24 years, its name was changed to Sri Lanka.

7. Ms. Johnson regularly answers her email messages as soon as she receives them.

8. Tarik will be able to work more efficiently once he becomes familiar with the new computer program.

PRACTICE 3 ▶ Periods and commas. (Chart 17-1)
Add periods and commas as necessary. Do not change, add, or omit any words. Capitalize as necessary.

1. The lake was calm Tom went fishing.

2. Because the lake was calm Tom went fishing.

3. Tom went fishing because the lake was calm he caught two fish.

4. When Tom went fishing the lake was calm he caught two fish.

5. The lake was calm so Tom went fishing he caught two fish.

6. Because the lake was calm and quiet Tom went fishing.

7. The lake was calm quiet and clear when Tom went fishing.

8. Because Mr. Hood has dedicated his life to helping the poor he is admired in his community.

9. Mr. Hood is admired because he has dedicated his life to helping the poor he is well known for his work on behalf of homeless people.

10. Microscopes automobile dashboards and cameras are awkward for left-handed people to use they are designed for right-handed people when "lefties" use these items they have to use their right hand to do the things that they would normally do with their left hand.

PRACTICE 4 ▶ Using adverb clauses to show time relationships. (Charts 17-1 and 17-2)
Choose the correct completions.

1. After Ismael _____ his degree, he plans to seek employment in an engineering firm.
   a. will finish   b. finishes   c. is going to finish   d. is finishing

2. By the time Colette leaves work today, she _____ the budget report.
   a. will finish   b. finishes   c. will have finished   d. had finished

3. When my aunt _____ at the airport tomorrow, I'll be at work, so I can't pick her up.
   a. will arrive   b. arrived   c. will have arrived   d. arrives

4. Natasha heard a small "meow" and looked down to discover a kitten at her feet. When she saw it, she _____.
   a. is smiling   b. had smiled   c. smiled   d. smiles

5. Ahmed has trouble keeping a job. By the time Ahmed was 30, he _____ eight different jobs.
   a. has   b. was having   c. had had   d. had been having

6. Maria waits until her husband, Allen, _____ to work before she calls her friends on the phone.
   a. will go   b. went   c. will have gone   d. goes

7. I went to an opera at Lincoln Center the last time I _____ to New York City.
   a. go   b. went   c. had gone   d. have gone

8. When the police arrived, the building was empty. The thieves _____ and escaped through an unlocked window.
   a. will have   b. have entered   c. had entered   d. were entering

9. It seems that whenever I try to take some quiet time for myself, the phone _____.
   a. has been ringing   b. rings   c. is ringing   d. has rung

10. I'll invite the Thompsons to the potluck dinner the next time I _____ them.
    a. see   b. will see   c. will have seen   d. have seen

11. I _____ hard to help support my family ever since I was a child.
    a. worked   b. work   c. am working   d. have worked

12. A small rabbit ran across the path in front of me as I _____ through the woods.
    a. was walking   b. had walked   c. am walking   d. had been walking

PRACTICE 5 ▶ Using adverb clauses to show time relationships. (Chart 17-2)

Write "1" before the event that happened first. Write "2" before the event that happened second.
Write "S" for *same* if the events happened at the same time.

1. As soon as it stopped snowing, the kids ran out to go sledding in the fresh snow.

   _1_ It stopped snowing.

   _2_ The kids ran out to go sledding.

2. I'll call you as soon as we arrive at the motel.

   _____ I'll call you.

   _____ We arrive at the hotel.

3. We turned on the heat when it got cold.

   _____ It got cold.

   _____ We turned on the heat.

4. We will turn on the heat when it gets cold.

   _____ We will turn on the heat.

   _____ It will get cold.

5. By the time Sharon gets home from Africa, she will have been away for two years.

   _____ Sharon gets home.

   _____ She will have been away.

6. By the time Marc graduated from medical school, he had been studying for 20 years.

   _____ He had been studying.

   _____ Marc graduated from medical school.

7. We were crying while we were watching the movie.

   _____ We were crying.

   _____ We were watching the movie.

8. When I have some news, I'll tell you.

   _____ I have some news.

   _____ I'll tell you.

PRACTICE 6 ▸ Using adverb clauses to show cause and effect. (Chart 17-3)
Complete the sentences in Column A with a clause from Column B.

Column A

1. I left a message on Jane's voicemail because _____.

2. Since everybody in my office dresses informally, _____.

3. Now that it's summer, _____.

4. Our carpool was late because _____.

5. Because the temperature dropped

   below 0 degrees C (32 degrees F), _____.

6. Olivia hopes to find a good job now that _____.

7. I'm not going to the party since _____.

8. We had to eat dinner by candlelight because _____.

9. Since their favorite restaurant was closed, _____.

10. I prefer a small car because _____.

Column B

a. the days are longer

b. they went to another one

c. I wasn't invited

d. she didn't answer her phone

e. there was a big traffic jam

f. the power went out

g. it uses less gasoline

h. the water in the lake froze

i. I usually wear jeans to work

j. she has received her master's degree
   in business

PRACTICE 7 ▸ Using adverb clauses to show cause and effect. (Chart 17-3)
Combine the sentences. Write one clause in each blank.

1. My registration was canceled. I didn't pay the registration fee on time.

   _____ because _____ .

2. I'm late. There was a lot of traffic.

   _____ because _____ .

3. Harry lost 35 pounds. He was on a strict weight-loss diet.

   Because _____ , _____ .

4. We can't have lunch at Mario's tomorrow. It is closed on Sundays.

   Since _____ , _____ .

5. Jack drives to work. He has a car.

   Now that _____ , _____ .

6. Natalie should find another job. She is very unhappy in this job.

   _____ since _____ .

7. David knows the way. He will lead us.

   _____ because _____ .

8. Frank has graduated from law school. He is looking for a job in a law office.

   _____ now that _____ .

PRACTICE 8 ▶ Even though vs. because. (Chart 17-4)
Choose the correct completions.

1. I put on my raincoat   even though / because   it was a bright, sunny day.

2. I put on my raincoat   even though / because   it was raining.

3. Even though / Because   Sue is a good student, she received a scholarship.

4. Even though / Because   Ann is a good student, she didn't receive a scholarship.

5. Even though / Because   I was so tired, I didn't want to walk all the way home. I took a taxi.

6. Even though / Because   I was dead tired, I walked all the way home.

7. This letter was delivered   even though / because   it didn't have enough postage.

8. That letter was returned to the sender   even though / because   it didn't have enough postage.

PRACTICE 9 ▶ Even though vs. because. (Chart 17-4)
Complete the sentences with **even though** or **because**.

1. a. I'm going horseback riding with Judy this afternoon _____ I'm afraid

   of horses.

   b. I'm going horseback riding with Judy this afternoon _____ I enjoy it.

2. a. _____ the economy is not good right now, people are not buying new

   cars and other expensive items.

   b. _____ the economy is not good right now, the supermarket is still

   a profitable business. People always have to eat.

3. a. Members of the Polar Bear Club are swimmers who go swimming in the ocean

   _____ the temperature may be freezing.

   b. Members of the Polar Bear Club are swimmers who swim in the ocean every day in

   summer and winter _____ they love to swim in the ocean.

4. a. Janet got a grade of 98% on her history test _____ she studied hard.

   b. Mike got a grade of 98% on his history test _____ he didn't study

   at all. I wonder how that happened.

PRACTICE 10 ▶ Showing direct contrast: while. (Chart 17-5)
Choose the phrase that shows direct contrast.

1. Larry and Barry are twins, but they are very different. Larry never studies, while Barry _____.
   a. rarely studies
   b. sleeps all day
   c. is very studious

2. My roommate and I disagree about the room temperature. While she likes it warm, I _____.
   a. prefer cold temperatures
   b. have trouble when it is cool
   c. don't like my roommate

3. Athletes need to be strong, but they may need different physical characteristics for different sports.

   For example, weight-lifters have well-developed chest muscles, while _____.
   a. basketball players' muscles are strong
   b. basketball players should be tall
   c. basketball players' chest muscles are very large

4. Portland, Maine, is on the East Coast of the United States, while Portland, Oregon, _____.
   a. is on the East Coast too
   b. lies on the West Coast
   c. is another medium-sized city

5. Crocodiles and alligators look a lot alike, but they have certain differences.

   While a crocodile has a very long, narrow, V-shaped snout, the alligator's
   snout is _____.
   a. wider and U-shaped
   b. long, narrow, and V-shaped
   c. large and green

6. The Earth is similar to Venus in some ways, but their atmospheres are different. While the Earth's atmosphere contains mostly nitrogen and oxygen, _____.
   a. Venus has mainly nitrogen and oxygen
   b. Venus' air is very cold
   c. Venus' atmosphere consists mostly of the gas carbon dioxide

7. Polar bears live near the North Pole, while _____.
   a. penguins live there too
   b. penguins live at the South Pole
   c. they live in the South Pole

8. Potatoes and tomatoes originated in the Americas, while _____.
   a. mangos and bananas come from Asia
   b. corn and chocolate come from the Americas
   c. turkeys first lived in North America

PRACTICE 11 ▸ *If*-clauses. (Chart 17-6)

Underline the entire *if*-clause. Correct any errors in verb forms. Some sentences have no errors.

1. We won't go to the beach if it ~~will rain~~ *rains* tomorrow.

2. If my car doesn't start tomorrow morning, I'll take the bus to work.

3. If I have any free time during my workday, I'll call you.

4. I'll text you if my phone won't die.

5. If we don't leave within the next ten minutes, we are late for the theater.

6. If we will leave within the next ten minutes, we will make it to the theater on time.

7. The population of the world will be 9.1 billion in 2050 if it will continue to grow at the present rate.

PRACTICE 12 ▶ Shortened *if*-clauses. (Chart 17-7)
First, complete the sentences in two ways:
    a. Use *so* or *not*.
    b. Use a helping verb or main verb *be*.
Second, give the full meaning of the shortened *if-clause*.

1. Does Asraf live near you?

    a. If _____*so*_____, ask him to pick you up at 5:30.

    b. If he _____*does*_____, ask him to pick you up at 5:30.

    Meaning: _____*If Asraf lives near you*_____

2. Are you a resident of Springfield?

    a. If _____, you can get a library card for the Springfield Library.

    b. If you _____, you can get a library card for the Springfield Library.

    Meaning: _____

3. Do you have enough money to go out to dinner?

    a. If _____, I'll pay for you.

    b. If you _____, I'll pay for you.

    Meaning: _____

4. Are you going to do the laundry?

    a. If _____, I have some things that need washing too.

    b. If you _____, I have some things that need washing too.

    Meaning: _____

5. I think I left the water running in the sink.

    a. If _____, we'd better go home and turn it off.

    b. If I _____, we'd better go home and turn it off.

    Meaning: _____

PRACTICE 13 ▶ Using *whether or not* and *even if*. (Chart 17-8)
Complete the sentences using the given information.

1. Juan is going to major in photography no matter what. He doesn't care if his parents approve. In other words, Juan is going to major in photography even if his parents _____*don't approve*_____. He's going to get a degree in photography whether his parents _____*approve*_____ or not.

2. Fatima is determined to buy an expensive car. It doesn't matter to her if she can't afford it. In other words, Fatima is going to buy an expensive car whether she _____ it or not. She's going to buy one even if she _____ it.

3. William wears his raincoat every day. He wears it when it's raining. He wears it when it's not raining. In other words, William wears his raincoat whether it _____ or not. He wears it even if it _____ .

4. Some students don't understand what the teacher is saying, but still they smile and nod. In other words, even if they _____ what the teacher is saying, they smile and nod. They smile and nod whether they _____ what the teacher is saying or not.

5. Everybody has to pay taxes. It doesn't matter whether you want to or not. In other words, even if you _____, you have to pay them. You have to pay your taxes _____ or not.

PRACTICE 14 ▸ Adverb clause of condition: using *in case*. (17-9)
Complete the sentences in Column A with a clause from Column B.

Column A

1. You should take a jacket _____.

2. Be sure to save your work _____.

3. I brought a charger _____.

4. Here's my number _____.

5. I picked up some local travel brochures _____.

6. Dr. Kennedy is on call tonight _____.

7. I put the salad dressing on the side _____.

8. Take your car to the mechanic before you leave for your trip _____.

Column B

a. in case my phone dies.

b. in case you need to reach me

c. in case you're interested in taking a day trip

d. in case a patient has a medical emergency

e. in case it gets cold tonight

f. just in case your computer crashes

g. just in case it has any problems

h. in case you don't like it

PRACTICE 15 ▸ Adverb clauses of condition: using *unless*. (Chart 17-10)
The sentences in *italics* are well-known proverbs or sayings. Write sentences with the same meaning as the sentences in *italics*. Use ***unless***.

1. *If you can't stand the heat, get out of the kitchen.*

   This means that if you can't take the pressure, then you should remove yourself from the situation.

   _____ *Get out of the kitchen unless you can stand the heat* _____.

2. *If it isn't broken, don't fix it.* This is often said as *If it ain't broke, don't fix it.*

   This means that any attempt to improve something that already works is pointless and may even hurt it.

   Don't fix it _____.

3. *If you can't beat them, join them.*

   This means if you can't beat your opponents, you can join them.

   You might not be successful _____.

4. *If you scratch my back, I'll scratch yours.*

   This means that if you help me, I'll help you too.

   I might not help you _____.

5. *If you're in a hole, stop digging.*

   This means that you should try not to make a problem worse than it already is.

   A hole will continue to get bigger _____.

PRACTICE 16 ▸ Adverb clauses of condition: using *only if*. (Chart 17-11)
Complete the sentences with the information in the given sentence.

1. Jason never calls his uncle unless he wants something.

   Jason calls his uncle only if _____.

2. When Helen runs out of clean clothes, she does her laundry. Otherwise, she never does laundry.

   Helen does laundry only if _____.

3. José doesn't like to turn on the heat in his house unless the temperature outside goes below
   50 degrees F (10 degrees C).

   José turns on the heat only if _____.

4. Zach hates to fly. He usually travels by car or train except when it is absolutely necessary to get
   somewhere quickly.

   Zach flies only if _____.

5. Most applicants cannot get into Halley College. You probably won't get in. Only the top students
   will get in.

   Only if you are a top student _____.

6. I could never afford a big house like that! Well, maybe if I win the lottery. That would be the only way.

   Only if I win the lottery _____.

PRACTICE 17 ▸ Review: adverb clauses of condition. (Charts 17-8 → 17-11)
Choose the word to logically complete each sentence.

1. I'll pass the course only if I   pass / don't pass   the final examination.

2. I'm   going to go / not going to go   to the park unless the weather is nice.

3. I'm going to the park unless it   rains / doesn't rain.

4. I'm sorry that you won't be able to join us on Saturday. But please call us   in case / even if   you
   change your mind.

5. Roberto doesn't like to work. He'll get a job   unless / only if   he has to.

6. I   always eat / never eat   breakfast unless I get up late and don't have enough time.

7. I always finish my homework   even if / only if   I'm sleepy and want to go to bed.

8. Ali is at his desk at 8:00 A.M. sharp   whether / unless   his boss is there or not.

9. You   will / won't   learn to play the guitar well unless you practice every day.

10. Even if the president calls,   wake / don't wake   me up. I don't want to talk to anyone.
    I need to sleep.

11. Burt is going to come to the game with us today   if / unless   his boss gives him the afternoon off.

12. Only if people succeed in reducing greenhouse gases   we can / can we   avoid the effects
    of global warming.

PRACTICE 18 ▸ Chapter review.
Complete each conversation with the correct phrase from the list. Write the letter.

a. her friend goes with her
b. I don't eat meat
c. I don't have an 8:00 A.M. class anymore
d. I eat meat

e. I work weekends now
f. none of her friends will go with her
g. you have a real emergency
h. you promise to keep it a secret

1. A: Won't you tell me about Emma and Tom? Oh, please tell me!

   B: Well, OK, I'll tell you, but only if _____ .

2. A: Hello, 911? Police? I want to report a barking dog.

   B: This is 911. You've dialed the wrong number. Call this number only in case _____ .

3. A: Isn't Sara coming to the party?

   B: I don't think so. She's too shy to come alone. She doesn't go anyplace unless _____ .

4. A: Your grandmother has traveled to 32 countries all by herself?

   B: Yes, she has! She loves to travel to exotic places even if _____ .

5. A: Do you want to go to Johnson's Steak House or Vernon's Vegetable Stand for lunch?

   B: Definitely Vernon's Vegetable Stand since _____ .

6. A: They say that people who don't eat meat live longer than people who do.

   B: Well, I think that I will live a certain number of years whether or not _____ .

7. A: You haven't come to our book club for months! How come?

   B: Oh, I can't come on Saturdays anymore because _____ .

8. A: Hi, Kevin. ... Oh, did I wake you up? It's 7:30 already! You need to get up.

   B: I sleep later now, Andy, since _____ .

PRACTICE 19 ▸ Chapter review.
Choose the correct completions.

1. Alice will tutor you in math _____ you promise to show up promptly every day.
   a. unless   b. only if   c. whereas   d. even though

2. Oscar won't pass his math course _____ he gets a tutor.
   a. in case   b. unless   c. only if   d. because

3. Most people you meet will be polite to you _____ you are polite to them.
   a. in case   b. even though   c. unless   d. if

4. I'm glad that my mother made me take piano lessons when I was a child _____ I hated it at the time.
   Now, I enjoy playing the piano every day.
   a. even though   b. because   c. unless   d. if

5. Chicken eggs will not hatch _____ they are kept at the proper temperature.
   a. because   b. unless   c. only if   d. even though

6. You'd better take your raincoat with you _____ the weather changes. It could rain before you get
   home again.
   a. now that   b. even if   c. in case   d. only if

7. Vanessa got the research fellowship _____ she had the best qualifications of all the applicants.
   a. although   b. whereas   c. if   d. since

8. My sister can fall asleep under any conditions, but I can't get to sleep _____ the light is off and the room is perfectly quiet.
   a. if   b. unless   c. in case   d. now that

9. In a democratic government, a leader is directly responsible to the people, _____ in a dictatorship, a leader has no direct responsibility to the people.
   a. because   b. even though   c. while   d. unless

10. Parents love and support their children _____ the children misbehave or do foolish things.
    a. even if   b. since   c. if   d. only if

CHAPTER 18

Reduction of Adverb Clauses to Modifying Adverbial Phrases

PRACTICE 1 ▶ Preview.

Underline the ten adverb clause or phrases.

> **Coloring Books for Adults**
>
> Coloring books for children have always been popular, but lately many adults have been buying coloring books for themselves. These days, it's not unusual to see an adult coloring pages while waiting for a doctor's appointment or sitting on a bus. Looking for an easy activity to relieve stress, some people turn to coloring. Research has shown that anxiety levels drop when people color. Coloring is similar to meditation because it helps people focus on the moment while allowing the brain to switch off other thoughts or worries. Other people enjoy coloring because they feel that they can be creative even if they don't have the artistic ability to draw something from scratch. Still others are looking for an escape from technology. Constantly staring at screens all day, adults need a chance to "unplug." Nostalgia is yet another reason for the sudden popularity of adult coloring books. Wanting to feel like a kid again, an adult might open up a coloring book. Since becoming a trend, adult coloring books have become widely available. They can be found in almost any bookstore and have even been included on bestseller lists.

PRACTICE 2 ▶ Modifying adverbial phrases. (Chart 18-2)

Check (✓) the grammatically correct sentences.

1. _____ While watching an exciting program, the TV suddenly went off.

2. _____ While starting up, my computer suddenly crashed.

3. _____ While listening to a podcast, I fell asleep.

4. _____ Before going to bed, I always open the bedroom windows.

5. _____ Before going to bed, the bedroom windows are always open.

6. _____ After opening the bedroom windows, I crawl into bed for the night.

7. _____ Since graduating from college, nobody has offered me a job.

8. _____ Since graduating from college, I haven't found a job.

9. _____ After sitting on her eggs for four weeks, we saw the mother duck welcome her baby ducklings.

10. _____ After sitting on her eggs for four weeks, the mother duck welcomed her baby ducklings.

PRACTICE 3 ▸ Changing time clauses to modifying adverbial phrases. (Chart 18-2)
Change the adverb clause to a modifying phrase.

1. Since ~~he opened~~ *opening* his new business, Liam has been working 16 hours a day.
2. I shut off the lights before I left the room.
3. After I had met the movie star in person, I understood why she was so popular.
4. After I searched through all my pockets, I found my keys.
5. While he was herding his goats in the mountains, an Ethiopian named Kaldi discovered the coffee plant more than 1,200 years ago.
6. Before they marched into battle, ancient Ethiopian soldiers ate a mixture of coffee beans and fat for extra energy.
7. While she was flying across the Pacific Ocean in 1937, the famous pilot Amelia Earhart disappeared.
8. After they imported rabbits to Australia, the settlers found that these animals became pests.

PRACTICE 4 ▸ Adverb clauses and modifying phrases. (Charts 18-1 → 18-3)
Complete the sentences with the correct form of the verbs in parentheses.

1. a. Before (*leave*) _____ *leaving* _____ on his trip, Tom renewed his passport.

   b. Before Tom (*leave*) _____ *left* _____ on his trip, he renewed his passport.

2. a. After Thomas Edison (*invent*) _____ *invented / had invented* _____ the light bulb, he went on to create many other useful inventions.

   b. After (*invent*) _____ *inventing / having invented* _____ the light bulb, Thomas Edison went on to create many other useful inventions.

3. a. While (*work*) _____ with uranium ore, Marie Curie discovered two new elements, radium and polonium.

   b. While she (*work*) _____ with uranium ore, Marie Curie discovered two new elements, radium and polonium.

4. a. Before an astronaut (*fly*) _____ on a space mission, she will have undergone thousands of hours of training.

   b. Before (*fly*) _____ on a space mission, an astronaut will have undergone thousands of hours of training.

5. a. After they (*study*) _____ the stars, the ancient Maya in Central America developed a very accurate solar calendar.

   b. After (*study*) _____ the stars, the ancient Maya in Central America developed a very accurate solar calendar.

6. a. Since (*learn*) _____ that cigarettes cause cancer, the medical profession has encouraged people to quit smoking.

   b. Since they (*learn*) _____ that cigarettes cause cancer, the medical profession has encouraged people to quit smoking.

7. a. When (take) _____ any medication, you should be sure to follow the directions on the label.

   b. When you (take) _____ any medication, you should be sure to follow the directions on the label.

8. a. While I (drive) _____ to my uncle's house, I took a wrong turn and ended up back where I had started.

   b. While (drive) _____ to my uncle's house, I took a wrong turn and ended up back where I had started.

PRACTICE 5 ▶ Adverb clauses and modifying phrases. (Charts 18-1 → 18-3)

Underline the subject of the adverb clause and the subject of the main clause. Change the adverb clauses to modifying phrases if possible.

1. While Sam was driving to work in the rain, his car got a flat tire.

   _____ (no change) _____

2. While Sam was driving to work, he had a flat tire.

   _____ While driving to work, Sam had a flat tire. _____

3. Before Nick left on his trip, his son gave him a big hug and a kiss.

   _____

4. Before Nick left on his trip, he gave his itinerary to his secretary.

   _____

5. After Tom had worked hard in the garden all afternoon, he took a shower and then went to the movies with his friends.

   _____

6. After Sunita had made a delicious chicken curry for her friends, they wanted the recipe.

   _____

7. Emily always clears off her desk before she leaves the office at the end of each day.

   _____

PRACTICE 6 ▶ Expressing the idea of "during the same time" and cause/effect in modifying adverbial clauses. (Charts 18-3 and 18-4)

Underline the modifying adverbial phrase in each sentence. Then choose the meaning of each modifying phrase. In some sentences, both meanings may be given.

1. Riding his bicycle to school, Enrique fell off and scraped his knee.
   a. while   b. because

2. Being seven feet tall, the basketball player couldn't sit in a regular airplane seat.
   a. while   b. because

3. Driving to work this morning, I remembered that I had already missed the special 8:00 A.M. breakfast meeting.
   a. while   b. because

4. Running five miles on a very hot day, James felt exhausted.
   a. while   b. because

5. Having run for 26 miles in the marathon, the runners were exhausted at the end of the race.
   a. while   b. because

6. Drinking a tall glass of refreshing iced tea, Ann felt her tired muscles relax.
   a. while   b. because

7. Clapping loudly at the end of the game, the fans showed their appreciation of the team.
   a. while   b. because

8. Speaking with her guidance counselor, Clara felt that she was being understood.
   a. while   b. because

9. Knowing that I was going to miss the plane because of heavy traffic, I contacted the airline about taking a later flight.
   a. while   b. because

10. Having missed my plane, I had to wait four hours to take the next one.
    a. while   b. because

11. Waiting for my plane to depart, I watched thousands of people walking through the airport.
    a. while   b. because

PRACTICE 7 ▶ Expressing the idea of "during the same time" and cause/effect in modifying adverbial phrases. (Charts 18-3 and 18-4)

Complete the sentences in Column A with a clause from Column B.

Column A

1. Rushing to the airport, _____ .

2. While watching an old movie on TV _____ .

3. Drinking a big glass of water in four

   seconds, _____ .

4. Because I like old movies, _____ .

5. Since receiving a big job promotion, _____ .

6. Having finished my long report, _____ .

7. Unable to reach my friend by phone, _____ .

8. Being a shy person, _____ .

9. Having lived in Rome for two years, _____ .

10. Wanting to get home quickly, _____ .

Column B

a. I handed it in to my supervisor this morning

b. I watch a lot of them on TV late at night

c. I decided to email her

d. I have more responsibility

e. I can speak Italian

f. I don't like to go to parties alone

g. I ran all the way

h. I forgot my passport at home

i. I fell asleep

j. I quenched my thirst

PRACTICE 8 ▶ Modifying phrases and clauses. (Charts 18-2 → 18-4)

Choose all the possible completions for each sentence. More than one answer may be possible.

1. Before _____ you, I had not known such a wonderful person existed!
   a. met   b. meeting   c. I met

2. After _____ what the candidate had to say, I am considering voting for him.
   a. I heard   b. having heard   c. hearing

3. Since _____ married, Fred seems very happy and content.
   a. he got   b. getting   c. got

4. _____ through outer space at a speed of 25,000 miles per hour (40,000 kilometers), the astronauts were able to see the Earth.
   a. Speeding   b. While speeding   c. Sped

5. _____ president of his new country, George Washington had been a general in its army.
   a. Before becoming   b. While becoming   c. Before he became

6. _____ rap music before, our grandparents wondered why it was so popular.
   a. Had never heard   b. Because they had never heard   c. Never having heard

7. _____ the English faculty, Professor Wilson has become the most popular teacher at our university.
   a. Since joining   b. While joining   c. Since he joined

PRACTICE 9 ▸ Modifying phrases with *upon*. (Chart 18-5)
Rewrite the sentences with the given words.

1. When Sarah received her acceptance letter for medical school, she shouted for joy.

   a. Upon _____ .

   b. On _____ .

2. On hearing the sad news, Kathleen began to cry.

   a. Upon _____ .

   b. When _____ .

3. Upon looking at the accident victim, the paramedics decided to transport him to the hospital.

   a. On _____ .

   b. When _____ .

PRACTICE 10 ▸ Modifying phrases with *upon*. (Chart 18-5)
Complete the sentences using the ideas from the list.

   a. She learned the problem was not at all serious.
   b. She was told she got it.
   c. She discovered a burned-out wire.
   d. She arrived at the airport.
   e. She reached the other side of the lake.

1. It had been a long, uncomfortable trip. Upon _____*arriving at the airport*_____, Sue quickly
   unfastened her seat belt and stood in the aisle waiting her turn to disembark.

2. Kim rented a small fishing boat last weekend, but she ended up doing more rowing than fishing.
   The motor died halfway across the lake, so she had to row to shore. It was a long distance away.
   Upon _____, she was exhausted.

3. At first, we thought the fire had been caused by lightning. However, upon
   _____, the fire chief determined it had been
   caused by faulty electrical wiring.

4. Amy felt terrible. She was sure she had some terrible disease, so she went to the doctor for some
   tests. Upon _____, she was extremely relieved.

5. Vanessa wanted that scholarship with all her heart and soul. Upon
   _____, she jumped straight up in the air and let
   out a scream of happiness.

PRACTICE 11 ▸ Modifying phrases. (Charts 18-1 → 18-5)
Write the letter of the clause from the list that logically follows the modifying phrase.

a. the desperate woman grasped a floating log after the boat turned over
b. the taxi driver caused a multiple-car accident
c. carefully proofread all your answers
d. the doctor asked the patient more questions
e. the athletes waved to the cheering crowd
f. the student raised her hand
g. the manager learned of their dissatisfaction with their jobs
h. the passengers angrily walked back to the ticket counter
i. Margo hasn't been able to play tennis
j. Micah requested to meet with the Teaching Assistant.

1. Trying to better understand the problem, _____.

2. Fighting for her life, _____.

3. Wanting to ask her professor a question, _____.

4. After having injured her ankle, _____.

5. Not wanting to bother his professor, _____.

6. Upon hearing the announcement that their plane was delayed, _____.

7. Talking with the employees after work, _____.

8. Attempting to get onto the freeway, _____.

9. Stepping onto the platform to receive their medals, _____.

10. Before turning in your exam paper, _____.

PRACTICE 12 ▸ Chapter review.
The following sentences contain popular expressions. Change the adverb clauses to modifying phrases if possible.

1. Before a friend tries to do something hard, you may say "Break a leg!" to wish him or her good luck.

   _____

2. After you finish something very easy, you can say it was a "piece of cake."

   _____

3. When something is very expensive, you can say it "costs an arm and a leg."

   _____

4. When you do or say something exactly right, you can say you "hit the nail on the head."

   _____

5. While you are working late in the night, you are "burning the midnight oil."

   _____

6. After you wake up in a bad mood, you can say you "woke up on the wrong side of the bed."

   _____

7. Because I lost all my work when my computer crashed, I went "back to square one."

   _____

8. Because our original plans didn't work, we went "back to the drawing board."

   _____

PRACTICE 1 ▶ Preview.
Underline the ten connecting words. Then answer the questions.

Language and Toys

Parents often buy noisy electronic toys for their babies because these toys
seem educational. If a toy talks or plays music, many parents believe that
the toy is teaching the sounds and structure of language. However, some
researchers believe electronic toys actually delay language development
in small children. They believe this happens due to a lack of human
interaction. Because of their busy schedules, parents often buy electronic
toys to keep their children occupied. Consequently, these parents might
spend less time talking to and interacting with their children. While electronic toys are entertaining, the
most important skill for babies to learn is how to communicate with other people. Even if electronic toys
sing the alphabet or say the names of shapes and colors, they do not promote communication. On the
other hand, more traditional toys such as puzzles and blocks seem to encourage babies to communicate.
Studies have found that books produce the most communication between parents and babies. Whether or
not parents buy electronic toys, they should try to interact with their babies as much as possible.

---

1. Which connecting words express cause and effect?

   _____

2. Which connecting words express contrast?

   _____

3. Which connecting words express condition?

   _____

PRACTICE 2 ▶ Using *because of* and *due to*. (Chart 19-2)
Choose the correct completions. More than one answer may be correct.

1. The plane was delayed because _____.
   a. bad weather
   b. the weather was bad
   c. there was heavy air traffic
   d. heavy air traffic
   e. mechanical difficulty
   f. the mechanics had to make a repair

2. The plane was delayed because of _____.
   a. bad weather
   b. the weather was bad
   c. there was heavy air traffic
   d. heavy air traffic
   e. mechanical difficulty
   f. the mechanics had to make a repair

3. The burglar was caught because _____.
   a. the police responded quickly
   b. the quick police response
   c. he left fingerprints
   d. the fingerprints on the door
   e. there was a security video
   f. a security video

4. The burglar was caught due to _____.
   a. the police responded quickly
   b. the quick police response
   c. he left fingerprints
   d. the fingerprints on the door
   e. there was a security video
   f. a security video

PRACTICE 3 ▸ Using because of and due to. (Chart 19-2)
Choose the correct completions. More than one answer may be correct.

1. We delayed our trip   because / because of / due to   Dad was sick with the flu.
2. Claire's eyes were red   due to / because of / because   she had been crying.
3. The water in most rivers is unsafe to drink   because / due to / because of   pollution.
4. The water in most rivers is unsafe to drink   because / due to / because of   it is polluted.
5. Some people think Harry succeeded in business   due to / because of / because   his charming personality rather than his business skills.
6. You can't enter this secured area   because of / because / due to   you don't have proper ID.
7. My lecture notes were incomplete   due to / because of / because   the instructor talked too fast.
8. It's unsafe to travel in that country   because / due to / because of   the ongoing civil war.

PRACTICE 4 ▸ Using because of and due to. (Chart 19-2)
Use the ideas in parentheses to complete the sentences.

1. (*There was heavy traffic.*) We were late due to ____heavy trafic____ .
2. (*There was heavy traffic.*) We were late because _____ .
3. (*Grandpa is getting old.*) Grandpa doesn't like to drive at night anymore because

   _____ .

4. (*Our history professor is quite old.*) Our history professor is going to retire because of

   _____ .

5. (*Sarah is afraid of heights.*) She will not walk across a bridge because

   _____ .

6. (*Sarah is afraid of heights.*) She will not walk across a bridge because of

   _____ .

7. (*There was a cancellation.*) Due to _____ , you can have an

   appointment with the doctor this afternoon.

8. (*There was a cancellation today.*) Because _____ , you can

   have an appointment with the doctor this afternoon.

PRACTICE 5 ▸ Cause and effect: using therefore, consequently, and so. (Chart 19-3)
Punctuate the sentences in Column B. Add capital letters if necessary.

Column A	Column B
1. adverb clause:	Because she had a headache she took some aspirin.
2. adverb clause:	She took some aspirin because she had a headache.
3. prepositional phrase:	Because of her headache she took some aspirin.
4. prepositional phrase:	She took some aspirin because of her headache.
5. transition:	She had a headache therefore she took some aspirin.
6. transition:	She had a headache she therefore took some aspirin.
7. transition:	She had a headache she took some aspirin therefore.
8. conjunction:	She had a headache so she took some aspirin.

PRACTICE 6 ▸ Cause and effect: using *therefore*, *consequently*, and *so*. (Chart 19-3)
Each sentence in *italics* is followed by sentences that refer to it. Choose the word that logically
completes each sentence. Notice the punctuation and capitalization.

SENTENCE 1: *Water boils when its temperature reaches 212 degrees Fahrenheit (100 degrees Celsius).*

1. The water in the pot had reached 212 degrees Fahrenheit. _____, it started to boil.
   a. Therefore   b. So   c. Because

2. The water in the pot started to boil _____ it had reached 212 degrees Fahrenheit.
   a. so   b. because   c. therefore

3. The water in the pot had reached 212 degrees Fahrenheit, _____ it started to boil.
   a. because   b. therefore   c. so

SENTENCE 2: *The main highway is closed.*

1. The main highway is closed. _____, we are going to take another road.
   a. Therefore   b. Because   c. So

2. We are going to take another road _____ the main highway is closed.
   a. so   b. because   c. therefore

3. The main highway is closed. We are going to take another road, _____.
   a. therefore   b. Therefore   c. so

4. The main highway is closed, _____ we are going to take another road.
   a. So   b. so   c. therefore

PRACTICE 7 ▸ Cause and effect: using *therefore*, *consequently*, and *so*. (Chart 19-3)
Combine the two sentences in *italics* in four different ways. Notice the punctuation and capitalization.

1. *The store didn't have orange juice. I bought lemonade instead.*

   a. _____I bought lemonade_____ because ____the store didn't have any orange juice____.

   b. Because _____, _____.

   c. _____. Therefore, _____

   _____.

   d. _____, so _____.

2. *Max has excellent grades. He will go to a top university.*

   a. _____. Therefore, _____.

   b. _____. He, therefore, _____.

   c. _____. _____, therefore.

   d. _____, so _____.

3. *There had been no rain for several months. The crops died.*

   a. Because _____, _____.

   b. _____. Consequently, _____.

   c. _____. _____, therefore,

   _____.

   d. _____, so _____.

PRACTICE 8 ▸ Showing cause and effect. (Charts 19-2 and 19-3)

Part I. Complete the sentences with *because of, because,* or *therefore.* Add any necessary punctuation and capitalization.

1. _____Because_____ it rained we stayed home.

2. It rained. _____Therefore,_____ we stayed home.

3. We stayed home _____because of_____ the bad weather.

4. The weather was bad. _____ we stayed home.

5. The typhoon was moving directly toward a small coastal town. _____ all residents were advised to move inland until it passed.

6. The residents moved inland _____ the typhoon.

7. _____ the typhoon was moving directly toward the town all residents were advised to move inland.

8. Giraffes, which are found in the African plains, are the tallest of all animals. Although their bodies are not extremely large, they have very long necks. _____ their long necks, they are tall enough to eat the leaves from the tops of the trees.

Part II. Complete the sentence with *due to, since,* or *consequently.* Add any necessary punctuation and capitalization.

9. _____ his poor eyesight John has to sit in the front row in class.

10. _____ John has poor eyesight he has to sit in the front row.

11. John has poor eyesight _____ he has to sit in the front row.

12. Sarah is afraid of heights _____ she will not walk across a bridge.

13. Sarah will not walk across a bridge _____ her fear of heights.

14. Mark is overweight _____ his doctor has advised him to exercise regularly.

15. _____ a diamond is extremely hard it can be used to cut glass.

PRACTICE 9 ▸ Summary of patterns and punctuation. (Chart 19-4)

Punctuate the sentences properly, using periods and commas. Add capital letters if necessary.

1. Edward missed the final exam. ~~therefore~~ *Therefore,* he failed the course.

2. Edward failed the course because he missed the final exam. (*no change*)

3. Edward missed the final exam. he simply forgot to go to it.

4. Because we forgot to make a reservation we couldn't get a table at our favorite restaurant last night.

5. The server kept coming to work late or not at all therefore she was fired.

6. The server kept forgetting customers' orders so he was fired.

7. Ron is an unpleasant dinner companion because of his terrible table manners.

8. The needle has been around since prehistoric times the button was invented about 2,000 years ago the zipper wasn't invented until 1890.

9. It is possible for wildlife observers to identify individual zebras because the patterns of stripes on each zebra are unique no two zebras are alike.

10. When students in the United States are learning to type, they often practice this sentence because it contains all the letters of the English alphabet: The quick brown fox jumps over the lazy dog.

Connectives That Express Cause and Effect, Contrast, and Condition 179

PRACTICE 10 ▸ Summary of patterns and punctuation. (Chart 19-4)
Combine the two sentences in *italics*. Use the words in parentheses in the new sentences.

SENTENCE 1: *Kim ate some bad food. She got sick.*

a. (*because*) _____

b. (*because of*) _____

c. (*so*) _____

d. (*due to*) _____

SENTENCE 2: *Adam was exhausted. He had driven for 13 hours.*

a. (*therefore*) _____

b. (*since*) _____

c. (*due to the fact that*) _____

d. (*so*) _____

PRACTICE 11 ▸ Such ... that and so ... that. (Chart 19-5)
Write **such** or **so** to complete the sentences.

1. It was _____*such*_____ a hot day that we canceled our tennis game.

2. The test was _____*so*_____ easy that everyone got a high score.

3. The movie was _____ bad that we left early.

4. It was _____ a bad movie that we left early.

5. Professor James is _____ a demanding teacher that many students refuse to take his class.

6. The line at the post office was _____ long that I decided to leave and go back another day.

7. The intricate metal lacework on the Eiffel Tower in Paris was _____ complicated that the structure took more than two and a half years to complete.

8. Charles and his brother are _____ hard-working carpenters that I'm sure they'll make a success of their new business.

9. The kids had _____ much fun at the amusement park that they begged to go again.

10. I feel like I have _____ little energy that I wonder if I'm getting sick.

PRACTICE 12 ▸ Using such ... that and so ... that. (Chart 19-5)
Combine the two sentences. Use **so ... that** or **such ... that**.

1. We took a walk. It was a nice day.

   It was _____*such a nice day that we took a walk*_____.

2. Jeff was late. He missed the meeting.

   Jeff was _____.

3. I couldn't understand her. She talked too fast.

   She talked _____.

4. It was an expensive car. We couldn't afford to buy it.

   It was _____.

5. There were few people at the meeting. It was canceled.

   There were _____.

6. Ted couldn't fall asleep last night. He was worried about the exam.

Ted was _____.

7. The tornado struck with great force. It lifted cars off the ground.

The tornado _____.

8. I can't figure out what this sentence says. Joe's handwriting is illegible.

Joe's handwriting _____.

9. David has too many girlfriends. He can't remember all of their names.

David has _____.

10. Too many people came to the meeting. There were not enough seats for everyone.

There were _____.

PRACTICE 13 ▸ Expressing purpose. (Chart 19-6)
Check (✓) the sentences that express purpose.

1. _____ Ali changed jobs in order to be closer to his family.

2. _____ Ali changed jobs, so he has a lot of new information to learn.

3. _____ Ali changed jobs so he could be involved in more interesting work.

4. _____ Ali changed jobs so that he could be closer to his family.

5. _____ The highway will be closed tomorrow so that road crews can make repairs to the road.

6. _____ The highway will be closed tomorrow, so you will need to take a detour.

7. _____ The highway will be closed tomorrow so the road can be repaired.

8. _____ The highway will be closed tomorrow in order for road crews to make repairs.

9. _____ The highway will be closed tomorrow, so we can expect long delays.

10. _____ The highway will be closed tomorrow, so let's do our errands today.

PRACTICE 14 ▸ Expressing purpose: using *so that*. (Chart 19-6)
Complete the sentences in Column A with a clause from Column B.

Column A	Column B
1. Please open the windows so that _____.	a. my roommate wouldn't wake up
2. Sam put on his boots so that _____.	b. he can be a translator
3. I spoke softly on the phone so that _____.	c. it will sell more quickly
4. Li bought a compact car so that _____.	d. we can have some fresh air
5. Aiden stayed up all night so that _____.	e. it will be safer for drivers and pedestrians
6. You could lower the price on the house you are trying to sell so that _____.	f. he would save money on gasoline
7. The city has put up a traffic light at the busy intersection so that _____.	g. it will look bright and cheerful
8. We are painting the kitchen yellow so that _____.	h. he would look professional
9. Sid wore a suit and tie for his interview so that _____.	i. he could go hiking in the mountains
10. Mr. Kim studies advanced Russian so that _____.	j. he could finish writing his essay

PRACTICE 15 ▸ Expressing purpose: using *so that*. (Chart 19-6)
Combine the sentences by using *so* (*that*).

1. Rachel wanted to watch the news. She turned on the TV.

   Rachel turned on the TV so that she could watch the news. _____

2. Alex wrote down the time and date of his appointment. He didn't want to forget to go.

   _____

3. Nancy is taking extra courses every semester. She wants to graduate early.

   _____

4. Amanda didn't want to disturb her roommate. She turned down the TV.

   _____

5. Chris took some change from his pocket. He wanted to buy a snack from the vending machine.

   _____

6. I wanted to listen to the news while I was making dinner. I turned on the TV.

   _____

7. I turned off my phone. I didn't want to be interrupted while I was working.

   _____

8. It's a good idea for you to learn keyboarding skills. You'll be able to use your computer more efficiently.

   _____

9. Lynn wanted to make sure that she didn't forget to take her book back to the library. She tied a string around her finger.

   _____

10. Wastebaskets have been placed throughout the park. The department wants to make sure people don't litter.

    _____

PRACTICE 16 ▸ Showing contrast (unexpected result). (Chart 19-7)
Make logical completions by completing the sentences with *is* or *isn't*.

1. It's the middle of the summer, but the weather _____ very cold.

2. It's the middle of the summer; nevertheless, the weather _____ very cold.

3. The weather _____ warm today even though it's the middle of summer.

4. Although it's the middle of the summer, the weather _____ very cold today.

5. Even though it's the middle of summer, the weather _____ very cold today.

6. It's the middle of summer in spite of the fact that the weather _____ very warm today.

7. Despite the fact that it is the middle of summer, the weather _____ very cold today.

8. It's the middle of summer. However, the weather _____ warm today.

9. It's the middle of summer, yet the weather _____ very warm today.

10. Despite the cold weather, it _____ the middle of summer.

PRACTICE 17 ▸ *Despite, in spite of vs. even though, although.* (Chart 19-7)

Choose the correct completions.

1. a. Even though / Despite   her doctor has prescribed frequent exercise for her, Carol never does any exercise at all.

   b. Even though / Despite   her doctor's orders, Carol has not done any exercise at all.

   c. Even though / Despite   the orders her doctor gave her, Carol still hasn't done any exercise.

   d. Even though / Despite   the dangers of not exercising, Carol still doesn't exercise.

   e. Even though / Despite   she has been warned about the dangers of not exercising by her doctor, Carol still hasn't begun to exercise.

2. a. Although / In spite of   an approaching storm, the two climbers continued their trek up the mountain.

   b. Although / In spite of   a storm was approaching, the two climbers continued their trek.

   c. Although / In spite of   there was an approaching storm, the two climbers continued up the mountain.

   d. Although / In spite of   the storm that was approaching the mountain area, the two climbers continued their trek.

   e. Although / In spite of   the fact that a storm was approaching the mountain area, the two climbers continued their trek.

3. a. Although / Despite   his many hours of practice, George failed his driving test for the third time.

   b. Although / Despite   he had practiced for many hours, George failed his driving test for the third time.

   c. Although / Despite   practicing for many hours, George failed his driving test again.

   d. Although / Despite   his mother and father spent hours with him in the car trying to teach him how to drive, George failed his driving test repeatedly.

   e. Although / Despite   his mother and father's efforts to teach him how to drive, George failed his driving test.

4. a. Even though / In spite of   repeated crop failures due to drought, the villagers are refusing to leave their traditional homeland for resettlement in other areas.

   b. Even though / In spite of   their crops have failed repeatedly due to drought, the villagers are refusing to leave their traditional homeland for resettlement in other areas.

   c. The villagers refuse to leave   even though / in spite of   the drought.

   d. The villagers refuse to leave   even though / in spite of   the drought seriously threatens their food supply.

   e. The villagers refuse to leave   even though / in spite of   the threat to their food supply because of the continued drought.

   f. The villagers refuse to leave   even though / in spite of   the threat to their food supply is serious because of the continued drought.

   g. The villagers refuse to leave   even though / in spite of   their food supply is threatened.

   h. The villagers refuse to leave   even though / in spite of   their threatened food supply.

PRACTICE 18 ▸ Showing contrast. (Chart 19-7)
Complete each sentence with the correct phrase from the list. Write the letter.

   a. an inability to communicate well in any language besides English
   b. he had the necessary qualifications
   c. he is afraid of heights
   d. he is normally quite shy and sometimes inarticulate
   e. his fear of heights
   f. his parents were worried about his intelligence because he didn't speak until he was four years old
   g. it has been shown to be safe
   h. they have been shown to cause birth defects and sometimes death
   i. its many benefits
   j. his competence and experience

1. In spite of _____, Carl enjoyed his helicopter trip over the Grand Canyon in Arizona.

2. Although _____, Mark rode in a cable car to the top of Sugar Loaf mountain in Rio de Janeiro for the magnificent view.

3. Because of his age, John was not hired even though _____.

4. Although _____, many people avoid using a microwave oven for fear of its radiation.

5. Jack usually has little trouble making new friends in other countries despite _____.

6. In spite of _____, the use of chemotherapy to treat cancer has many severe side effects.

7. Though _____, Bob managed to give an excellent presentation at the board meeting.

8. Jerry continued to be denied a promotion despite _____.

9. Dangerous pesticides are still used in many countries even though _____.

10. Despite the fact that Einstein turned out to be a genius _____.

PRACTICE 19 ▸ Showing contrast. (Chart 19-7)
Combine the two *italicized* sentences. Add any other necessary punctuation.

1. *It was night. We could see the road very clearly.*

   a. Even though _____.

   b. Although _____.

   c. _____, but _____.

2. *Helena has a fear of heights. She enjoys skydiving.*

   a. Despite the fact that _____, _____.

   b. Despite _____, _____.

   c. _____; nevertheless _____.

3. *Millie has the flu. She is working at her computer.*

   a. Though _____, _____.

   b. _____, but _____ anyway.

   c. _____, but _____ still _____

   _____.

PRACTICE 20 ▸ Showing direct contrast. (Chart 19-8)

Connect the given ideas using the words in parentheses. Add punctuation and capital letters as necessary.

1. (*while*) red is bright and lively gray is a dull color

   ___Red is bright and lively, while gray is a dull color.___ OR

   ___While red is bright and lively, gray is a dull color.___

2. (*on the other hand*) Jane is insecure and unsure of herself her sister is full of self-confidence

   _____

3. (*while*) a rock is heavy a feather is light

   _____

4. (*however*) some children are unruly others are quiet and obedient

   _____

5. (*on the other hand*) language and literature classes are easy and enjoyable for Alex math and science courses are difficult for him

   _____

6. (*however*) strikes can bring improvements in wages and working conditions they can also cause loss of jobs and bankruptcy

   _____

PRACTICE 21 ▸ Expressing condition: using *otherwise*. (Chart 19-9)

Make sentences with the same meaning as the given sentence. Use ***otherwise***.

1. If I don't call my mother, she'll start worrying about me.

   ___I should / had better / have to call my mother. Otherwise, she'll start worrying about me.___

2. If the bus doesn't come soon, we'll be late to work.

   _____

3. Unless you've made a reservation, you won't get seated at the restaurant.

   _____

4. If Beth doesn't stop complaining, she will lose the few friends she has.

   _____

5. You can't get on the plane unless you have a government-issued ID.

   _____

6. Louis can replace his driver's license only if he applies for it in person.

   _____

7. Only if you are a registered voter can you vote in the general election.

   _____

8. If you don't clean up the kitchen tonight, you'll have to clean it up early tomorrow.

   _____

PRACTICE 22 ▸ Expressing cause and effect. (Chart 19-9)
Complete the sentences in Column A with a phrase from Column B.

Column A

1. We see lightning first and then hear the thunder because _____ .

2. Plants need light to live. These plants didn't have light; therefore, _____ .

3. Halley's Comet appears in the sky every 76 years, so _____ .

4. Children in Scandinavia go to school in darkness in the winter since _____ .

5. Objects fall to the ground because of _____ .

6. Now that _____ , newspapers are not as necessary as they used to be.

7. People get their news faster than they used to due to _____ .

8. Because _____ , people can heat the air in a balloon and make it fly.

Column B

a. faster means of communication

b. gravity

c. hot air rises to the top

d. it will next be seen in 2061

e. light travels faster than sound

f. people can get their news instantly on the Internet

g. there is almost no daylight then

h. they died

PRACTICE 23 ▸ Expressing contrast. (Chart 19-9)
Choose the correct completions.

1. Colombia exports a lot of emeralds, while South Africa   exports / doesn't export   gold.

2. Even though Colombia exports some precious stones, it   exports / doesn't export   diamonds.

3. Although Japan   uses / doesn't use   a lot of oil, oil isn't found in Japan.

4. Despite the declining population of Japan, Tokyo's population   is / isn't   getting larger.

5. Most people believe that the pineapple is native to Hawaii, a state in the middle of the Pacific Ocean; however, pineapples   originated / didn't originate   in South America.

6. China   is / isn't   the largest producer of pineapples today. Nevertheless, Hawaii still produces a lot of pineapples.

PRACTICE 24 ▸ Expressing condition. (Chart 19-9)
Write the correct form of the verb **pass** in each sentence.

1. Keith will graduate if he _____ *passes* _____ all of his courses.

2. Sam won't graduate if he _____ *doesn't pass* _____ all of his courses.

3. Brad won't graduate unless he _____ all of his courses.

4. Joslyn will graduate only if she _____ all of her courses.

5. Jessica will graduate even if she _____ all of her courses.

6. Alex won't graduate even if he _____ all of his courses.

7. Jennifer will graduate unless she _____ all of her courses.

PRACTICE 25 ▸ Chapter review.
Complete the sentences logically using the ideas from the list. Write each verb in its correct tense.
Punctuate and capitalize correctly.

   a. take care of the garden (or not)
   b. the flowers bloom (or not)
   c. my care

1. Because I took good care of the garden, _____ *the flowers bloomed* _____.

2. The flowers bloomed because _____ *I took good care of the garden* _____.

3. The flowers bloomed because of _____ *my care* _____.

4. The flowers didn't bloom in spite of _____.

5. Although I took good care of the garden _____.

6. I did not take good care of the garden therefore _____.

7. I didn't take good care of the garden however _____.

8. I took good care of the garden nevertheless _____.

9. I did not take good care of the garden so _____.

10. Even though I did not take good care of the garden _____.

11. Since I did not take good care of the garden _____.

12. I didn't take good care of the garden, but _____ anyway.

13. If I take good care of the garden _____.

14. Unless I take good care of the garden _____.

15. I must take good care of the garden otherwise _____.

16. I did not take good care of the garden consequently _____.

17. I did not take good care of the garden nonetheless _____.

18. I have to take good care of the garden so that _____.

19. Only if I take good care of the garden _____.

20. I took good care of the garden yet _____.

21. You'd better take good care of the garden or else _____.

22. The flowers will probably bloom whether _____.

CHAPTER 20 · Conditional Sentences and Wishes

PRACTICE 1 ▸ Preview.
Read the passage. <u>Underline</u> the eight conditional clauses.

Coral Reefs

If you have ever been snorkeling or scuba diving, you may have seen a coral reef. Coral reefs look like rocks, but they are actually living creatures. Because reefs are so colorful and are home to such a large number of sea creatures, some people describe them as cities or rain forests of the ocean.

Unfortunately, coral reefs all around the world are dying. If a reef dies, so will a lot of the sea life around the reef. Coral reefs are an important part of the ocean food chain. They also provide shelter for many animals, such as fish, sponges, eels, jellyfish, sea stars, and shrimp. If there were no coral reefs, many species would simply not exist. If these creatures no longer existed, millions of people who depend on fish for their main food supply and livelihood would go hungry.

There are actions we can take to protect coral reefs. Pollution is one of the biggest problems for all sea life. If we choose to walk or bike instead of driving cars, there will be fewer pollutants. Another major problem is overfishing. If governments restrict or limit fishing around reefs, the reefs might have a chance of survival. Most importantly, we need to raise awareness. If more people were aware of the dangers of dying reefs, the reefs would probably not be in such bad condition. With greater awareness, more people will volunteer with beach and reef cleanup and be careful when swimming or diving near fragile reefs. If we follow these actions, we can keep our reefs around for future generations.

PRACTICE 2 ▸ Introduction to conditional sentences. (Chart 20-1)
Read the sentences under the given sentence. Choose *yes* if the sentence describes the situation. Choose *no* if the sentence doesn't describe the situation.

1. If Sophie didn't have the flu, she would be at work today.

   a. Sophie has the flu.   yes no

   b. Sophie is at work today.   yes no

2. If Evan didn't take his allergy medication, he would sneeze and cough all day.

   a. Evan takes his allergy medication.   yes no

   b. Evan sneezes and coughs all day.   yes no

3. If our first flight had been on time, we would not have missed our connecting flight.

   a. The first flight was on time.   yes no

   b. We missed our connecting flight.   yes no

4. If we had a reliable car, we would drive from the East Coast to the West Coast.

    a. We have a reliable car.   yes no

    b. We are going to drive from the East Coast to the West Coast   yes no

    c. We would like to drive from the East Coast to the West Coast.   yes no

5. Tim would have married Tina if she had accepted his proposal of marriage.

    a. Tina accepted Tim's marriage proposal.   yes no

    b. Tina and Tim got married.   yes no

    c. Tim wanted to marry Tina.   yes no

    d. Tina wanted to marry Tim.   yes no

PRACTICE 3 ▶ Overview of basic verb forms in conditional sentences. (Chart 20-1)
Choose the correct completions.

Group 1

1. Present real: If it snows, __c__.

2. Present unreal: If it snowed, __a__.

3. Past unreal: If it had snowed, __b__.

a. I would walk to work

b. I would have walked to work

c. I will walk to work

Group 2

1. Present real: If you come early, _____.

2. Present unreal: If you came early, _____.

3. Past unreal: If you had come early, _____.

a. we wouldn't be late

b. we wouldn't have been late

c. we won't be late

Group 3

1. Present unreal: If Professor Smith were absent, _____.

2. Present real: If Professor Smith is absent, _____.

3. Past unreal: If Professor Smith had been absent, _____.

a. class would have been canceled.

b. class will be canceled.

c. class would be canceled

Group 4

1. Present real: If John finds a better job, _____.

2. Past unreal: If John had found a better job, _____.

3. Present unreal: If John found a better job, _____.

a. he will take it.

b. he would take it.

c. he would have taken it.

PRACTICE 4 ▶ Real conditions in the present or future. (Chart 20-2)
Read the given sentence and the two sentences that follow. Complete the sentences with the verbs in the box.

be, be	forget, look	heat, boil
eat, feel	have, call	pet, purr

1. Water boils at 100 degrees C. (212 degrees F.)

    (General truth) If you _____ water to 100 degrees C.,

    it _____.

    (Future) If you _____ the water in that pot to 100 degrees C.,

    it _____.

2. Sometimes I forget my own schedule.

(Habitual activity) If I _____ my schedule, I _____ at my appointment calendar.

(Future) If I _____ my schedule tomorrow, I _____ at my appointment calendar.

3. Sometimes the cat purrs.

(Habitual situation) If you _____ the cat gently, she _____.

(Future) If you _____ the cat gently right now, she _____.

4. I might have some news tomorrow.

(Future) If I _____ any news tomorrow, I _____ you.

(Habitual situation) If I _____ any news, I _____ you.

5. You eat too much junk food.

(Future) If you _____ too much junk food, you _____ energetic.

(Predictable fact) If you _____ too much junk food, you _____ energetic.

6. It might be cloudy tonight.

(Predictable fact) If it _____ cloudy, the stars _____ visible.

(Future) If it _____ cloudy tonight, the stars _____ visible.

PRACTICE 5 ▸ Unreal (contrary to fact) in the present or future. (Chart 20-3)
Choose the sentence that describes the real situation.

1. If I had a million dollars, I would travel around the world.
   a. I have a million dollars.   b. I don't have a million dollars.

2. If I didn't have a bad cold, I'd go swimming with you.
   a. I have a bad cold.   b. I don't have a bad cold.

3. If Jenny were here, she could help us.
   a. Jenny is here.   b. Jenny isn't here.

4. If Henry weren't in charge here, nothing would ever get done.
   a. Henry is in charge here.   b. Henry isn't in charge here.

5. If I spoke Chinese, I could converse with your grandmother.
   a. I speak Chinese.   b. I don't speak Chinese.

6. If I knew the answer, I would tell you.
   a. I know the answer.   b. I don't know the answer.

PRACTICE 6 ▸ Unreal (contrary to fact) in the present or future. (Chart 20-3)

Read the given sentence(s) and the sentence that follows. Complete the second sentence with the verbs in the box.

be, be	have, go	have, travel
be, can have	have, like	like, cook

1. There aren't any trees on our street, and consequently, there is no shade.

   If there _____ trees on our street, there _____ shade.

2. We don't have enough money to travel abroad.

   If we _____ enough money, we _____ abroad.

3. The students don't have a good history teacher. They don't like history because of her.

   If the students _____ a better history teacher, they _____

   history.

4. Sam doesn't like fish, so his mother doesn't cook it for him.

   If Sam _____ fish, his mother _____ fish for him.

5. The weather is bad. We can't have our picnic at the lake today.

   If the weather _____ bad, we _____ our picnic at the lake

   today.

6. I have so much work to do. I will not go out with you tonight.

   If I _____ so much work, I _____ out with you tonight.

PRACTICE 7 ▸ Real vs. unreal in the present or future. (Charts 20-2 and 20-3)

Complete the sentences in Column A with a clause in Column B.

Column A

1. If the temperature goes below freezing, _____.
2. If the temperature were below freezing right now, _____.
3. If the baby is hungry, _____.
4. If the baby were hungry, _____.
5. If this fish were not fresh, _____.
6. If fish is not fresh, _____.
7. If a car runs out of gas, _____.
8. If this car had more power, _____.
9. If you threw a rock into the water, _____.
10. If you throw a life ring into the water, _____.

Column B

a. it stops
b. he cries
c. it smells bad
d. we would be very cold
e. it would go faster
f. it floats
g. it would sink
h. we will be very cold
i. it would smell bad
j. he would cry

PRACTICE 8 ▸ Unreal (contrary to fact) in the past. (Chart 20-4)
Choose the completions that describe the real situation.

1. If you had been here last night, you would have had a wonderful time. But _____.
   a. you were here   b. you weren't here

2. If I hadn't been rude, Jenna wouldn't have gotten angry. But _____.
   a. I was rude   b. I wasn't rude

3. If Anna hadn't been late, we could have seen the beginning of the movie. But _____.
   a. Anna was late   b. Anna wasn't late

4. If Rudi hadn't fallen asleep, he wouldn't have crashed into the tree. But _____.
   a. he fell asleep   b. he didn't fall asleep

5. If Alexi had studied, he might have passed the test. But _____.
   a. he studied   b. he didn't study

6. If I had known the password, I would have told you. But _____.
   a. I knew the password   b. I didn't know the password

PRACTICE 9 ▸ Unreal (contrary to fact) in the past. (Chart 20-4)
Using the information in the first sentence, complete the conditional sentences with the correct form of the verbs in parentheses.

1. Adam met his future wife, Alice, on a flight to Tokyo. (*take / meet*)

   If Adam (*not*) _____ that flight to Tokyo, he (*not*) _____

   Alice.

2. I forgot my credit card, so I couldn't pay for my groceries. (*forget / can pay*)

   If I (*not*) _____ my credit card, I _____ for my groceries.

3. I didn't know Jane was in the hospital, so I didn't visit her. (*know / visit*)

   If I _____ that Jane was in the hospital, I _____ her.

4. Alex didn't pay the electric bill. The electric company cut off his power. (*pay / cut off*)

   If Alex _____ the bill, the electric company (*not*) _____ his

   electricity.

5. The weather was bad. The outdoor concert was canceled. (*be / be*)

   If the weather _____ good, the outdoor concert

   (*not*) _____ canceled.

6. Alexander Fleming accidentally discovered the medical usefulness of a certain kind of mold.

   Scientists developed penicillin from that mold. (*discover / develop*)

   If Fleming (*not*) _____ the usefulness of that mold, scientists

   (*not*) _____ penicillin.

PRACTICE 10 ▸ Conditional sentences: present, future, or past. (Charts 20-2 → 20-4)
Complete each conversation with the correct phrase from the list. Write the letter.

a. I can join you   d. I had joined one
b. I could have joined you   e. I join one
c. I could join you   f. I joined one

1. A: Hi, Kim! Can you have lunch with us?

   B: I'm sorry, I can't. If _____, I would, but I have another appointment.

2. A: Hi, Sid! Would you like to join us for tomorrow?

   B: Maybe. I might have to work through lunch, but if _____, I will.

3. A: Hey, Mary! What happened? Why didn't you have lunch with us?

   B: Oh, if _____, I would have, but I had an emergency at my office.

4. A: Mr. Simmons, you should exercise more.

   B: I'll try, Dr. Scott. Maybe I'll join a gym. If _____, I'll get more exercise.

5. A: Ms. Mora, you need to exercise. Why don't you join a gym?

   B: Oh, Doctor, if _____, it would be a waste of money. I would never use it.

6. A: Mrs. Smith, you said you were going to join a gym, but you didn't. What happened?

   B: Right, I didn't. If _____, it would have been a waste of money. I would never have used it.

PRACTICE 11 ▸ Conditional sentences: present, future, or past. (Charts 20-2 → 20-4)
Write the correct form of the verbs in parentheses.

1. We're going to be stuck in this traffic jam for an hour. It's too bad we don't have wings. If we
   (*have*) _____ wings, we (*can, fly*) _____ over all this traffic instead
   of being stuck in it.

2. If we (*can, fly*) _____ over all this traffic, we (*get*) _____ where we
   need to be very quickly.

3. Maybe we'll get there before noon. If we (*get*) _____ there before noon, I
   (*have*) _____ a chance to talk with Olga before lunch.

4. I might have a chance to talk with Olga before we have lunch. If I (*have*) _____ a
   chance to talk with her before lunch, I (*tell*) _____ her about the job opening in
   our department.

5. I didn't have a chance to talk to John yesterday. If I (*have*) _____ a chance to talk to
   him, I (*tell*) _____ him about the job opening.

6. You didn't tell John about the job opening at the meeting yesterday. But, even if you
   (*tell*) _____ him, I'm sure that he (*be, not*)_____ interested
   at all. He wasn't looking for a new job.

PRACTICE 12 ▸ Conditional sentences. (Charts 20-2 → 20-4)
Write a conditional sentence with *if* for each given sentence.

1. I was sick yesterday, so I didn't go to class.
   If _____ *I hadn't been sick yesterday, I would have gone to class.* _____

2. Because Alan never eats breakfast, he always overeats at lunch.
   If _____

3. Kostas was late to his own wedding because his watch was slow.
   If _____

4. I don't ride the bus to work every morning because it's always so crowded.
   If _____

5. Sara didn't know that Highway 57 was closed, so she didn't take an alternative route.

   If _____

6. Camille couldn't finish unloading the truck because no one was there to help her.

   If _____

PRACTICE 13 ▸ Progressive verb forms in conditional sentences. (Chart 20-5)

Write a conditional sentence with *if* for each given sentence.

1. The wind is blowing so hard. We can't go sailing.

   If the wind weren't blowing so hard, we could go sailing.

2. The wind was blowing so hard. We couldn't go sailing.

   _____

3. The water is running. I can't hear you.

   _____

4. The water was running. I couldn't hear the phone.

   _____

5. The baby is hungry. That's why she's crying.

   _____

6. Jude was sleeping soundly, so he didn't hear his alarm clock.

   _____

7. I was watching an exciting mystery on TV, so I didn't answer the phone.

   _____

8. I'm trying to concentrate, so I can't talk to you now.

   _____

PRACTICE 14 ▸ Using "mixed time" in conditional sentences. (Chart 20-6)

Choose all the sentences that describe each situation.

1. If I hadn't stayed up late last night, I wouldn't be tired this morning.
   a. I went to bed late.
   b. I went to bed early.
   c. I am tired this morning.
   d. I am not tired this morning.

2. If Luke had saved some money, he could buy a house now.
   a. Luke saved some money.
   b. Luke didn't save any money.
   c. Luke can buy a house.
   d. Luke can't buy a house.

3. If I hadn't apologized to Ben, he would still be angry at me.
   a. I apologized to Ben.
   b. I didn't apologize to Ben.
   c. Ben is still angry at me.
   d. Ben is not angry at me anymore.

4. If I had taken Grandpa's advice, I wouldn't be in this mess now!
   a. I took Grandpa's advice.
   b. I didn't take Grandpa's advice.
   c. I am in a mess now.
   d. I am not in a mess now.

5. If Laura hadn't been wearing her seat belt, she would have been severely injured.
   a. Laura was wearing her seat belt.
   b. Laura wasn't wearing her seat belt.
   c. Laura was severely injured.
   d. Laura was not severely injured.

6. If new houses had not been built near the campgrounds, the area would still be wilderness.
   a. New houses have been built near the campgrounds.
   b. New houses have not been built near the campgrounds.
   c. The area is still wilderness.
   d. The area is not wilderness anymore.

PRACTICE 15 ▶ Using progressive forms and "mixed time" in conditional sentences. (Charts 20-5 and 20-6)

Write a conditional sentence with *if* for each given sentence.

1. It is raining, so we won't finish the game.

   _____*If it weren't raining, we would finish the game.*_____

2. I didn't eat lunch, and now I'm hungry.

   If _____

3. Bob left his wallet at home this morning, and now he doesn't have money for lunch.

   If _____

4. Bryce is always daydreaming, so he never gets his work done.

   If _____

5. My muscles hurt today because I played basketball for three hours last night.

   If _____

6. I couldn't hear what you said because the band was playing so loud.

   If _____

7. Because Diana asked the technician a lot of questions, she understands how to fix her computer now.

   If _____

8. Sasha and Ivan weren't paying attention, so they didn't see the exit sign on the highway.

   If _____

9. I really don't know what the test results mean because the doctor didn't explain them to me.

   If _____

10. We were sleeping last night, so we didn't feel the earthquake.

    If _____

PRACTICE 16 ▸ Omitting *if*. (Chart 20-7)
Write sentences with the same meaning by omitting *if*.

1. If I were you, I wouldn't go there.
   _____*Were I you,*_____ I wouldn't go there.

2. If you should need my help, please call.
   _____*Should you need*_____ my help, please call.

3. If I had known about her accident, I would have gone to the hospital immediately.
   _____ about her accident, I would have gone to the hospital immediately.

4. If I had been offered a job at the law office, I would have gladly accepted.
   _____ a job at the law office, I would have gladly accepted.

5. If anyone should call, would you please take a message?
   _____, would you please take a message?

6. (Directions on the pizza box) "If this pizza needs reheating, place it in a hot oven for five minutes. "
   _____, place it in a hot oven for five minutes.

7. (Directions on a medicine bottle) "If you feel any dizziness, nausea, or muscle pain, discontinue taking this medicine and call your doctor immediately. "
   _____ any dizziness, nausea, or muscle pain, discontinue taking this
   medicine and call your doctor immediately.

8. If you were really a lawyer, I would take your advice.
   _____, I would take your advice.

PRACTICE 17 ▸ Omitting *if*. (Chart 20-7)
Choose the one sentence that has the same meaning as the given sentence.

1. Had she not been texting and walking, she wouldn't have tripped and fallen down.
   a. She had to text and walk.
   b. She was texting and walking.
   c. She didn't trip.
   d. She has to text and fall down.

2. Should you have further questions, please don't hesitate to contact us again.
   a. You should ask more questions.
   b. You might have more questions.
   c. You will certainly have more questions.
   d. Don't bother calling us again.

3. Had the building been properly built, it would have withstood the hurricane.
   a. The building was properly built.
   b. The building survived the hurricane.
   c. The building wasn't properly built.
   d. The building was built after the hurricane.

4. If you were rich, you could fly across the ocean to visit your family every week.
   a. Are you rich?
   b. You are not rich.
   c. You visit your family every week.
   d. You used to be rich, but you are not anymore.

5. Had I known how much work would be involved, I never would have remodeled my kitchen.
   a. I expected it to be a lot of work.
   b. I remodeled my kitchen.
   c. I didn't remodel my kitchen.
   d. I knew how much work would be involved.

PRACTICE 18 ▸ Implied conditions. (Chart 20-8)
Rewrite the sentences with *if*-clauses.

1. Sara's dad would have picked her up, but I forgot to tell him that she needed a ride.

   Sara's dad would have picked her up if _____ *I hadn't forgotten to tell him that she needed a ride.* _____

2. I couldn't have finished the project without your help.

   I couldn't have finished the project if _____.

3. I opened the door slowly. Otherwise, I could have hit someone.

   If _____, I could have hit

   someone.

4. Dave would have gone on vacation with me, but he couldn't get time off from work.

   Dave would have gone with me if _____.

5. CAROL: Why didn't Oscar tell his boss about the problem?

   ALICE: He would have gotten into a lot of trouble.

   Oscar would have gotten into a lot of trouble if _____

   _____.

PRACTICE 19 ▸ Review: conditional sentences. (Charts 20-1 → 20-8)
Choose the correct completions.

1. If I spoke Spanish, I _____ abroad in Spain next year.
   a. will study   c. had studied
   b. would have studied   d. would study

2. It would have been a much more serious accident _____ fast at the time.
   a. had she been driving   c. she had driven
   b. was she driving   d. if she drove

3. A: Can I borrow your car for this evening?

   B: Sure, but Nora's using it right now. If she _____ it back in time, you're welcome to borrow it.
      a. brought   c. brings
      b. would bring   d. will bring

4. I didn't get home until well after midnight last night. Otherwise, I _____ your call.
   a. returned   c. would return
   b. had returned   d. would have returned

5. If energy _____ inexpensive and unlimited, many things in the world would be different.
   a. is   c. were
   b. will be   d. would be

6. We _____ the game if we'd had a few more minutes.
   a. will win   c. had won
   b. won   d. could have won

7. I _____ William with me if I had known you and he didn't get along with each other.
   a. hadn't brought   c. wouldn't have brought
   b. didn't bring   d. won't bring

8. Dr. Mason was out of town, so a guest lecturer gave the talk. It was boring and I almost fell asleep.

If Dr. Mason _____, I would have paid attention and not fallen asleep.
a. lectured
b. had been lecturing
c. was lecturing
d. would lecture

9. If you _____ to my advice in the first place, you wouldn't be in so much trouble right now.
a. listen
b. had listened
c. will listen
d. listened

10. _____ interested in that subject, I would try to learn more about it.
a. Were I
b. Should I
c. I was
d. If I am

11. If I _____ the problems you had as a child, I might not have succeeded in life as well as you have.
a. have
b. would have
c. had had
d. should have

12. I _____ your mother to dinner if I had known she was visiting you.
a. invite
b. invited
c. had invited
d. would have invited

13. _____ more help, I can call my neighbor.
a. Needed
b. Should I need
c. I have needed
d. I should need

14. _____ then what I know today, I would have saved myself a lot of time and trouble over the years.
a. If I know
b. Did I know
c. If I would know
d. Had I known

15. Do you think there would be less conflict in the world if all people _____ the same language?
a. speak
b. will speak
c. spoke
d. had spoken

16. If you can tell me why I wasn't included, _____ this incident again.
a. I don't mention
b. I will never mention
c. I never mention
d. will I never mention

17. I didn't know you were asleep. Otherwise, I _____ so much noise when I came in.
a. didn't make
b. wouldn't have made
c. won't make
d. don't make

18. Unless you _____ all of my questions, I can't do anything to help you.
a. answered
b. answer
c. would answer
d. are answering

19. Had you told me that this was going to happen, I _____ it.
a. never would have believed
b. don't believe
c. hadn't believed
d. can't believe

20. If Jake _____ to go on the trip, would you have gone alone?
a. doesn't agree
b. didn't agree
c. hadn't agreed
d. wouldn't agree

PRACTICE 20 ▸ Wishes about the present and past. (Chart 20-9)
Choose the sentence that describes the real situation.

1. I wish that you were my true friend.
   a. You are my true friend.
   b. You are not my true friend.

2. I wish I had known the truth.
   a. I knew the truth.
   b. I didn't know the truth.

3. I wish you hadn't lied to me.
   a. You lied to me.
   b. You didn't lie to me.

4. I wish we were going on vacation.
   a. We are going on vacation.
   b. We are not going on vacation.

5. I wish I had a motorcycle.
   a. I have a motorcycle.
   b. I don't have a motorcycle.

6. I wish John could have met my father.
   a. John was able to meet my father.
   b. John was not able to meet my father.

PRACTICE 21 ▸ Wishes about the present and the past. (Chart 20-9)
Make wishes. Complete the sentences with a verb.

1. The sun isn't shining.

   I wish the sun _____*were shining*_____ right now.

2. You didn't go to the concert with us last night.

   I wish you _____ with us to the concert last night.

3. Spiro didn't drive to this party.

   I wish Spiro _____ to the party. I'd ask him for a ride home.

4. I can't swim.

   I wish I _____ so I would feel safe in a boat.

5. Our team didn't win.

   I wish our team _____ the game last night.

6. Bill didn't get the promotion.

   I wish Bill _____ the promotion. He feels bad.

7. I quit my job.

   I wish I _____ my job until I'd found another one.

8. It isn't winter.

   I wish it _____ winter so that I could go skiing.

PRACTICE 22 ▸ Verb forms following *wish*. (Chart 20-9)
Write the correct form of the verbs in parentheses.

1. Heinrich doesn't like his job as a house painter. He wishes he (*go*) _____ to art

   school when he was younger. He wishes he (*can, paint*) _____ canvasses instead

   of houses for a living.

2. I don't like living here. I wish I (*move, not*) _____ to this

   big city. I can't seem to make any friends, and everything is so crowded. I wish I

   (*take*) _____ the job I was offered before I moved here.

3. I know I shouldn't eat junk food every day, but I wish you (*stop*) _____ nagging me about it.

4. I wish you (*invite, not*) _____ the neighbors over for dinner when you talked to them earlier this afternoon. I don't feel like cooking a big dinner.

5. A: Did you get your car back from the garage?

   B: Yes, and it still isn't fixed. I wish I (*pay, not*) _____ them in full when I picked the car up. I should have waited to make sure that everything was all right.

6. A: I wish you (*hurry*) _____! We're going to be late.

   B: I wish you (*relax*) _____. We've got plenty of time.

7. A: How do you like the new apartment manager?

   B: Not much. I wish she (*choose, not*) _____.

   A: Me too. She's not very helpful. I wish the owners (*pick*) _____ someone else.

8. A: My thirteen-year-old daughter wishes she (*be, not*) _____ so tall and that her hair (*be*) _____ black and straight.

   B: Really? My daughter wishes she (*be*) _____ taller and that her hair (*be*) _____ blond and curly.

9. A: I can't go to the game with you this afternoon.

   B: Really? That's too bad. But I wish you (*tell*) _____ me sooner so that I could have invited someone else to go with me.

10. A: How long have you been sick?

    B: For over a week.

    A: I wish you (*go*) _____ to see a doctor later today. You should find out what's wrong with you.

    B: Maybe I'll go tomorrow.

PRACTICE 23 ▸ Wishes about the future. (Chart 20-10)
Make wishes about the future using the verbs in the box.

cook	end	get	hang up	leave	snow

1. A: So, Mom, how do you like my haircut?

   B: You got a haircut? Your hair is still long. I wish you _____ a real haircut.

2. A: Aren't you going on your annual ski trip this year?

   B: No, not unless it snows. There hasn't been any snow this year. I wish it _____ so we could go skiing.

3. A: Helen! How long are our guests going to stay? It's almost midnight.

   B: I don't know. I wish they _____, but Henry just keeps on talking. Everyone is falling asleep.

4. A: I love you, Pat, but I wish you were neater.

   B: Neater? What do you mean? I pick up everything, I clean up everything ...

   A: Well, I mean I wish you _____ your clothes instead of leaving them on a chair.

5. A: What's the matter? Don't you like the movie?

   B: Not at all! I wish it _____. We have to stay, though because the kids are enjoying it so much.

6. A: Meatballs again?

   B: Don't you like meatballs?

   A: You know I do, but sometimes I wish you _____ something else.

PRACTICE 24 ▶ Wishes about the past, present, and future. (Charts 20-9 and 20-10)

Complete the sentences with the correct form of the verbs in parentheses.

At the Pet Store

LAILA: Look at these puppies! They're so cute. I wish my apartment manager

(*allow*) _____ dogs.

REAGAN: Really? I have a dog, but I wish I (*get*) _____ a cat instead. Dogs need a lot of attention. You have to play with them and take them for walks every day. I go to school all day and work in the evenings, so my dog gets very lonely. I wish I (*think*) _____ of that before. I feel guilty now.

LAILA: Don't cats need attention too?

REAGAN: Of course, but not nearly as much as dogs. Cats can take care of themselves a lot of the time. Does your apartment manager allow cats?

LAILA: Yes, cats are allowed, but I live with my sister. She's allergic to cats. I wish she

(*have*) _____ so many allergies.

REAGAN: Yeah, that's too bad. Hey, look at all these colorful fish! They're beautiful. I wish I

(*get*) _____ a big aquarium and fill it with lots of fish, but I already have more responsibilities than I can take care of.

LAILA: Maybe, I'll get some fish. It's not the same as a cuddly cat or dog, but it's better than nothing.

REAGAN: I really wish someone (*take*) _____ my dog for walks on the days when I'm too busy. Would you be interested?

LAILA: I'd love to!

PRACTICE 25 ▶ Chapter review.
Complete the sentences with the correct form of the verb in parentheses.

RYAN: What's wrong, Gavin? You look awful!

GAVIN: Yeah, you (*look*) _____ bad too if you (*have*) _____ a day like
　　　1　　　　　　　　　　　　　　　　　　　　　　　2
mine yesterday. My car slid into a tree because the roads were icy.

RYAN: Really? What happened?

GAVIN: Well, I guess if I (*drive, not*) _____ so fast,
　　　　　　　　　　　　　　　　　3
I (*slide, not*) _____ into the tree.
　　　　　　　　　4

RYAN: Seriously? Speeding again, Gav? Don't you know that if a driver (*step*) _____
　　　　　　　　　　　　　　　　　　　　　　　　　　　　　　　　　　　　5
on the gas on ice, the car will spin around in a circle?

GAVIN: I know that now, but I didn't know that yesterday! If I (*know*) _____ that
　　　　　　　　　　　　　　　　　　　　　　　　　　　　　　　　　6
yesterday, I (*not, crash*) _____. And if that weren't bad enough,
　　　　　　　　　　　　　　　7
I didn't have my driver's license with me, so I'll have to pay an extra fine for that when I go to
court next month.

RYAN: You were driving without your license? Are you crazy?

GAVIN: Yeah. It fell out of my pocket.

RYAN: You sure have bad luck! If you (*lose, not*) _____ your wallet, you
　　　　　　　　　　　　　　　　　　　　　　　8
(*have*) _____ your driver's license with you when you hit a
　　　　9
tree. If you (*have*) _____ your license with you, you (*have to pay, not*)
　　　　　　　　　10
_____ a steep fine when you go to court next week. And of course,
　　　11
if you hadn't been driving too fast, you (*run into, not*) _____ a tree,
　　　　　　　　　　　　　　　　　　　　　　　　　　　12
and you (*be, not*) _____ in this awful situation now. If I
　　　　　　　　　13
(*be*) _____ you, I (*take*) _____ it easy and just
　　　14　　　　　　　　　　　　　　15
(*stay*) _____ home where you'll be no danger to yourself or to anyone else.
　　　16

GAVIN: Yeah, thanks for the advice. Enough about me! How about you?

RYAN: Everything's going pretty well. I'm planning to take off for Florida soon. I'm sick of all this cold,
rainy weather. I (*stay*) _____ here for vacation if the weather
　　　　　　　　　　　　17
(*be, not*) _____ so bad. But I need some sun!
　　　　18

GAVIN: I wish I (*can, go*) _____ with you. How are you planning on getting there?
　　　　　　　　　19

RYAN: If I have enough money, I (*fly*) _____. Otherwise,
　　　　　　　　　　　　　　　　20
I (*take*) _____ the bus. I wish I (*can, drive*) _____ my
　　　21　　　　　　　　　　　　　　　　　　　　22
own car there because it (*be*) _____ nice to have it to drive around in once I
　　　　　　　　　　　　23
get there, but it's such a long trip. I wish I (*have*) _____ someone to go with me
　　　　　　　　　　　　　　　　　　　24
and share the driving.

GAVIN: Hey, what about me? Why don't I go with you? I can share the driving. I'm a great driver!

RYAN: Didn't you just get through telling me that you'd wrapped your car around a tree?

Appendix
Supplementary Grammar Units

PRACTICE 1 ▶ Subjects, verbs, and objects. (Chart A-1)
Underline and identify the subject (**S**), verb (**V**), and object of the verb (**O**) in each sentence.

       S   **V**   **O**
1. Airplanes have wings.
2. The teacher explained the problem.
3. Children enjoy games.
4. Jack wore a blue suit.
5. Some animals eat plants. Some animals eat other animals.
6. According to an experienced waitress, you can carry full cups of coffee without spilling them just by never looking at them.

PRACTICE 2 ▶ Transitive vs. intransitive verbs. (Chart A-1)
Underline and identify the verb in each sentence. Write **VT** if it is transitive. Write **VI** if it is intransitive.

        VI
1. Alice arrived at six o'clock.

        VT
2. We drank some tea.
3. I agree with you.
4. I waited for Sam at the airport for two hours.
5. They're staying at a resort hotel in San Antonio, Texas.
6. Mr. Chan is studying English.
7. The wind is blowing hard today.
8. I walked to the theater, but Janice rode her bicycle.
9. Crocodiles hatch from eggs.
10. Rivers flow toward the sea.

PRACTICE 3 ▶ Adjectives and adverbs. (Charts A-2 and A-3)
Underline and identify the adjectives (**ADJ**) and adverbs (**ADV**) in these sentences.

        ADJ   **ADV**
1. Jack opened the heavy door slowly.
2. Chinese jewelers carved beautiful ornaments from jade.
3. The old man carves wooden figures skillfully.
4. A busy executive usually has short conversations on the telephone.
5. The young woman had a very good time at the picnic yesterday.

PRACTICE 4 ▸ Adjectives and adverbs. (Charts A-2 and A-3)
Complete each sentence with the correct adjective or adverb.

1. *quick, quickly* We ate _____ quickly _____ and ran to the theater.
2. *quick, quickly* We had a _____ quick _____ dinner and ran to the theater.
3. *polite, politely* I've always found Fred to be a _____ person.
4. *polite, politely* He responded to my question _____.
5. *regular, regularly* Mr. Thomas comes to the store _____ for cheese and bread.
6. *regular, regularly* He is a _____ customer.
7. *usual, usually* The teacher arrived at the _____ time.
8. *usual, usually* She _____ comes to class five minutes before it begins.
9. *good, well* Jennifer Cooper paints _____.
10. *good, well* She is a _____ artist.
11. *gentle, gently* A _____ breeze touched my face.
12. *gentle, gently* A breeze _____ touched my face.
13. *bad, badly* The audience booed the actors' _____ performance.
14. *bad, badly* The audience booed and whistled because the actors performed

    _____ throughout the show.

PRACTICE 5 ▸ Midsentence adverbs. (Chart A-3)
Put the adverb in parentheses in its usual midsentence position.

1. (*always*) Ana ₐ takes a walk in the morning.   *[always inserted above]*
2. (*always*) Tim is a hard worker.
3. (*always*) Beth has worked hard.
4. (*always*) Carrie works hard.
5. (*always*) Do you work hard?
6. (*usually*) Taxis are available at the airport.
7. (*rarely*) Yusef takes a taxi to his office.
8. (*often*) I have thought about quitting my job and sailing to Alaska.
9. (*probably*) Yuko needs some help.
10. (*ever*) Have you attended the show at the Museum of Space?
11. (*seldom*) Brad goes out to eat at a restaurant.
12. (*hardly ever*) The students are late.
13. (*usually*) Do you finish your homework before dinner?
14. (*generally*) In India, the monsoon season begins in April.
15. (*usually*) During the monsoon season, Mr. Singh's hometown receives around 610 centimeters
    (240 inches) of rain, which is an unusually large amount.

PRACTICE 6 ▸ Identifying prepositions. (Chart A-4)
Underline the prepositions.

1. Jim came to class <u>without</u> his books.

2. We stayed at home during the storm.

3. Sonya walked across the bridge over the Cedar River.

4. When Alex walked through the door, his little sister ran toward him and put her arms around his neck.

5. The two of us need to talk to Tom too.

6. Animals live in all parts of the world. Animals walk or crawl on land, fly in the air, and swim in the water.

7. Scientists divide living things into two main groups: the animal kingdom and the plant kingdom.

8. Asia extends from the Pacific Ocean in the east to Africa and Europe in the west.

PRACTICE 7 ▸ Sentence elements. (Charts A-1 → A-4)
Underline and identify the subject (**S**), verb (**V**), object (**O**), and prepositional phrases (**PP**) in the following sentences.

      S   **V**   **O**   **PP**

1. <u>Harry</u> <u>put</u> the <u>letter</u> <u>in the mailbox</u>.

2. The kids walked to school.

3. Caroline did her homework at the library.

4. Chinese printers created the first paper money in the world.

5. Dark clouds appeared on the horizon.

6. Rhonda filled the shelves of the cabinet with boxes of old books.

PRACTICE 8 ▸ Preposition combinations. (Chart A-5)
Choose <u>all</u> the correct completions for each sentence.

1. Max is known for his (*honesty* / *fairness* / *famous*).

2. Several students were absent from (*yesterday* / *school* / *class*).

3. Has Maya recovered from (*her illness* / *her husband's death* / *the chair*)?

4. The criminal escaped from (*jail* / *the key* / *prison*).

5. Do you believe in (*ghosts* / *UFOs* / *scary*)?

6. Anthony is engaged to (*my cousin* / *a friend* / *marriage*).

7. Chris excels in (*mathematics* / *sports* / *his cousins*).

8. I'm very fond of (*you* / *exciting* / *your children*).

9. Henry doesn't approve of (*smoking* / *cigarettes* / *rain*).

10. I subscribe to (*magazines* / *a newspaper* / *websites*).

PRACTICE 9 ▸ Preposition combinations. (Chart A-5)
Choose the correct prepositions in parentheses.

1. Water consists (*of* / *with*) oxygen and hydrogen.

2. I am uncomfortable because that man is staring (*to* / *at*) me.

3. Ella hid the candy (*from* / *back*) the children.

4. I arrived (*in* / *to*) this country two weeks ago.

5. We arrived (*to* / *at*) the airport ten minutes late.

6. I am envious (*in* / *of*) people who can speak three or four languages fluently.

7. The students responded (*at* / *to*) the teacher's questions.

8. The farmers are hoping (*on* / *for*) rain.

9. I'm depending (*on* / *in*) you to finish this work for me.

10. Tim wore sunglasses to protect his eyes (*for* / *from*) the sun.

PRACTICE 10 ▸ Preposition combinations. (Chart A-5)
Complete the sentences with appropriate prepositions.

SITUATION 1: Mr. and Mrs. Jones just celebrated their 50th wedding anniversary.

1. They have been married _____*to*_____ each other for 50 years.

2. They have always been faithful _____ each other.

3. They are proud _____ their marriage.

4. They are polite _____ one another.

5. They are patient _____ each other.

6. They are devoted _____ one another.

7. They have been committed _____ their marriage.

SITUATION 2: Jacob and Emily have been together for five months. They don't have a healthy relationship, and it probably won't last long.

1. They are often annoyed _____ each other's behavior.

2. They argue _____ each other every day.

3. They are bored _____ their relationship.

4. They are tired _____ one another.

5. Jacob is jealous _____ Emily's friends.

6. Emily is sometimes frightened _____ Jacob's moods.

PRACTICE 11 ▸ Preposition combinations. (Chart A-5)
Complete each sentence in Column A with the correct phrase from Column B.

Column A	Column B
1. My boots are made __*c*__ .	a. from the burning building
2. We hope you succeed _____ .	b. for telling a lie
3. She forgave him _____ .	✓c. of leather
4. I'm going to take care _____ .	d. from entering the tunnel
5. The firefighters rescued many people _____ .	e. in winning the scholarship
6. I pray _____ .	f. of the children tonight
7. Trucks are prohibited _____ .	g. for peace

PRACTICE 12 ▸ Preposition combinations. (Chart A-5)

Complete the sentences with appropriate prepositions.

1. Andrea contributed her ideas _____*to*_____ the discussion.
2. Ms. Kleeman substituted _____ our regular teacher.
3. I can't distinguish one twin _____ the other.
4. Children rely _____ their parents for food and shelter.
5. I'm worried _____ this problem.
6. I don't care _____ spaghetti. I'd rather eat something else.
7. Charles doesn't seem to care _____ his bad grades.
8. I'm afraid I don't agree _____ you.
9. We decided _____ eight o'clock as the time we should meet.
10. I am not familiar _____ that author's works.
11. Do you promise to come? I'm counting _____ you to be here.
12. The little girl is afraid _____ an imaginary bear that lives in her closet.

PRACTICE 13 ▸ Preposition combinations. (Chart A-5)

Complete the sentences with appropriate prepositions.

1. We will fight _____*for*_____ our rights.
2. Who did you vote _____ in the last election?
3. Jason was late because he wasn't aware _____ the time.
4. I am grateful _____ you _____ your assistance.
5. Elena is not content _____ the progress she is making.
6. Paul's comments were not relevant _____ the topic under discussion.
7. Have you decided _____ a date for your wedding yet?
8. Patricia applied _____ admission _____ the university.
9. Daniel dreamed _____ some of his childhood friends last night.
10. Mr. Miyagi dreams _____ owning his own business someday.
11. The accused woman was innocent _____ the crime with which she was charged.
12. Ms. Sanders is friendly _____ everyone.
13. The secretary provided me _____ a great deal of information.
14. Ivan compared the wedding customs in his country _____ those in the United States.

PRACTICE 14 ▶ Review: basic question forms. (Chart B-1)

From the underlined sentences, make questions for the given answers. Fill in the blank spaces with the appropriate words. If no word is needed, write Ø.

1. *Chris can live there.*

	Question word	Auxiliary verb	Subject	Main verb	Rest of question	→	Answer
1a.	Ø	Can	Chris	live	there	? →	Yes.
1b.	Where	can	Chris	live	Ø	? →	There.
1c.	Who	can	Ø	live	there	? →	Chris.

2. *Ron is living there.*

	Question word	Auxiliary verb	Subject	Main verb	Rest of question	→	Answer
2a.	Ø				there	? →	Yes.
2b.	Where				Ø	? →	There.
2c.	Who				there	? →	Ron.

3. *Kate lives there.*

	Question word	Auxiliary verb	Subject	Main verb	Rest of question	→	Answer
3a.	Ø				there	? →	Yes.
3b.	Where				Ø	? →	There.
3c.	Who				there	? →	Kate.

4. *Anna will live there.*

	Question word	Auxiliary verb	Subject	Main verb	Rest of question	→	Answer
4a.	Ø				there	? →	Yes.
4b.	Where				Ø	? →	There.
4c.	Who				there	? →	Anna.

5. *Jack lived there.*

	Question word	Auxiliary verb	Subject	Main verb	Rest of question	→	Answer
5a.					there	? →	Yes.
5b.					Ø	? →	There.
5c.					there	? →	Jack.

6. *Mary has lived there.*

	Question word	Auxiliary verb	Subject	Main verb	Rest of question	→	Answer
6a.						? →	Yes.
6b.						? →	There.
6c.						? →	Mary.

PRACTICE 15 ▸ Yes / no and information questions. (Charts B-1 and B-2)

Make questions to fit the conversations. Notice in the examples that there is a short answer and then in parentheses a long answer. Your questions should produce those answers.

1. A: _____*When are you going to the zoo?*_____

   B: Tomorrow. (*I'm going to the zoo tomorrow.*)

2. A: _____*Are you going downtown later today?*_____

   B: Yes. (*I'm going downtown later today.*)

3. A: _____

   B: Yes. (*I live in an apartment.*)

4. A: _____

   B: In a condominium. (*Alex lives in a condominium.*)

5. A: _____

   B: Janice. (*Janice lives in that house.*)

6. A: _____

   B: Yes. (*I can speak French.*)

7. A: _____

   B: Jeff. (*Jeff can speak Arabic.*)

8. A: _____

   B: Two weeks ago. (*Ben arrived two weeks ago.*)

9. A: _____

   B: Mazzen. (*Mazzen arrived late.*)

10. A: _____

    B: The window. (*Ann is opening the window.*)

11. A: _____

    B: Opening the window. (*Ann is opening the window.*)

12. A: _____

    B: Her book. (*Mary opened her book.*)

13. A: _____

    B: Ramzy. (*Ramzy opened the door.*)

14. A: _____

    B: Yes. (*The mail has arrived.*)

15. A: _____

    B: Yes. (*I have a bicycle.*)

16. A: _____

    B: A pen. (*Zach has a pen in his hand.*)

17. A: _____

    B: Yes. (*I like ice cream.*)

18. A: _____

    B: Yes. (*I would like an ice cream cone.*)

19. A: _____

    B: A candy bar. (*Scott would like a candy bar.*)

20. A: _____

    B: Isabel. (*Isabel would like a soft drink.*)

PRACTICE 16 ▸ Information questions. (Charts B-1 and B-2)

Make questions from these sentences. The *italicized* words in parentheses should be the answers to your questions.

1. I take my coffee (*black*). → *How do you take your coffee?*

2. I have (*an English-Spanish*) dictionary.

3. He (*runs a grocery store*) for a living.

4. Margaret was talking to (*her uncle*).

5. (*Only ten*) people showed up for the meeting.

6. (*Because of heavy fog*), none of the planes could take off.

7. She was thinking about (*her experiences as a rural doctor*).

8. I was driving (*sixty-five miles per hour*) when the police officer stopped me.

9. I like (*hot and spicy Mexican*) food best.

10. (*The*) apartment (*at the end of the hall on the second floor*) is mine.

11. Oscar is (*friendly, generous, and kindhearted*).

12. Oscar is (*tall and thin and has short black hair*).

13. (*Taylor's*) dictionary fell to the floor.

14. Abby isn't here (*because she has a doctor's appointment*).

15. All of the students in the class will be informed of their final grades (*on Friday*).

16. I feel (*awful*).

17. Of those three books, I preferred (*the one by Tolstoy*).

18. I like (*rock*) music.

19. The plane is expected to be (*an hour*) late.

20. The driver of the stalled car lit a flare (*in order to warn oncoming cars*).

21. I want (*the felt-tip*) pen, (*not the ballpoint*).

22. The weather is (*hot and humid*) in July.

23. I like my steak (*medium rare*).

24. I did (*very well*) on the test.

25. There are (*31,536,000*) seconds in a year.

PRACTICE 17 ▶ Information questions. (Charts B-1 and B-2)
Make questions from the following sentences. The words in parentheses should be the answers to your questions.

1. I need (*five dollars*). → *How much money do you need?*

2. Roberto was born (*in Panama*).

3. I go out to eat (*at least once a week*).

4. I'm waiting for (*Maria*).

5. (*My sister*) answered the phone.

6. I called (*Benjamin*).

7. (*Benjamin*) called.

8. She bought (*twelve gallons of*) gas.

9. "Deceitful" means (*"dishonest"*).

10. An abyss is (*a bottomless hole*).

11. He went (*this*) way, (*not that way*).

12. These are (*Scott's*) books and papers.

13. They have (*four*) children.

14. He has been here (*for two hours*).

15. It is (*two hundred miles*) to Madrid.

16. The doctor can see you (*at three on Friday*).

17. Her roommate is (*Jane Peters*).

18. Her roommates are (*Jane Peters and Ellen Lee*).

19. My parents have been living there (*for three years*).

20. This is (*Alice's*) book.

21. (*David and George*) are coming over for dinner.

22. Caroline's dress is (*blue*).

23. Caroline's eyes are (*brown*).

24. (*Andrew*) can't go on the picnic.

25. Andrew can't go (*because he is sick*).

26. I didn't answer the phone (*because I didn't hear it ring*).

27. I like (*classical*) music.

28. I don't understand (*the chart on page 50*).

29. Janie is (*studying*) right now.

30. You spell "sitting" (*with two "t's"—S-I-T-T-I-N-G*).

31. Xavier (*is about medium height and has red hair and freckles*).

32. Xavier is (*very serious and hard-working*).

33. Ray (*works as a civil engineer for the railroad company*).

34. Mexico is (*eight hundred miles*) from here.

35. I take my coffee (*black with sugar*).

36. Of Stockholm and Moscow, (*Stockholm*) is farther north.

37. (*Fine.*) I'm getting along (*just fine*).

PRACTICE 18 ▸ Shortened Yes/No Questions. (Chart B-3)

Make full questions from the shortened questions.

1. Find your keys? → *Did you find your keys?*

2. Want some coffee?

3. Need help?

4. Leaving already?

5. Have any questions?

6. (On an elevator) Going up?

7. Make it on time?

PRACTICE 19 ▸ Negative questions. (Chart B-4)

In these dialogues, make negative questions from the words in parentheses, and determine the expected response.

1. A: Your infected finger looks terrible. (*you, see, not*) ____*Haven't you seen*____ a doctor yet?

   B: ___*No*___. But I'm going to. I don't want the infection to get any worse.

2. A: You look pale. What's the matter? (*you, feel*) _____ well?

   B: _____. I think I might be coming down with something.

3. A: Did you see Mark at the meeting?

   B: No, I didn't.

   A: Really? (*he, be, not*) _____ there?

   B: _____.

   A: That's funny. I've never known him to miss a meeting before.

4. A: Why didn't you come to the meeting yesterday afternoon?

   B: What meeting? I didn't know there was a meeting.

   A: (*Dana, tell, not*) _____ you about it?

   B: _____. No one said a word to me about it.

5. A: I have a package for Jill. (*Jill and you, work, not*) _____

   _____ in the same building?

   B: _____. I'd be happy to take the package to her tomorrow when I go to work.

6. A: Kevin didn't report all of his income on his tax forms.

   B: (*that, be, not*) _____ against the law?

   A: _____. And that's why he's in a lot of legal trouble. He might even go to jail.

7. A: Did you give Miranda my message when you went to class this morning?

   B: No. I didn't see her.

   A: Oh? (*she, be*) _____ in class?

   B: _____. She didn't come today.

8. A: Do you see that woman over there, the one in the blue dress? (*she, be*) _____

   Mrs. Robbins?

   B: _____.

   A: I thought so. I wonder what she is doing here.

PRACTICE 20 ▶ Tag questions. (Chart B-5)

Add tag questions to the following.

1. You live in an apartment, ___don't you___?

2. You've never been in Italy, ___have you___?

3. Sara turned in her report, _____?

4. There are more countries north of the equator than south of it, _____?

5. You've never met Jack Freeman, _____?

6. You have a ticket to the game, _____?

7. You'll be there, _____?

8. John knows Claire Reed, _____?

9. We should call Rhonda, _____?

10. Ostriches can't swim, _____?

11. These books aren't yours, _____?

12. That's Charlie's, _____?

13. Your neighbors died in the accident, _____?

14. I'm right, _____?

15. This grammar is easy, _____?

PRACTICE 21 ▶ Contractions. (Chart C)

Write the contraction of the pronoun and verb if appropriate. Write Ø if the pronoun and verb cannot be contracted.

1. He is (___He's___) in my class.

2. He was (___Ø___) in my class.

3. He has (___He's___) been here since July.

4. He has (___Ø___) a Volvo.*

5. She had (_____) been there for a long time before we arrived.

6. She had (_____) a bad cold.

7. She would (_____) like to go to the zoo.

8. I did (_____) well on the test.

9. We will (_____) be there early.

10. They are (_____) in their seats over there.

11. It is (_____) going to be hot tomorrow.

12. It has (_____) been a long time since I've seen him.

13. A bear is a large animal. It has (_____) four legs and brown hair.*

14. We were (_____) on time.

15. We are (_____) always on time.

16. She has (_____) a good job.*

17. She has (_____) been working there for a long time.

*NOTE: **has, have,** and **had** are NOT contracted when they are used as main verbs. They are contracted only when they are used as helping verbs.

18. She had (_____) opened the window before class began.

19. She would (_____) have helped us if we had (_____) asked her.

20. He could have helped us if he had (_____) been there.

PRACTICE 22 ▸ Using *not* and *no*. (Chart D-1)

Change each sentence into the negative in two ways: use *not . . . any* in one sentence and *no* in the other.

1. I have some problems. → *I don't have any problems. I have no problems.*

2. There was some food on the shelf.

3. I received some letters from home.

4. I need some help.

5. We have some time to waste.

6. You should have given the beggar some money.

7. I trust someone. → *I don't trust anyone. I trust no one.***

8. I saw someone.

9. There was someone in his room.

10. She can find somebody who knows about it.

PRACTICE 23 ▸ Avoiding double negatives. (Chart D-2)

Correct the errors in these sentences, all of which contain double negatives.

1. We don't have no time to waste.

    → *We have no time to waste.* OR *We don't have any time to waste.*

2. I didn't have no problems.

3. I can't do nothing about it.

4. You can't hardly ever understand her when she speaks.

5. I don't know neither Joy nor her husband.

6. Don't never drink water from that river without boiling it first.

7. Because I had to sit in the back row of the auditorium, I couldn't barely hear the speaker.

PRACTICE 24 ▸ Beginning a sentence with a negative word. (Chart D-3)

Change each sentence so that it begins with a negative word.

1. I had hardly stepped out of bed when the phone rang.

    → *Hardly had I stepped out of bed when the phone rang.*

2. I will never say that again.

3. I have scarcely ever enjoyed myself more than I did yesterday.

4. She rarely makes a mistake.

5. I will never trust him again because he lied to me.

6. It is hardly ever possible to get an appointment to see him.

7. I seldom skip breakfast.

8. I have never known a more generous person than Samantha.

***They're, their,** and **there** all have the same pronunciation.

****Also spelled with a hyphen in British English: *no-one*

PRACTICE 25 ▸ Spelling of *-ing* forms. (Chart E-2)

Write the *-ing* form of each verb in the correct column.

	Just add *-ing* to the simple form.	Drop the final *-e* and add *-ing*.	Double the final letter and add *-ing*.
1. arrive		*arriving*	
2. copy	*copying*		
3. cut			*cutting*
4. enjoy			
5. fill			
6. happen			
7. hope			
8. leave			
9. make			
10. rub			
11. stay			
12. stop			
13. take			
14. win			
15. work			

PRACTICE 26 ▸ Spelling of *-ed* forms. (Chart E-2)

Write the *-ed* form for each verb in the correct column.

	Just add *-ed* to the simple form.	Add *-d* only.	Double the final letter and add *-ed*.	Change the *-y* to *-i* and add *-ed*.
1. bother	*bothered*			
2. copy				*copied*
3. enjoy				
4. snore				
5. fear				
6. occur				
7. pat				
8. play				
9. rain				
10. refer				
11. reply				
12. return				
13. scare				
14. try				
15. walk				

PRACTICE 27 ▸ The simple tenses and the progressive tenses. (Chart E-3)
Circle the correct verb to complete each sentence.

1. It (*is raining / rains*) every day in August.

2. Uncle Joe (*visited / visits*) us last month.

3. Our team (*will win / wins*) the soccer game tomorrow.

4. Nick (*watches / is watching*) an action movie on TV now.

5. Tomorrow at this time we (*will be flying / are flying*) over the Atlantic Ocean.

6. Tina! I (*was thinking / am thinking*) of you just a minute ago when the phone rang!

7. I know you, Aunt Martha. You're never going to retire. You (*are working / will be working*) at your computer even when you are 90 years old.

8. At 9:00 P.M. last night, all the children (*go / went*) to bed. At 10:00 P.M. they (*slept / were sleeping*).

9. Uh-oh. Look! Mr. Anton (*fell / was falling*) down on the ice. Mr. Anton! Don't move! We (*help / will help*) you!

10. A: Why is the beach closed today?

    B: There are sharks in the water! They (*swim / are swimming*) near the shore!

PRACTICE 28 ▸ The perfect tenses. (Chart E-3)
Circle the correct verb to complete each sentence.

1. I (*have / had*) already seen the movie twice.

2. I (*have / had*) already seen the movie, so I didn't want to see it again.

3. Matthew (*has been / was*) a professor at this university since 2001. He's going to be chairman of the English department next year.

4. Fred (*has been / was*) a judge in the Supreme Court of this state for 21 years until he retired last year.

5. On the 14th of next month, my grandparents are going to celebrate their 50th wedding anniversary. They (*will have been / had been*) married for 50 years.

6. Rafael and Julie live in Springfield. They (*lived / have lived*) there all their lives.

7. Susanna and Jeff moved to Chicago. Before that, they (*have / had*) lived in this town all their lives.

8. Sorry, Mr. Wu. You (*have / will have*) missed your flight! The plane left just two minutes ago.

9. Javier speaks excellent English. He (*had / has*) studied English in school for twelve years before he came here.

10. We were too late to have dinner at the restaurant. When we got there, it (*has / had*) already closed for the night.

PRACTICE 29 ▸ The perfect progressive tenses. (Chart E-3)
Circle the correct verb to complete each sentence.

1. I'm thirsty, aren't you? We (*have / had*) been driving for four hours. Let's stop for a cold drink soon.

2. When is the rain going to stop? It (*has been / was*) raining for two days.

3. When Greta graduates from medical school next year, she (*will be / will have been*) studying for twenty years!

4. After Jim and Kim (*have / had*) been going out together for seven years, they finally got married last month.

5. You (*has / have*) been working in this office for only two months, and you've already gotten a raise? That's great!

6. Stan finally quit playing professional tennis after he broke his ankle two months ago. He (*has / had*) been playing for twenty years.

7. Well, it's good to be on this plane. Finally! We (*have been waiting / will have been waiting*) almost two hours!

8. Wake Maria up now. She (*had / has*) been sleeping for three hours. That's a very long nap.

9. The police officer gave Pedro a ticket because he (*has / had*) been speeding.

PRACTICE 30 ▶ Summary of verb tenses. (Charts E-4)
Write the correct form of the verbs in parentheses to complete the sentences.

	SIMPLE	PROGRESSIVE
PRESENT	1. Tom has regular habits. He (*eat*) _____ dinner every day. He has eaten dinner every day since he was a child. He ate dinner every day last month. He ate dinner yesterday. He will eat dinner tomorrow. He will probably eat dinner almost every day until the end of his life.	4. At 7:00 this evening, Tom started to eat dinner. It is now 7:15. Tom is on the phone because Mary called him. He says, "Can I call you back? I (*eat*) _____ dinner right now. I'll finish soon and will call you back. I don't want my dinner to get cold." Tom's dinner is in progress when Mary calls.
PAST	2. Tom eats dinner every day. Usually he eats at home, but yesterday, he (*eat*) _____ dinner at a restaurant.	5. Last week Tom went to a restaurant. He began to eat at 7:00. At 7:15 Mary came into the restaurant, saw Tom, and walked over to say hello. Tom's dinner was still in front of him. He hadn't finished it yet. In other words, when Mary walked into the restaurant, Tom (*eat*) _____ dinner. Tom's dinner was in progress when Mary arrived.
FUTURE	3. Tom ate dinner yesterday. He eats dinner every day. In all probability, he (*eat*) _____ dinner tomorrow.	6. Tom will begin his dinner at 7:00 tonight. Mary will arrive at 7:15. It takes Tom 30 minutes to eat his dinner. In other words, when Mary arrives tonight, Tom (*eat*) _____ his dinner. Tom's dinner will be in progress when Mary arrives.

	PERFECT	PERFECT PROGRESSIVE
PRESENT	7. Tom finished eating dinner at 7:30 tonight. It is now 8:00, and his mother has just come into the kitchen. She says, "What would you like for dinner? Can I cook something for you?" Tom says, "Thanks Mom, but I (*eat, already*) _____ dinner."	10. Tom began to eat dinner at 7:00 tonight. It is now, at this moment, 7:15. Tom (*eat*) _____ _____ his dinner for 15 minutes, but he hasn't finished yet. In other words, his dinner has been in progress for 15 minutes.
PAST	8. Yesterday Tom cooked his own dinner. He began at 7:00 and finished at 7:30. At 8:00 his mother came into the kitchen. She offered to cook some food for Tom, but he (*eat, already*) _____ . In other words, Tom had finished his dinner before he talked to his mother.	11. Last week Tom went to a restaurant. He began to eat at 7:00. At 7:15 Mary came into the restaurant, saw Tom, and walked over to say hello. Tom's dinner was still in front of him. He hadn't finished it yet. In other words, when Mary walked into the restaurant, Tom (*eat*) _____ dinner. Tom's dinner was in progress when Mary arrived.
FUTURE	9. Tomorrow Tom will begin dinner at 7:00 and finish at 7:30. His mother will come into the kitchen at 8:00. In other words, Tom (*eat, already*) _____ dinner by the time his mother walks into the kitchen.	12. Tonight Tom will go to a restaurant. He will begin to eat at 7:00. At 7:15 Mary will come into the restaurant, see Tom, and walk over to say hello. Tom's dinner will still be in front of him. He won't have finished it yet. In other words, when Mary walks into the restaurant, Tom (*eat*) _____ dinner for 15 minutes. Tom's dinner will have been in progress for 15 minutes by the time Mary arrives.

PRACTICE 31 ▶ Linking verbs. (Chart E-7)

Some of the *italicized* words in the following are used as linking verbs. Identify which ones are linking verbs by underlining them. Also underline the adjective that follows the linking verb.

1. Olivia *looked* at the fruit. (*no underline*)

2. It *looked* fresh.

3. Dan *noticed* a scratch on the door of his car.

4. Morris *tasted* the candy.

5. It *tasted* good.

6. The crowd *grew* quiet as the official began her speech.

7. Felix *grows* tomatoes in his garden.

8. Bella *grew* up in Florida.

9. I can *smell* the chicken in the oven.

10. It *smells* delicious.

11. Dahlia *got* a package in the mail.

12. Allie *got* sleepy after dinner.

13. During the storm, the sea *became* rough.

14. Vanessa *became* a doctor after many years of study.

15. Diana *sounded* her horn to warn the driver of the other car.

16. Helen *sounded* happy when I talked to her.

17. The weather *turns* hot in July.

18. When Aiden entered the room, I *turned* around to look at him.

19. I *turned* a page in the book.

20. It *appears* certain that Mary Hanson will win the election.

21. Cameron's story *seems* strange. Do you believe it?

PRACTICE 32 ▶ Linking verbs; adjectives and adverbs. (Chart E-7)
Complete each sentence with the correct adjective or adverb.

1. *clean, cleanly*   The floor looks _____ clean _____.

2. *slow, slowly*   The bear climbed _____ slowly _____ up the tree.

3. *safe, safely*   The plane landed _____ on the runway.

4. *anxious, anxiously*   When the wind started to blow, I grew _____.

5. *complete, completely*   This list of names appears _____. No more names need to be added.

6. *wild, wildly*   The crowd yelled _____ when we scored a goal.

7. *honest, honestly*   The clerk looked _____, but she wasn't. I discovered when I got home that she had cheated me.

8. *thoughtful, thoughtfully*   Jane looked at her book _____ before she answered the teacher's question.

9. *good, well*   Most of the students did _____ on their tests.

10. *fair, fairly*   The contract offer sounded _____ to me, so I accepted the job.

11. *terrible, terribly*   Jim felt _____ about forgetting his son's birthday.

12. *good, well*   A rose smells _____.

13. *light, lightly*   As dawn approached, the sky became _____.

14. *confident, confidently*   Kennedy spoke _____ when she delivered her speech.

15. *famous, famously*   The actor became _____ throughout much of the world.

16. *fine, finely*   I don't think this milk is spoiled. It tastes _____ to me.

PRACTICE 33 ▶ Troublesome verbs. (Chart E-8)
Choose the correct verb in parentheses.

1. The student (*raised*/ *rose*) his hand in class.

2. Hot air (*raises* / *rises*).

3. Natasha (*set* / *sat*) in a chair because she was tired.

4. I (*set* / *sat*) your dictionary on the table a few minutes ago.

5. Hens (*lay / lie*) eggs.

6. Sara is (*laying / lying*) on the grass in the park right now.

7. Jan (*laid / lay*) the comb on top of the dresser a few minutes ago.

8. If you are tired, you should (*lay / lie*) down and take a nap.

9. San Francisco (*lays / lies*) to the north of Los Angeles.

10. Mr. Faust (*raises / rises*) many different kinds of flowers in his garden.

11. The student (*raised / rose*) from her seat and walked to the front of the auditorium to receive her diploma.

12. Hiroki is a very methodical person. Every night before going to bed, he (*lays / lies*) his clothes for the next day on his chair.

13. Where are my keys? I (*lay / laid*) them here on the desk five minutes ago.

14. Fahad (*set / sat*) the table for dinner.

15. Fahad (*set / sat*) at the table for dinner.

16. The fulfillment of all your dreams (*lies / lays*) within you — if you just believe in yourself.

Special Workbook Section

Phrasal Verbs

PHRASAL VERBS (TWO-WORD AND THREE-WORD VERBS)

The term *phrasal verb* refers to a verb and particle which together have a special meaning. For example, ***put + off*** means "postpone." Sometimes a phrasal verb consists of three parts. For example, ***put + up + with*** means "tolerate." Phrasal verbs are also called *two-word verbs* or *three-word verbs*.

SEPARABLE PHRASAL VERBS (a) ***I handed*** *my paper* ***in*** yesterday. (b) ***I handed in*** *my paper* yesterday. (c) ***I handed*** *it* ***in*** yesterday. (*INCORRECT:* I *handed in it* yesterday.)	A phrasal verb may be either *separable* or *nonseparable*. With a separable phrasal verb, a noun may come either between the verb and the preposition or after the preposition, as in (a) and (b). A pronoun comes between the verb and the preposition if the phrasal verb is separable, as in (c).

NONSEPARABLE PHRASAL VERBS
(d) ***I ran into*** *an old friend* yesterday.
(e) ***I ran into*** *her* yesterday.
    (*INCORRECT:* I *ran* an old friend *into.*)
    (*INCORRECT:* I *ran* her *into* yesterday.)
	With a nonseparable phrasal verb, a noun or pronoun must follow the preposition, as in (d) and (e).

Phrasal verbs are especially common in informal English. Following is a list of common phrasal verbs and their usual meanings. This list contains only those phrasal verbs used in the exercises in the text. The phrasal verbs marked with an asterisk (*) are nonseparable.

A   ask out . . . . *ask someone to go on a date*

B   bring about, bring on . . . . *cause*
        bring up . . . . *(1) rear children; (2) mention or introduce a topic*

C   call back . . . . *return a telephone call*
        call in . . . . *ask to come to an official place for a specific purpose*
        call off . . . . *cancel*
        *call on . . . . *ask to speak in class*
        call up . . . . *call on the telephone*
        *catch up (with) . . . . *reach the same position or level*
        *check in, check into . . . . *register at a hotel*
        check into . . . . *investigate*
        check out . . . . *(1) borrow a book from the library; (2) investigate*
        check out (of) . . . . *leave a hotel*
        cheer up . . . . *make (someone) feel happier*
        clean up . . . . *make clean and orderly*
        *come across . . . . *meet / find by chance*
        cross out . . . . *draw a line through*
        cut out . . . . *stop an annoying activity*

D   do over . . . . *do again*
        *drop by, drop in (on) . . . . *visit informally*
        drop off . . . . *leave something / someone at a place*
        *drop out (of) . . . . *stop going to school, to a class, to a club, etc.*

F	figure out	*find the answer by reasoning*
	fill out.	*write the answers to a questionnaire or complete an official form*
	find out	*discover information*
G	*get along (with)	*have a good relationship with*
	get back (from).	*(1) return from a place; (2) receive again*
	*get in, get into.	*(1) enter a car; (2) arrive*
	*get off.	*leave an airplane, a bus, a train, a subway, a bicycle*
	*get on	*enter an airplane, a bus, a train, a subway, a bicycle*
	*get out of	*(1) leave a car; (2) avoid work or an unpleasant activity*
	get over.	*recover from an illness*
	get through (with).	*finish*
	*get up (from)	*arise from a bed, a chair*
	give back	*return an item to someone*
	give up	*stop trying, quit*
	*go over	*review or check carefully*
	*grow up	*become an adult*
H	hand in.	*submit an assignment*
	hang up	*(1) conclude a telephone conversation; (2) put clothes on a hanger or a hook*
	have on.	*wear*
K	keep out (of)	*not enter*
	*keep up (with)	*stay at the same position or level*
	kick out (of).	*force (someone) to leave*
L	*look after	*take care of*
	*look into.	*investigate*
	*look out (for)	*be careful*
	look over.	*review or check carefully*
	look up	*look for information in a reference book, on the internet, etc.*
M	make up	*(1) invent; (2) do past-due work*
N	name after, name for	*give a baby the name of someone else*
P	*pass away, pass on	*die*
	pass out	*distribute*
	*pass out	*lose consciousness*
	pick out	*select*
	pick up	*(1) go to get someone (e.g., in a car); (2) take in one's hand*
	point out	*call attention to*
	put away.	*remove to a proper place*
	put back.	*return to the original place*
	put off	*postpone*
	put on	*put clothes on one's body*
	put out	*extinguish a cigarette, cigar, fire*
	*put up with.	*tolerate*
R	*run into, *run across	*meet by chance*
	*run out (of)	*finish a supply of something*
S	*show up	*appear, come*
	shut off.	*stop a machine, light, faucet*

T   *take after . . . .* resemble
     take off . . . . *(1) remove clothing; (2) leave on a trip*
     take out . . . . *(1) take someone on a date; (2) remove*
     take over . . . . *take control*
     take up . . . . *begin a new activity or topic*
     tear down . . . . *demolish; reduce to nothing*
     tear up . . . . *tear into many little pieces*
     think over . . . . *consider carefully*
     throw away, throw out . . . . *discard, get rid of*
     throw up . . . . *vomit; regurgitate food*
     try on . . . . *put on clothing to see if it fits*
     turn down . . . . *decrease volume or intensity*
     turn in . . . . *(1) submit an assignment; (2) go to bed*
     turn off . . . . *stop a machine, light, faucet*
     turn on . . . . *start a machine, light, faucet*
     turn out . . . . *extinguish a light*
     turn up . . . . *increase volume or intensity*

PRACTICE 1 ▸ Phrasal verbs.

Complete each sentence with the appropriate preposition(s). The meaning of the phrasal verb is in parentheses.

1. Lara looked . . .

     a. __*after*__ her father when he was sick. (*took care of*)

     b. _____ her children's homework. (*reviewed*)

     c. _____ some information on the Internet. (*looked for information*)

     d. _____ an unusual situation at work. (*investigated*)

2. The tourists checked . . .

     a. _____ travel DVDs from the library before their trip. (*borrowed*)

     b. _____ their hotel. (*registered at*)

     c. _____ a famous archeological site. (*investigated*)

     d. _____ _____ their hotel rooms. (*left*)

3. Mrs. Jenkins got . . .

     a. _____ a serious illness. (*recovered from*)

     b. _____ _____ her planning for her daughter's wedding. (*finished*)

     c. _____ _____ doing an unimportant project at work. (*avoided*)

     d. _____ _____ her summer vacation early. (*returned*)

     e. _____ the subway at an unfamiliar stop. (*left*)

4. The school principal called . . .

     a. _____ the school assembly. (*canceled*)

     b. _____ some parents. (*telephoned*)

     c. _____ a few students to answer questions while visiting a class. (*asked them to speak*)

     d. _____ a teacher who was sick. (*returned a phone call*)

     e. _____ a student for discipline. (*asked the student to come to his/her office*)

PRACTICE 2 ▶ Phrasal verbs.

Complete each sentence with the correct form of a phrasal verb from the list. One phrasal verb is used twice.

get along with	pass out (2)	put up with	take after	turn in
pass away	pick out	show up	think over	

1. The flight attendants gave one snack to passengers during the flight. They __*passed* *out*__ small bags of peanuts.

2. You choose the vegetables for dinner. _____ _____ whatever you like.

3. You look like your mother, but your brother _____ _____ your father.

4. I have three good job offers to consider. I need some time to _____ them _____.

5. Nathan tolerates his roommate's messy habits. I wonder how he _____ _____ _____ them.

6. Mary's elderly mother died last week. She _____ _____ after a long illness.

7. Julianna was two hours late for the dinner party. When she finally appeared, her friends told her it was rude to _____ _____ so late.

8. The Smiths are a friendly couple and people really like them. They seem to _____ _____ _____ everyone.

9. Good night. It's bedtime. I'm going to _____ _____ now.

10. Hannah got hit in the head with a golf ball, but fortunately didn't lose consciousness. The ball was traveling so fast that it was a miracle she didn't _____ _____ .

PRACTICE 3 ▶ Phrasal verbs.

Choose the correct completions. More than one completion may be correct.

1. When do we turn in   (our assignment?)   the dinner?   yesterday?
2. Mario made up   a lie.   a story.   a flower.
3. The government took over   the city.   the banks.   the trees.
4. Please put out   your cigarette.   the lights.   the fire.
5. What brought about   the war?   the package?   the crisis?
6. Did you figure out   working?   the problem?   the puzzle?
7. How do I turn on   the lights?   the music?   the printer?
8. Hugo asked out   his classmate.   a question.   a girl.
9. Jill is going to give up   a present.   chocolate.   smoking.
10. At the airport, I came across   a friend.   a classmate.   to fly.
11. Tina dropped out of   high school.   the ball.   college.

PRACTICE 4 ▶ Phrasal verbs.

Complete each sentence with an appropriate preposition from the list to form a two-word verb. Some prepositions may be used more than once.

| back | into | off | on | out | up |

1. A: Guess who I ran ___*into*___ today as I was walking across campus. Ann Keefe!

   B: You're kidding!

2. A: There will be a test on Chapters 8 and 9 next Friday.

   B: Oh, no! Couldn't you put it _____ until Monday?

3. A: You'd better put _____ your coat before you leave. It's chilly out.

   B: What's the temperature?

4. A: I smell something burning in the kitchen. Can I call you _____ in a minute?

   B: Sure. I hope your dinner hasn't burned.

   A: So do I! Bye.

5. A: I think that if I learn enough vocabulary I won't have any trouble using English.

   B: That's not necessarily so. I'd like to point _____ that language consists of much more than just vocabulary.

6. A: Your children certainly love the outdoors.

   B: Yes, they do. We brought them _____ to appreciate nature.

7. A: What forms do I have to fill out to change my tourist visa to a student visa?

   B: I don't know, but I'll look _____ it first thing tomorrow and try to find _____. I'll let you know.

8. A: How long were you in the hospital?

   B: About a week. But I've missed almost two weeks of classes.

   A: It's going to be hard for you to make _____ all the work you've missed, isn't it?

   B: Very.

9. A: Could you pick _____ a newspaper on your way home from work tonight? There's a story I want to read.

   B: Sure.

10. A: I like your new shoes.

    B: Thanks. I had to try _____ almost a dozen pairs before I decided to get these.

PRACTICE 5 ▶ Phrasal verbs.

Complete each sentence with an appropriate preposition from the list to form a two-word verb. Some prepositions may be used more than once.

about	away	in	of	off	on	out	up

1. A: I'm trying to find yesterday's newspaper. Have you seen it?

   B: I'm afraid I threw it ___*away / out*___. I thought you had finished reading it.

2. A: Where did you grow _____?

   B: In Seattle, Washington.

3. A: Don't forget to turn the lights _____ before you go to bed.

   B: I won't.

4. A: I have a car, so I can drive us to the festival.

   B: Good.

   A: What time should I pick you _____?

   B: Any time after five would be fine.

5. A: We couldn't see the show at the outdoor theater last night.

   B: Why not?

   A: It was called _____ on account of rain.

6. A: Thomas looks sad.

   B: I think he misses his girlfriend. Let's try to cheer him _____.

7. A: What brought _____ your decision to quit your present job?

   B: I was offered a better job.

8. A: Why did you come back early from your trip?

   B: Unfortunately, I ran _____ _____ money.

9. A: Thanks for the ride. I appreciate it.

   B: Where should I drop you _____?

10. A: What time does your plane take _____?

    B: 10:40.

    A: How long does the flight take?

    B: I think we get _____ around 12:30.

PRACTICE 6 ▶ Phrasal verbs.

Complete the sentences with appropriate prepositions to form two-word or three-word verbs.

1. A: Look ___*out*___! A car is coming!

2. A: May I borrow your dictionary?

   B: Sure. But please be sure to put it _____ on the shelf when you're finished.

3. A: I'm going to be in your neighborhood tomorrow.

   B: Oh? If you have time, why don't you drop _____ to see us?

4. A: How does this tape recorder work?

   B: Push this button to turn it _____ and push that button to shut it _____.

5. A: Did you hear what started the forest fire?

   B: Yes. Some campers built a fire, but when they left their campsite, they didn't _____ it

   _____ completely.

6. A: I need to talk to Karen.

   B: Why don't you call her _____? She's probably at home now.

7. A: Uh-oh. I made a mistake on the check I just wrote.

   B: Don't try to correct the mistake. Just tear _____ the check and throw it

   _____.

8. A: Are you here to apply for a job?

   B: Yes.

   A: Here is an application form. Fill it _____ and then give it _____ to me when

   you are finished.

9. A: Look. There's Mike.

   B: Where?

   A: At the other end of the block, walking toward the administration building. If we run, we can

   catch _____ with him.

10. A: Is your roommate here?

    B: Yes. She decided to come to the party after all. Have you ever met her?

    A: No, but I'd like to.

    B: She's the one standing over there by the far window. She has a blue dress _____.

    Come on. I'll introduce you.

PRACTICE 7 ▶ Phrasal verbs.
Complete each sentence with an appropriate preposition.

1. A: What time did you get _____*up*_____ this morning?

   B: I slept late. I didn't drag myself out of bed until after nine.

2. A: How did you do on your composition?

   B: Not well. It had a lot of spelling mistakes, so I have to do it _____.

3. A: What's the baby's name?

   B: Helen. She was named _____ her paternal grandmother.

4. A: I need to get more exercise.

   B: Why don't you take _____ tennis?

5. A: You can't go in there.

B: Why not?

A: Look at that sign. It says, "Keep _____. No trespassing."

6. A: The radio is too loud. Would you mind if I turned it _____ a little?

B: No.

7. A: I can't hear the radio. Could you turn it _____ a little?

B: Sure.

8. A: What are you doing Saturday night, Bob?

B: I'm taking Virginia _____ for dinner and a show.

9. A: Don't you think it's hot in here?

B: Not especially. If you're hot, why don't you take your sweater _____?

10. A: How do you spell *occasionally*?

B: I'm not sure. You'd better look it _____ in your dictionary.

11. A: I'm tired. I wish I could get _____ of going to the meeting tonight.

B: Why do you have to go?

PRACTICE 8 ▸ Phrasal verbs.

Complete each sentence with an appropriate preposition.

1. A: I need my dictionary, but I lent it to José.

B: Why don't you get it _____*back*_____ from him?

2. A: Cindy is only three. She likes to play with the older kids, but when they're running and playing, she can't keep _____ with them.

B: She doesn't seem to mind, does she?

3. A: I made a mistake in my composition. What should I do?

B: Since it's an in-class composition, just cross it _____.

4. A: What happened when the pilot of the plane passed out during the flight?

B: The co-pilot took _____.

5. I took a plane from Atlanta to Miami. I got _____ the plane in Atlanta. I got _____ the plane in Miami.

6. It was a snowy winter day, but I still had to drive to work. First I got _____ the car to start the engine. Then I got _____ of the car to scrape the snow and ice from the windows.

7. Last year I took a train trip. I got _____ the train in Chicago. I got _____ the train in Des Moines.

8. Jessica takes the bus to work. She gets _____ the bus at Lindbergh Boulevard and gets _____ the bus about two blocks from her office on Tower Street.

9. A: Do you like living in the dorm?

   B: It's OK. I've learned to put _____ _____ all the noise.

10. A: What brought _____ your decision to quit your job?

   B: I couldn't get _____ _____ my boss.

11. A: Did you go _____ your paper carefully before you handed it _____?

   B: Yes. I looked it _____ carefully.

Index

Answer Key

CHAPTER 1: PRESENT AND PAST; SIMPLE AND PROGRESSIVE

PRACTICE 1, p. 1

Many people <u>keep</u> indoor house plants for their natural beauty, but these plants also <u>create</u> a healthier living space. While scientists at NASA (National Aeronautics and Space Administration) <u>were researching</u> air quality in space stations, they <u>discovered</u> that common indoor house plants actually <u>clean</u> the air. The plants <u>absorb</u> carbon dioxide and <u>release</u> oxygen. NASA scientists <u>found</u> that plants also <u>eliminate</u> harmful chemicals in the air. In 1989, NASA <u>published</u> the first results of the NASA Clean Air Study. Today, scientists <u>are still learning</u> about the many benefits of houseplants.

1. keep, create, clean, absorb, release, eliminate
2. discovered, found, published
3. are learning
4. were researching

PRACTICE 2, p. 1

1. a. sets
   b. is setting
2. a. is raining / 's raining
   b. rains
3. a. listen
   b. am listening / 'm listening
4. a. form
   b. is forming
5. a. melts
   b. is melting

PRACTICE 3, p. 2

1. a. fall
   b. are falling
2. a. grows
   b. are growing
3. a. shines
   b. is shining … are singing
4. a. beats
   b. is beating
5. a. sleep
   b. is sleeping

PRACTICE 4, p. 2

1. Does
2. Is
3. Do
4. Is
5. Does
6. Do
7. Are

PRACTICE 5, p. 2

1. doesn't rise
2. is revolving
3. live
4. is raining / isn't raining
5. freezes
6. make / don't make
7. are making / aren't making

PRACTICE 6, p. 3

1. a
2. b
3. a
4. b
5. a
6. a
7. b
8. a
9. a
10. a

PRACTICE 7, p. 3

1. a
2. b
3. b
4. a
5. b
6. a

PRACTICE 8, p. 4

Part I.
changed … launched … was … weighed … took … ushered … was … marked

Part II.
1. T
2. F
3. T
4. F
5. T

PRACTICE 9, p. 4

Part I.
1. rained
2. snowed
3. listened

Part II.
1. hit
2. woke
3. rose
4. set

PRACTICE 10, p. 4

1. ran
2. drank
3. swam
4. won
5. lost
6. took
7. began
8. taught
9. went
10. bought
11. cost
12. ate
13. gave
14. made
15. felt

PRACTICE 11, p. 5

1. sold
2. bought
3. began
4. had
5. caught
6. quit
7. found
8. made
9. took
10. broke
11. came
12. lost
13. slept
14. built
15. fought
16. understood
17. spent
18. let
19. saw
20. taught
21. spoke
22. went
23. paid
24. forgot
25. wrote
26. fell
27. felt
28. left
29. upset
30. flew

PRACTICE 12, p. 5

1. broke
2. stole
3. knew
4. heard
5. came
6. shook
7. hid
8. found
9. fought
10. ran
11. shot
12. caught

PRACTICE 13, p. 6

1. bit
2. held
3. meant
4. blew
5. quit
6. felt
7. stung
8. swam
9. paid
10. caught

PRACTICE 14, p. 7

1. spent
2. led
3. bet
4. wept
5. sank
6. flew
7. spun
8. rang
9. chose
10. froze

PRACTICE 15, p. 7

1. called
2. were watching
3. was humming
4. met
5. saw
6. was cleaning
7. was driving ... got
8. was blowing ... were bending
9. were playing ... was pulling

PRACTICE 16, p. 8

1. 2, 1
2. 2, 1
3. 1, 2
4. 2, 1
5. 1, 2
6. 2, 1
7. 1, 2
8. 2, 1

PRACTICE 17, p. 8

1. had
2. were having
3. stopped ... fell ... spilled
4. served ... came

5. looked ... was sleeping ... was dreaming ... was smiling
6. was working ... exploded
7. caused ... dropped

PRACTICE 18, p. 9

1. c
2. e
3. b
4. a
5. d
6. g
7. f
8. h

PRACTICE 19, p. 9

1. a
2. a, b
3. a

PRACTICE 20, p. 10

1. 2   take ... rains
2. 4   was riding ... heard
3. 1   am riding ... is repairing
4. 3   rode ... forgot
5. 4   was having ... crashed
6. 3   had ... didn't eat
7. 1   is having
8. 2   has
9. 2   celebrate ... are
10. 4   were working ... called
11. 3   celebrated ... was

PRACTICE 21, p. 10

Across

2. listening
5. think
7. heard
8. thinking

Down

1. went
3. studying
4. ate
6. having
7. have

PRACTICE 22, p. 11

1. is
2. form
3. gather
4. rotate
5. is
6. lasts
7. moves
8. grow
9. damage
10. destroy
11. formed
12. moved
13. cost
14. caused
15. was
16. approached
17. tried
18. was
19. are studying
20. are learning
21. are discovering

PRACTICE 23, p. 12

1. Carole **visits** India every year.
2. In the past, no one **cared** about air pollution.
3. Today we **know** that air pollution is a serious health and environmental problem.
4. I **moved** to Houston two years ago.
5. I was eating dinner when you **called**.
6. The students **are** taking a test right now.
7. Judy **fell** on the slippery floor.
8. I was going **to be transferred** to another university, but I decided to stay here.

CHAPTER 2: PERFECT AND PERFECT PROGRESSIVE TENSES

PRACTICE 1, p. 13

Part I.
1. don't own, need, submit, use, is, use
2. have become, have praised, have expressed
3. has been expanding
4. began
5. had expanded

Part II.
1. T
2. F
3. T
4. T

PRACTICE 2, p. 14
1. shut, shut
2. brought, brought
3. hear, heard
4. lose, lost
5. taught, taught
6. begin, began
7. sang, sung
8. eat, eaten
9. saw, seen
10. throw, thrown
11. became, become
12. went, gone

PRACTICE 3, p. 14
1. a. for
   b. for
   c. since
   d. since
   e. for
   f. since
   g. since
2. a. since
   b. for
   c. since
   d. for
   e. since
   f. since
   g. for

PRACTICE 4, p. 15
1. three weeks ... April 1st ... three weeks
2. two months ago ... January 1st ... two months
3. two weeks ... February 14th
4. six years ... six years ... January, 2016

PRACTICE 5, p. 15
Answers will vary.
1. a. We have known Mrs. Jones for one month.
   b. We have known Mrs. Jones since last month.
2. a. They have lived there for (____) years.
   b. They have lived there since 2014.
3. a. I have liked foreign films since (____).
   b. I have liked foreign films for five years.
4. a. Jack has worked for a software company for one year.
   b. Jack has worked for a software company since last year.

PRACTICE 6, p. 16
1. eaten
2. visited
3. worked
4. liked
5. known
6. worn
7. taken
8. gone
9. ridden
10. been

PRACTICE 7, p. 16
1. have already eaten
2. have won
3. have not written
4. has improved
5. has not started
6. have already swept
7. have you known
8. have made
9. have never ridden
10. Have you ever swum

PRACTICE 8, p. 17
1. a
2. b
3. a
4. b
5. b
6. a
7. a
8. b
9. a
10. b
11. a
12. a

PRACTICE 9, p. 17
1. is
2. has
3. is
4. is
5. has
6. is
7. has
8. is
9. has

PRACTICE 10, p. 18
1. a. became
   b. has been
2. a. has been
   b. has rained
3. a. lived
   b. have lived
4. a. worked
   b. haven't worked

PRACTICE 11, p. 18
1. knew ... have known
2. agreed ... have agreed
3. took ... has taken
4. has played ... played
5. called ... has called
6. sent ... have sent
7. has flown ... flew
8. overslept ... has overslept

PRACTICE 12, p. 19
1. have been talking
2. have spoken
3. has won
4. have you been sitting
5. have sat

PRACTICE 13, p. 19
1. have been playing
2. has played
3. has raised
4. has been lecturing
5. has never missed
6. has slept
7. have been flying
8. has been sleeping
9. have been searching

PRACTICE 14, p. 20
Sample answers
1. In 1999, Janet moved to Canada.
2. In 2000, Janet joined Lingua Schools as a teaching assistant.
3. Janet has been a teacher since 2001.
4. Janet has been teaching / has taught her own class since 2001.
5. Janet has been working / has worked at Lingua Schools since 2000.

PRACTICE 15, p. 20
1. have had ... had been thinking ... been worried ... 've had ... has been ... taken
2. had warned ... has given ... has been crashing ... 've taken

PRACTICE 16, p. 21

1. We had driven only two miles = 1
   we got a flat tire = 2
2. Alan told me = 2
   he had written a book = 1
3. we arrived at the airport = 2
   the plane had already left = 1
4. the dog had eaten the entire roast = 1
   anyone knew it was gone = 2
5. We didn't stand in line for tickets = 2
   we had already bought them by mail = 1
6. Carl played the guitar so well = 2
   he had studied with a famous guitarist = 1
7. the movie ended = 2
   everyone had fallen asleep = 1
8. the professor had corrected the third paper = 1
   he was exhausted from writing comments on the
   students' papers = 2
9. I had just placed an order at the store for a new
   camera = 1
   I found a cheaper one online = 2

PRACTICE 17, p. 21

1. had not gotten
2. had not met
3. had never tried
4. had not eaten
5. had not had

PRACTICE 18, p. 21

1. b
2. a
3. b
4. b
5. a
6. b
7. b

PRACTICE 19, p. 22

1. went ... had never been ... didn't take ... was
2. ate ... had never eaten
3. saw ... did ... Had you ever acted ... started

PRACTICE 20, p. 22

1. have been studying
2. had been studying
3. have been waiting
4. had been waiting
5. had been working
6. has been working

PRACTICE 21, p. 23

1. had been listening ... have been dancing ... singing
2. have been waiting
3. had been waiting
4. has been training
5. had been running
6. had been trying ... has been teaching
7. has been performing

PRACTICE 22, p. 23

1. I've **seen** it ten times.
2. I've **been** reading it ...
3. Our guests **left** ...
4. We **have been** studying ...
5. I've been having ...
6. ... **had** eaten.
7. ..., so I **ran** ...
8. She **left** ...
9. ..., I **had** celebrated ...
10. B: ... **I have been** holding for more than half an hour!

CHAPTER 3: FUTURE TIME

PRACTICE 1, p. 24
Part I.

Welcome to your ski vacation at Yellowstone National
Park! According to the weather forecast, you <u>will have</u>
plenty of fresh snow to enjoy this weekend. Before you
begin your ski adventure, you need to be aware of possible
dangerous situations.

First, make sure you dress appropriately. Temperatures
can rise and fall dramatically. Dressing in layers <u>will help</u>
you avoid hypothermia and frostbite. A light inner layer of
clothing <u>will keep</u> you comfortable and dry. A middle layer
<u>will help</u> your body stay warm, and a waterproof outer layer
<u>will protect</u> you against rain or snow.

Second, you may encounter wild animals on the trails,
but do not approach or try to feed them. You <u>will scare</u>
them, and they may become aggressive. In general, animals
<u>won't bother</u> you if you don't bother them.

Finally, study a trail map of the ski area so you don't
get lost. Stay safe and enjoy your time here!

Part II.

1. T
2. F
3. F
4. F
5. T

PRACTICE 2, p. 24

1. are going to travel
2. are going to tour
3. are going to visit
4. is going to take
5. is going to study
6. is going to do
7. are going to return

PRACTICE 3, p. 25

1. a. will set
   b. is going to set
2. a. will arrive
   b. is going to arrive
3. a. will rain
   b. is going to rain
4. a. will bloom
   b. are going to bloom
5. a. will end
   b. is going to end
6. a. will ... buy
   b. are ... going to buy
7. a. will ... take
   b. am ... going to take

PRACTICE 4, p. 25

1. are
2. will
3. is
4. aren't
5. isn't
6. is
7. won't
8. will

PRACTICE 5, p. 26

1. willingness
2. prediction
3. prediction
4. prior plan
5. willingness
6. prior plan

PRACTICE 6, p. 26

1. a
2. b
3. b
4. a
5. a
6. b

PRACTICE 7, p. 26
1. I'll call him
2. She's going to be / She'll be
3. I'm going to fly
4. We're going to go to the game
5. I'll open it
6. I'm going to teach

PRACTICE 8, p. 27
1. will
2. are going to
3. will
4. A: Are you going to
   B: are going to
5. am going to
6. will
7. will
8. is going to
9. A: am going to
   B: will
10. B: am going to ... will

PRACTICE 9, p. 28
1. retire
2. rings
3. finish
4. take
5. arrives
6. graduates
7. is
8. hear
9. leave
10. get

PRACTICE 10, p. 28
1. b	3. b	5. a	7. a	9. a
2. a	4. a	6. a	8. b	10. a

PRACTICE 11, p. 28
1. will not return / are not going to return ... get
2. gets ... will be / is going to be
3. is not going to be / won't be ... learns ... comes ... asks
4. returns ... is going to work / will work
5. is going to build / will build ... is going to be / will be ... complete
6. hear ... will let
7. will lend ... finish
8. A: will be / is going to be
   B: will be / am going to be

PRACTICE 12, p. 29
1. 'm seeing / am seeing
2. is having / 's having
3. is opening / 's opening
4. are working / 're working
5. are having / 're having
6. are attending / 're attending

PRACTICE 13, p. 29
1. a, b, c	3. a, b	5. a, b
2. c	4. a, b, c	6. a

PRACTICE 14, p. 30
1. I'm sending
2. NC
3. I'm having
4. A: are you doing
   B: I'm studying
5. NC
6. are they getting
7. NC
8. we're moving
9. Is he teaching
10. A: I'm not sending ... I'm visiting

PRACTICE 15, p. 31
1. will be reading / 'll be reading
2. will be flying / we'll be flying
3. will be sleeping / 'll be sleeping
4. will be snowing / 'll be snowing
5. will be watching / 'll be watching

PRACTICE 16, p. 31
1. heals ... will be playing / 'll be playing
2. go ... will be standing / 'll be standing
3. start ... will be attending / 'll be attending
4. have ... will be shopping / 'll be shopping
5. will be attending / 'll be attending ... return

PRACTICE 17, p. 32
1. will already have risen
2. will have been riding
3. will already have landed
4. will have been listening
5. will have drunk
6. will have been flying
7. will have saved
8. will have taught

PRACTICE 18, p. 32
Note: *be going to* is also possible in place of *will*.
1. gets ... will be shining
2. will brush ... shower ... will make
3. eats ... will get
4. gets ... will have drunk
5. will answer ... will plan
6. will have called
7. will be attending
8. will go ... will have
9. finishes ... will take ... returns
10. will work ... goes
11. leaves ... will have attended
12. gets ... will be playing ... will be watching
13. will have been playing
14. will have ... will talk
15. will watch ... will put
16. goes ... will have had ... will be

PRACTICE 19, p. 34
1. Next month, I'm **traveling** / I'm **going to travel** to Europe with my sister.
2. My sister is going to **attend** an academic conference in Amsterdam.
3. While she is attending the conference, I'll **be** touring the city.
4. After Amsterdam, we are going **to** go to Ibiza.
5. When **I'm** there, I'm going to swim in the Mediterranean.
6. My sister and I are going to visit a few other cities in Spain before **we go** to Lisbon.
7. By the end of our trip, we'll have been **traveling** for two weeks.
8. When I return home, I'll have **visited** three European countries.
9. It's going **to** be an awesome vacation.

CHAPTER 4: REVIEW OF VERB TENSES

PRACTICE 1, p. 35

Central Market <u>is offering</u> two classes this month. If you <u>are</u> curious about Indian Food, then Tandoori Nights <u>is</u> the class for you. This class <u>will meet</u> every Friday night from 6:00–8:00. Instructor Elaine Adams <u>had owned</u> a small café in India for several years before she <u>returned</u> to the United States last year. She <u>is going to focus</u> primarily on chicken and vegetarian dishes from northern India. For Spanish food enthusiasts, we <u>are offering</u> Spanish Style Slow Cooking. This class <u>meets</u> Saturday afternoons 2:00–4:00. Instructor Ruben Reyes <u>has been teaching</u> classes at Central Market for nearly twenty years. He <u>has written</u> three cookbooks on Spanish and Mediterranean cuisine. His newest book <u>explores</u> the art of slow cooking. His class <u>introduces</u> students to several main dishes. If you <u>haven't registered</u>, there <u>is</u> still time, but classes <u>are getting</u> full.

1. are, is, meets, explores, introduces, is
2. are offering, are getting
3. returned
4. will meet, is going to focus
5. has written, haven't registered
6. has been teaching
7. had owned

PRACTICE 2, p. 36

1. eat
2. ate ... visited ... wrote
3. am talking ... am answering
4. was studying
5. have asked
6. have been talking
7. will be
8. will be sitting

PRACTICE 3, p. 36

1. has never flown
2. have been waiting ... hasn't arrived
3. are ... reach
4. didn't own ... had owned
5. are having ... has been
6. will have left ... get
7. went ... got ... were dancing ... were talking ... was standing ... had never met ... introduced
8. was sitting ... heard ... got ... looked ... had just backed

PRACTICE 4, p. 37

1. am taking ... leave ... 'm going ... leave ... am going to go ... is studying ... has lived ... knows ... has promised ... have never been ... am looking
2. had been raining ... dropped ... is going to be ... changes ... wake ... will be snowing

PRACTICE 5, p. 37

1. had been
2. met
3. had missed
4. was
5. got
6. took
7. was
8. had grown
9. was
10. was wearing
11. had changed
12. was still
13. asked
14. had gained
15. had turned
16. looked
17. were

PRACTICE 6, p. 38

1. haven't seen
2. is recuperating / 's recuperating
3. happened
4. broke
5. was playing
6. is / 's
7. doing
8. has
9. will / is going to be ... 'll / 's going to be

PRACTICE 7, p. 38

1. used
2. use
3. does it consist
4. do teachers use
5. doesn't give
6. doesn't make
7. knows
8. sounds
9. talked
10. fell
11. agree
12. think
13. am taking / 'm taking
14. always asks
15. has been using
16. didn't realize / hadn't realized

PRACTICE 8, p. 39

1. a. is waiting
   b. has been waiting
   c. will have been waiting
2. a. is standing
   b. has been standing
   c. will have stood / will have been standing
   d. will have been standing

PRACTICE 9, p. 39

1. d
2. c
3. a
4. b
5. c
6. c
7. a
8. c
9. b
10. d
11. a
12. d
13. a
14. b
15. c
16. d
17. b
18. d
19. c

PRACTICE 10, p. 41

1. a
2. a
3. b
4. c
5. a
6. c
7. b
8. b
9. d
10. c
11. a
12. a
13. a
14. c
15. c
16. d
17. b
18. a

CHAPTER 5: SUBJECT-VERB AGREEMENT

PRACTICE 1, p. 43

The key to success **is** a lot of practice and hard work. Malcolm Gladwell, in his book *Outliers,* **explains** the 10,000-hour rule. According to Gladwell, 10,000 hours of practice **is** enough to become an expert in almost any field. That's about three hours every single day for ten straight years. Gladwell **provides** several examples.

The Beatle**s were** one of the most successful musical groups in history. Before the Beatles became famous, the band members played near military bases in Germany for eight hours a day, seven days a week. They did this for a year and a half. They had performed about 1,200 times before they reached commercial success. That **is** more than most bands today perform in their entire career.

Another example **is** Bill Gates. Most people **agree** Gates is a computer genius. When Gates **was** in school in the 1960s, computer programming was not very popular. Most schools didn't have computer classes or clubs, but Gates **was** lucky. He attended a school that had advanced technology. He began programming in the eighth grade. By the time he finished high school, he had already completed several hundred hours of computer programming.

Is there a skill you have practiced for 10,000 hours? What do you think? **Is** 10,000 hours enough to make you an expert?

PRACTICE 2, p. 43

1. a.	floats	verb	singular
b.	Boats	noun	plural
2. a.	lives	verb	singular
b.	friends	noun	plural
3. a.	eats	verb	singular
b.	donuts	noun	plural
4. a.	babies	noun	plural
b.	cries	verb	singular

PRACTICE 3, p. 44

1. teach**es**
2. class**es** ... day**s**
3. us**es** ... song**s** ... game**s**
4. finish**es** ... **goes**
5. exercis**es** ... pick**s**

PRACTICE 4, p. 44

1. is
2. are
3. has
4. barks
5. bark
6. is
7. are
8. is
9. are
10. is

PRACTICE 5, p. 44

1. a. is
   b. is
   c. are
2. a. is
   b. are
   c. is
3. a. is
   b. are

PRACTICE 6, p. 44

1. a unit
2. a unit
3. the individual members
4. a unit
5. the individual members
6. a unit

PRACTICE 7, p. 45

1. a. is
   b. are
2. a. is
   b. are
3. a. is ... is
   b. are
4. a. are
   b. is
5. a. is
   b. are

PRACTICE 8, p. 45

1. has
2. were
3. was
4. was
5. is
6. is
7. has
8. has
9. have

PRACTICE 9, p. 45

1. is
2. are
3. are
4. is
5. weren't
6. was
7. aren't
8. isn't
9. has
10. have

PRACTICE 10, p. 46

1. are
2. is
3. is
4. is
5. is ... is ... is
6. isn't
7. isn't
8. is
9. are
10. is
11. are
12. are
13. are
14. are

PRACTICE 11, p. 46

1. is
2. like ... drive
3. is
4. are ... are
5. are ... contains ... are
6. costs
7. is ... is ... are
8. is ... reminds ... makes

PRACTICE 12, p. 47

1. has
2. takes
3. are ... have
4. was ... were
5. take
6. is
7. are ... is
8. has ... are ... were
9. is
10. is
11. is
12. is ... have
13. is
14. speak
15. use

PRACTICE 13, p. 48

1. vote
2. have participated
3. was
4. knows
5. speak ... understand
6. are
7. do ... broadcast
8. are
9. have been
10. has received ... have gone
11. confirms
12. is ... is
13. are
14. has
15. Aren't
16. is
17. begin *4 states begin with the letter A: Alabama, Arkansas, Alaska, Arizona.
18. consists
19. have
20. is
21. Was

PRACTICE 14, p. 48

1. My mother **wears** glasses.
2. Elephants **are** large animals.
3. Your heart **beats** faster when you exercise.
4. Healthy hearts **need** regular exercise.
5. Every child in the class **knows** the alphabet.
6. Some of the **magazines** at the dentist's office are two **years** old.
7. A number of the students in my class **are** from Mexico.
8. One of my favorite **subjects** in school is algebra.
9. **There are** many different **kinds** of insects in the world.
10. Writing compositions **is** difficult for me.
11. The United States **has** a population of over 300 million.
12. Most of the movie **takes** place in Paris.
13. Most of the people in my factory division **like** and **get** along with one another, but a few of the **workers don't fit** in with the rest of us very well.

CHAPTER 6: NOUNS

PRACTICE 1, p. 50

1. center
2. Residents, vegetables, eggs
3. cardboard, glass, metal, paper, fruit
4. Curitiba's
5. household, bus

PRACTICE 2, p. 50

1. cars
2. women
3. matches
4. mice
5. cities
6. donkeys
7. halves
8. chiefs
9. classes
10. feet
11. heroes
12. pianos
13. videos
14. bases
15. bacteria
16. series

PRACTICE 3, p. 51

1. potatoes
2. monkeys
3. thieves ... stereos
4. children
5. teeth
6. beliefs
7. fish
8. species ... kilos

PRACTICE 4, p. 51

1. cares ... feathers
2. occupations ... Doctors ... Pilots ... airplanes ... Professors ... classes ... Farmers ... crops
3. designs buildings ... digs ... objects
4. computers ... Computers
5. factories ... employs
6. Kangaroos ... animals ... continents ... zoos
7. Mosquitos / Mosquitoes
8. tomatoes

PRACTICE 5, p. 51

1. projects ... project
2. groceries ... grocery
3. tomato ... tomatoes
4. pictures ... picture
5. flower ... flowers
6. drugs ... drug
7. eggs ... egg
8. two lanes ... two-lane
9. five-minute ... five minutes
10. sixty-year-old ... sixty years old
11. truck ... truck
12. computers ... computer
13. peanut ... peanuts

PRACTCE 6, p. 52

1. a
2. c
3. b
4. a
5. b
6. c
7. a
8. b
9. a
10. c

PRACTICE 7, p. 52

1. student handbook
2. birthday party
3. government check
4. airplane seats
5. cotton pajamas
6. hotel rooms
7. ten-month-old baby
8. three-day trip
9. three-room apartment
10. five-page paper
11. opera singer
12. stamp collector

PRACTICE 8, p. 53

1. a. parents'
   b. more than one
   c. parents + house
2. a. parent's
   b. one
   c. parent + concern
3. a. cats'
   b. more than one
   c. cats + eyes
4. a. cat's
   b. one
   c. cat + eyes
5. a. Mary's
   b. brother
   c. Mary + brother
6. a. Mary's
   b. brothers
   c. Mary + brothers
7. a. brothers'
   b. more than one
   c. brothers + team
8. a. brother's
   b. one
   c. brother + team

PRACTICE 9, p. 54

1. one
2. more than one
3. more than one
4. one
5. more than one
6. more than one
7. one
8. one

PRACTICE 10, p. 54

1. a. secretary**'s**
   b. secreta**ries'**
2. a. cats**'**
   b. cat**'s**
3. a. supervisors**'**
   b. supervisor**'s**
4. a. bab**ies'**
   b. baby**'s**
5. a. child**'s**
   b. children**'s**
6. a. actors**'**
   b. actor**'s**

PRACTICE 11, p. 55

1. mother's
2. grandmothers'
3. teacher's
4. boss'
5. employee's ... employees'
6. men's ... women's ... children's ... girls' ... boys'

PRACTICE 12, p. 55

1. a
2. a
3. a
4. b
5. b
6. b
7. a

PRACTICE 13, p. 55

Count	Noncount
1. eggs ... bananas	food ... bread ... milk ... coffee
2. letters ... magazines ... catalogs ... bills	mail
3. Euros ... pounds ... dollars	money
4. ring ... earrings	jewelry
5. language	vocabulary ... grammar
6. table ... chairs ... umbrella	furniture

PRACTICE 14, p. 56

1. words
2. some
3. cars
4. much
5. sandwich
6. one
7. some
8. very

PRACTICE 15, p. 56

1. hair ... ey**es**
2. (*no change*)
3. (*no change*)
4. (*no change*)
5. (*no change*)
6. class**es**
7. messag**es**

PRACTICE 16, p. 56

1. courage
2. some
3. shoes
4. garbage
5. glasses ... glass
6. glasses ... glass
7. some ... many
8. much ... some
9. hills ... lovely ... damp
10. good

PRACTICE 17, p. 57

1. a ... b ... f ... g ... i
2. e ... h ... j ... l

PRACTICE 18, p. 57

1. many computers
2. much
3. many children are
4. many teeth
5. many countries
6. much
7. much ... much
8. many
9. is ... much
10. much
11. was ... much
12. much
13. many ... volcanoes are
14. many speeches

PRACTICE 19, p. 58

1. a, b, d
2. a, c
3. b, c
4. a, b, c
5. a, b, c
6. c
7. a, c
8. c, d
9. a, b, c
10. a, b, d

PRACTICE 20, p. 58

1. a
2. b
3. b
4. a
5. b

PRACTICE 21, p. 59

1. b
2. a
3. b
4. a
5. c
6. c
7. b

PRACTICE 22, p. 59

1. a little
2. a few
3. a few
4. a little
5. few
6. a few
7. little
8. a few
9. a little ... a little
10. a little ... a little

PRACTICE 23, p. 60

1. state
2. states
3. puppies
4. puppy
5. children
6. child ... chimpanzees
7. neighbors
8. man
9. goose
10. women

PRACTICE 24, p. 60

1. person
2. **the** rights
3. **the** states
4. **Each** senator
5. (*no change*)
6. small state**s**
7. **the** citizen**s** ... (*no change*)
8. citizen

PRACTICE 25, p. 61

1. of	7. Ø
2. Ø	8. Ø
3. of	9. Ø ... of ... of
4. Ø	10. Ø ... of
5. Ø	11. of ... Ø
6. of	

PRACTICE 26, p. 61

1. Last month, my brother and I cleaned out my **grandparents'** attic.
2. We found a lot of old **stuff**.
3. There **were** boxes and boxes of books.
4. We even found a 100-**year**-old copy of *The Adventures of Tom Sawyer*.
5. My brother was looking for old comic books, but he didn't find **many** comics.
6. He found a **few** of my uncle's old toys.
7. It was hard **work**, but we had a lot of fun.
8. My grandmother was happy to have a clean attic, and I was happy to have some of her old dishes and **furniture**.
9. One **person's** junk is another person's treasure.

PRACTICE 27, p. 62

Across
3. All
4. some
6. man
8. Every

Down
1. Two
2. One
3. An
5. mice
6. many
7. men

CHAPTER 7: ARTICLES

PRACTICE 1, p. 63

Worry dolls are tiny colorful dolls. They usually come in <u>a</u> group of six to eight dolls in <u>a</u> small wooden box. These dolls are <u>a</u> folk tradition from Guatemala. <u>The</u> dolls are about one-half inch tall. Guatemalan artisans use <u>a</u> short piece of wire to make <u>a</u> frame with legs, arms, <u>a</u> torso, and <u>a</u> head. <u>The</u> artisans wrap yarn around <u>the</u> frame for <u>the</u> shape, and they use pieces of traditional fabric for <u>the</u> costumes. In <u>the</u> folk tradition, children tell <u>a</u> worry to each doll before they go to bed. Then they put <u>the</u> dolls back in <u>the</u> box and close <u>the</u> lid. When <u>the</u> children wake up in <u>the</u> morning, <u>the</u> worries are gone. <u>The</u> dolls have taken away all of <u>the</u> worries.

PRACTICE 2, p. 63

1. indefinite	4. definite
2. indefinite	5. indefinite
3. indefinite	6. definite

PRACTICE 3, p. 63

1. (*no change*)
2. some ingredients
3. (*no change*)
4. some friends
5. some cake ... some music
6. some pictures

PRACTICE 4, p. 64

1. a	8. a
2. some	9. a
3. an	10. an
4. some	11. some
5. a	12. some
6. some	13. a
7. some	14. some

PRACTICE 5, p. 64

1. Ø ... The	5. The ... a
2. a ... the	6. the ... a
3. a ... The	7. a ... The
4. The ... a	

PRACTICE 6, p. 65

1. a. plural, generic
   b. singular, specific
2. a. plural, generic
   b. singular, generic
3. a. singular, generic
   b. singular, specific
4. a. plural, generic
   b. singular, specific

PRACTICE 7, p. 65

1. a. Baseball
   b. uniforms
2. a. A data analyst
   b. Data collection
3. a. The clarinet
   b. The violin
4. a. A pecan
   b. Pecans
5. a. A blog
   b. Bloggers
6. a. A meme
   b. Memes

PRACTICE 8, p. 65

1. a	3. b	5. a
2. b	4. a	6. b

PRACTICE 9, p. 66

1. A: a ... a
   B: a
   A: The
2. the
3. a
4. A: a
   B: the
5. a
6. A: the
   B: a
   A: the
   B: the

PRACTICE 10, p. 66

1. Ø Lightning ... a ... Ø
2. a ... the
3. Ø Circles ... Ø
4. A ... a ... the ... the
5. The ... the ... an
6. the ... a ... the ... a ... The ... Ø
7. a ... The

PRACTICE 11, p. 67

1. b	3. a	5. b
2. b	4. b	6. a

PRACTICE 12, p. 67

1. Ø ... the ... Ø	5. Ø
2. the ... Ø	6. A. the ... B. Ø
3. the	7. Ø ... the
4. Ø ... the ... the ... the	8. Ø ... Ø

PRACTICE 13, p. 68

Louis Braille was born in **Ø** France in 1809. He lost his eyesight due to **an** accident when he was **a** child. When he was 15 years old, he developed **a** writing system for **the** blind. **The** writing system consists of **Ø** raised dots. The number and patterns of **the** dots form characters. **The** system is called "Braille" after **the** inventor. Braille has spread from **Ø** France to many countries around **the** world.

PRACTICE 14, p. 68

1. It's beautiful today. **The s**un is shining and **the** sky is clear.
2. I read **a** good book about globalization.
3. **P**enguins live in Antarctica. **P**olar bears don't live in Antarctica.
4. Which is more important — **love or money**?
5. A: What does this word mean?
   B: Do you have **a** dictionary? Look up **the** word in **the** dictionary.
6. A: Watch out! There's a bee buzzing around!
   B: Where? I don't see it. Ouch! It stung me! I didn't see **the** bee, but I felt it!
7. Kevin is going to **the** grocery store. He's getting some ingredients for a pasta dish.
8. Every summer Yoko's family goes camping in **the** Canadian Rockies, but this summer they're going to **the** beach instead.

CHAPTER 8: PRONOUNS

PRACTICE 1, p. 69

1. people	8. one man
2. selfie sticks	9. Disneyland
3. selfie sticks	10. Disneyland's
4. Amanda Campbell	11. selfie sticks
5. the selfie	12. Museums
6. people's	13. visitors
7. many opponents	

PRACTICE 2, p. 69

1. He → Bob
2. They → Mr. and Mrs. Nobriega
3. her → teacher
4. She → baby
5. It → kind
6. them → hawks
7. him → Mr. Frank
8. They → a dog and a cat

PRACTICE 3, p. 70

1. I
2. me
3. them ... They
4. them
5. my ... yours
6. his ... hers ... their
7. She and I ... Our ... us
8. me ... its ... it
9. they ... They ... their
10. its ... its ... It's

PRACTICE 4, p. 70

1. b	5. a, b
2. a	6. a, b
3. a, b	7. a, b
4. a	

PRACTICE 5, p. 71

1. it ... them	5. his or her / their
2. their	6. their ... her
3. his ... her	7. his or her ... its / their
4. it ... They	

PRACTICE 6, p. 71

1. ourselves	5. myself
2. herself	6. yourselves
3. himself	7. yourself
4. themselves	

PRACTICE 7, p. 72

1. is angry at himself
2. introduce myself
3. help yourself
4. pat yourselves
5. talks to herself
6. fix itself
7. laugh at ourselves
8. feeling sorry for himself

PRACTICE 8, p. 72

1. c	3. a	5. c	7. a
2. b	4. a	6. b	

PRACTICE 9, p. 72

1. a	4. a	7. a	10. c
2. a	5. b	8. b	11. b*
3. a	6. c	9. b	

---

*Oregon, California, Alaska, Hawaii

PRACTICE 10, p. 73

1. another
2. another
3. another
4. another
5. another
6. another

PRACTICE 11, p. 74

1. d
2. f
3. a
4. e
5. b
6. c

PRACTICE 12, p. 74

Hackers look for weaknesses in a computer system. They use the weaknesses to break into computer systems or computer networks. Some hackers break into computer systems because **they** enjoys the challenge. ~~The~~ **O**thers work for large companies. These companies hire hackers to find weaknesses and point **them** out. Afterwards, the companies fix the weaknesses. **AnOther** hackers have criminal motivations. These hackers create viruses and worms. They steal important informations, such as the passwords and bank account numbers.

A computer virus is piece of code. Viruses attach themsel**ves** to files and programs. They copy themsel**ves** and spread to each computers they come in contact with. They often spread through email messages or Internet downloads. Some viruses slow down computers. ~~An~~**O**thers completely disable computers.

Worms are similar to viruses, but they do not need to attach to ~~a~~ files or programs. Worms use networks to send copies of **their** code to others computers.

There are **many** ways to protect your devices. To start with, keep your firewall on. A firewall is **a** software program or piece of hardware. It protects your device from hackers. Second, install anti-virus software. This software finds and removes viruses and worms. Next, keep your operating system up to date. Newer operating systems have fixed a lot of security problems from old versions. Finally, don't open ~~an~~ attachments or download anything from **an** unfamiliar person.

CHAPTER 9: MODALS, PART 1

PRACTICE 1, p. 75

Thank you for your interest in State University. You <u>must</u> meet certain entrance requirements before you <u>can</u> apply for admission. Each academic department has different requirements. You <u>should</u> read the specific requirements for your major. All applicants <u>must</u> submit a completed application form, entrance exam results, high school or college transcripts, and an application fee.

You <u>must</u> submit your application electronically. All students <u>must</u> take at least one entrance exam. Some majors <u>may</u> require more than one exam. The testing agency <u>will</u> send all entrance exam results directly to the university. Your high school or college <u>may</u> send your transcripts electronically or by mail in a sealed envelope. You <u>may</u> pay the application fee online with a credit card payment or mail a check or money order to the Office of Admissions.

PRACTICE 2, p. 75

1. b
2. a
3. b
4. a
5. c

PRACTICE 3, p. 75

1. a. don't have to
   b. must not
2. a. must not
   b. don't have to
3. a. must not
   b. don't have to
4. a. must not
   b. don't have to

PRACTICE 4, p. 76

1. necessity
2. prohibition
3. lack of necessity
4. necessity
5. lack of necessity
6. necessity
7. necessity
8. necessity
9. prohibition
10. lack of necessity

PRACTICE 5, p. 77

1. a
2. b
3. a
4. c
5. a
6. a
7. c
8. a
9. c
10. b

PRACTICE 6, p. 77

1. b
2. a
3. a
4. b
5. b
6. a
7. a
8. b

PRACTICE 7, p. 78

1. b
2. a
3. b, c
4. a
5. b
6. a

PRACTICE 8, p. 78

1. e
2. g
3. c
4. h
5. b
6. f
7. d
8. a

PRACTICE 9, p. 79

1. is supposed to arrive
2. am supposed to go
3. is supposed to be
4. was supposed to arrive
5. were supposed to come over
6. is supposed to run

PRACTICE 10, p. 79

1. It should be a good movie.
2. It should be available online now.
3. It should be funny.
4. He should appear in a new movie soon.

PRACTICE 11, p. 79

Part I.
1. Kevin is able to speak four languages.
2. Speak up! I am not able to hear you.
3. Are you able to arrive early tomorrow?
4. I am able to understand your point of view.

Part II.
1. Ikuko knows how to create a PowerPoint presentation.
2. Lucy doesn't know how to parallel park.
3. Mazzen knows how to code in JavaScript.
4. Do you know how to fix my computer?

PRACTICE 12, p. 80

1. may / might
2. may / might
3. can / may / might
4. may / might
5. can / may / might

PRACTICE 13, p. 80

1. could you help me
2. Can I help you
3. Would you please give me
4. May I borrow
5. Can you hurry
6. Could you please repeat

PRACTICE 14, p. 81

1. a. cooking
   b. if I cooked
2. a. taking
   b. if I took
3. a. if I opened
   b. opening
4. a. joining
   b. if we joined
5. a. writing
   b. if I wrote

PRACTICE 15, p. 81

1. closing
2. if I closed
3. taking
4. if I went
5. leaving / if we left
6. cooking
7. making / if I made
8. finishing
9. if I used
10. recommending

PRACTICE 16, p. 82

1. a, d
2. b
3. b
4. a, b
5. c
6. b

PRACTICE 17, p. 82

1. Our teacher **can speak** five languages.
2. Oh, this table is heavy! Jim, **can / could / would** you help me move it?
3. We come to class on weekdays. We **don't** have to come to class on weekends.
4. Park here. It's free. You **don't have to** pay anything.
5. When you speak in front of the judge, you **must tell** the truth. You must not tell lies.
6. Pat looks tired. She should **get** some rest.
7. I **am** not able to go to the party this weekend.
8. The children are **supposed** to be in bed by nine o'clock.
9. The Garcias **are** supposed to be here at 7:00, but I think they will be late, as usual.
10. We're going to make chicken for dinner. Why **don't you** join us?
11. Here's my advice about your diet, Mr. Jackson. You **should** not eat a lot of sugar and salt.
12. A: This is wonderful music. **Shall / Why don't** we dance?
    B: No, let's **not** dance. Let's just sit here and talk.

CHAPTER 10: MODALS, PART 2

PRACTICE 1, p. 83

Last Friday's soccer match <u>should have been</u> an easy game for the Wildcats. Their team had an undefeated record this season. However, fans <u>couldn't believe</u> it when the Falcons defeated the Wildcats 5-2. It was the first win of the season for the Falcons. The Falcons <u>must have practiced</u> very hard to achieve their surprise victory. The next Falcons game is this Friday at 6:00 P.M. on their home field. It <u>should be</u> an exciting game!

PRACTICE 2, p. 83

1. would fall ... would throw
2. would always say ... would come
3. would always bring
4. used to live ... would always wipe
5. used to have ... would stay ... would sleep
6. would tell ... would listen

PRACTICE 3, p. 84

1. You had to use blue ink on the form.
2. The students had to memorize 100 new words a week.
3. Sylvia had to cancel her summer vacation plans.
4. Who did you have to call?
5. The children had to get vaccinations.
6. The passengers had to fasten their seat belts because of the turbulent weather.

PRACTICE 4, p. 84

1. should have taken
2. should have turned
3. shouldn't have watched
4. should have visited
5. should have bought
6. should have ordered
7. shouldn't have come ... should have stayed
8. shouldn't have changed ... should have kept

PRACTICE 5, p. 85

1. should travel
2. should have gone
3. should paint ... should be
4. shouldn't have painted
5. shouldn't have eaten
6. shouldn't drink ... should drink
7. shouldn't have killed
8. should make

PRACTICE 6, p. 85

1. was supposed to arrive
2. were supposed to come over
3. was supposed to give
4. was supposed to snow
5. Were you supposed to turn in

PRACTICE 7, p. 86

1. can't
2. can't
3. can
4. couldn't
5. can't
6. could ... can't
7. couldn't ... Can

PRACTICE 8, p. 86

1. about 50% or less
2. about 95%
3. 100%
4. about 95%
5. about 50% or less
6. 100%
7. about 95%
8. about 50% or less
9. about 50% or less
10. about 50% or less

PRACTICE 9, p. 87

1. a
2. b
3. b
4. a
5. b
6. a
7. b
8. b
9. b
10. a
11. b
12. b

PRACTICE 10, p. 88

1. f
2. a
3. c
4. d
5. b
6. e

PRACTICE 11, p. 88

1. b
2. a
3. b
4. a
5. a
6. b

PRACTICE 12, p. 89

1. must not have remembered
2. couldn't have been
3. may / might not have left
4. must not have heard
5. may / might not have had
6. couldn't have happened

PRACTICE 13, p. 89

1. must have driven
2. must have been / must be
3. must not have known
4. must be
5. must have left
6. must have gone
7. must need
8. must have hurt

PRACTICE 14, p. 90

1. a
2. a
3. b
4. a
5. b
6. a

PRACTICE 15, p. 91

1. e
2. j
3. a
4. f
5. b
6. d
7. i
8. c
9. h
10. g

PRACTICE 16, p. 91

1. will
2. should
3. will
4. should
5. will
6. should
7. must
8. should

PRACTICE 17, p. 92

Modals may vary.

1. could be working
2. should be flying
3. might be sleeping
4. must be kidding
5. must have been kidding
6. might be hiking
7. may not be dating

PRACTICE 18, p. 92

1. have to get
2. should be able to complete
3. won't have to stand
4. will you be able to leave
5. am not going to be able to graduate
6. must not have been able to get

PRACTICE 19, p. 93

1. would rather not say
2. would rather have gone
3. would rather have studied
4. would rather not eat
5. would rather have
6. would rather be sailing

PRACTICE 20, p. 93

1. c
2. c
3. b
4. b
5. c
6. c
7. b
8. c
9. b
10. b

PRACTICE 21, p. 94

Answers may vary.

1. a. It should arrive soon.
   b. It may / might / could have taken off late.
   c. We should have called the airport.
2. a. It may be for me.
   b. It's for me.
   c. It can't be for me.
3. a. He should have responded.
   b. He may not have gotten it.
   c. He must not have gotten it.
   d. He couldn't have gotten it.

4. a. The dishwasher may / might / could be leaking.
   b. It can't be the dishwasher.
   c. A pipe must be broken.
   d. You should call a plumber.
   e. You don't have to call a plumber.

PRACTICE 22, p. 95

Distracted drivers often cause major traffic accidents. In the past, before the widespread use of smartphones, drivers **would / could** be distracted by eating, reading maps, or grooming. These activities **can / might** still cause problems, but one of the biggest issues today is cell phone use. People **can / might** use their phones to talk, text, engage in social media, play games, use navigation systems, check their bank accounts, write shopping lists, listen to music, or look up information on the Internet.

Joy has become a leading advocate against distracted driving since she had an accident last year. She hit another car and blacked out. She **can't / couldn't** remember anything about the accident. According to her phone records, she **must have been** talking on the phone when the accident occurred. Luckily, no one was injured. It **could have been** much worse. She still feels terrible about the accident. She **shouldn't have been using / shouldn't have used** her phone while she was driving.

Advocates like Joy are calling for stricter distracted-driving laws. Several places have already adopted laws against texting or using a cell phone at all while driving. With more distracted-driving laws, the roads **should / can / may** become much safer.

CHAPTER 11: THE PASSIVE

PRACTICE 1, p. 96

The National Weather Service has issued a winter storm warning. Heavy snowfall <u>is expected</u> early this evening. More than a foot of snow accumulation <u>is anticipated</u> by tomorrow morning. Because student safety is our top priority, classes <u>have been canceled</u> for the remainder of the day. The university's business offices <u>are also closed</u>. Residence and dining halls will remain open. Tonight's basketball game <u>has been postponed</u> to next Tuesday. Classes <u>will be canceled</u> all day tomorrow. The university is monitoring the weather closely and will notify the campus community with any additional updates. More details <u>can be found</u> on our school website.

PRACTICE 2, p. 96

1. are	10. has been
2. is being	11. was
3. has been	12. are being
4. was	13. will be
5. was being	14. had been
6. had been	15. will have been
7. will be	16. are
8. is going to be	17. is going to be
9. will have been	18. were being

PRACTICE 3, p. 97

1. a.	A	Henry	visited
b.	P	The park	was visited
2. a.	A	Olga	was reading
b.	A	Philippe	has read
c.	P	Bambi	has been read
3. a.	A	Whales	swim
b.	P	Whales	were hunted
4. a.	P	The answer	won't be known
b.	A	I	know
5. a.	P	Two new houses	were built
b.	A	A famous architect	designed
6. a.	P	The Internet	was invented
b.	A	The Internet	has expanded
7.	P	The World Cup	is seen
b.	A	Soccer fans	watch

PRACTICE 4, p. 98

1. is written	7. will be written
2. is being written	8. is going to be written
3. has been written	9. will have been written
4. was written	10. Was … written
5. was being written	11. Will … be written
6. had been written	12. Has … been written

PRACTICE 5, p. 98

Part I.
1. was painted by Picasso
2. are flown by experienced pilots
3. is going to be sung by a famous singer
4. has been accepted by Yale University
5. will be examined by the doctor
6. is being questioned by the defense attorney
7. was bitten by a dog
8. was being fed by the mother bird
9. won't be persuaded by his words
10. wasn't painted by me … painted by Laura
11. owned by Mrs. Crane… isn't owned by her father anymore
12. weren't signed by me … was signed by someone else

Part II.
13. is going to clean my teeth
14. Did … send that email
15. don't celebrate the Fourth of July
16. Has … sold your house yet
17. haven't caught the thief
18. are cleaning the carpets

PRACTICE 6, p. 99

Checked sentences: 2, 3, 6, 7, 8, 10

PRACTICE 7, p. 100

1. b	7. c
2. b	8. b
3. c	9. a
4. a	10. c
5. b	11. b
6. c	12. a

PRACTICE 8, p. 100

1. b	4. b
2. b	5. a
3. a	

PRACTICE 9, p. 101

1. was invented ... told
2. was established ... was given ... still attend
3. is known ... is related ... live ... became ...
   were killed ... were saved
4. originated ... like ... gives ... was valued ...
   was used ... were treated ... is believed

PRACTICE 10, p. 101

1. The chefs prepared the food.
2. The food was prepared yesterday.
3. The rain stopped.
4. A rainbow appeared in the sky.
5. The documents were sent to you yesterday.
6. My lawyer sent the documents to me.
7. The winner of the election was announced on TV.
8. I didn't agree with you about this.
9. What happened yesterday?
10. Something wonderful happened to me.
11. The trees died of a disease.
12. The trees were killed by a disease.
13. A disease killed the trees.
14. I was accepted at the University of Chicago.
15. I was recommended for a scholarship.

PRACTICE 11, p. 102

1. can't be
2. should be washed
3. should have been washed
4. to be finished
5. must have been built
6. have to be paid ... must be sent
7. be permitted
8. ought to be painted

PRACTICE 12, p. 102

1. a. should be made
   b. should make
2. a. should have been made
   b. should have made
3. a. couldn't be spoken
   b. couldn't speak
4. a. must be registered
   b. must register
5. a. has to be paid
   b. have to pay
6. a. must have been
   b. may have been

PRACTICE 13, p. 103

1. g	5. b
2. e	6. c
3. a	7. f
4. h	8. d

PRACTICE 14, p. 103

1. is interested in	6. are made of
2. depends on	7. is composed of
3. is married to	8. is located in
4. is scared of	9. is equipped with
5. bores	10. am prepared for

PRACTICE 15, p. 103

1. by	7. with
2. for	8. with
3. about	9. with
4. in	10. with
5. to	11. of
6. of	12. to

PRACTICE 16, p. 104

1. The plane **arrived** very late.
2. Four people **were** injured in the accident.
3. Bella is married **to** José.
4. People are worried **about** global warming.
5. Astronomers are **interested** in several new meteors.
6. We were **surprised** by Harold's announcement.
7. Spanish **is** spoken by people in Mexico.
8. This road is not the right one. We **are** lost.
9. Pat should try that new medicine. He might
   be helped.
10. Lunch is **being** served in the cafeteria right now.
11. Something unusual **happened** yesterday.
12. Will **the refrigerator be fixed** today?

PRACTICE 17, p. 104

1. crowded	6. hurt
2. hungry	7. invited
3. lost	8. chilly
4. scared	9. stopped
5. dressed	10. elected

PRACTICE 18, p. 104

1. a. excited
   b. exciting
2. a. shocking
   b. shocked
3. a. exhausting
   b. exhausted
4. a. boring
   b. bored
5. a. confused
   b. confusing
6. a. interesting
   b. interested
7. a. thrilling
   b. thrilled

PRACTICE 19, p. 105

1. a. fascinating
   b. fascinated
2. a. exhausting
   b. exhausted
3. a. disappointed
   b. disappointing

PRACTICE 20, p. 105

1. a, d	4. b, d
2. a, b	5. b, c
3. b, c	

PRACTICE 21, p. 106

1. frustrating
2. grown ... irritating
3. washing
4. writing
5. frozen
6. depressing ... depressed
7. entertaining
8. known ... spilt
9. comforting ... Barking
10. inspiring ... United ... divided

PRACTICE 22, p. 107

are usually considered ... unprotected ... of ... build
... must be kept ... can range ... is regulated ... maintain ...
was inspired ... drawn ... is warmed or cooled ... is called ...
amazing

CHAPTER 12: NOUN CLAUSES

PRACTICE 1, p. 108

The fact that Patrick is retiring soon is not a secret.
He has been teaching English at the community college for
35 years. He'll miss his students, but he's excited about
his retirement. He's especially excited that he'll be able to
travel more often. He told me that he's going to Greece
this summer. I wonder what other countries he'll visit. I
think that his wife is retiring soon too. We're having a
retirement dinner for Patrick at his favorite restaurant next
month. Everyone is invited to the dinner.

PRACTICE 2, p. 108

1. what he said
2. (none)
3. what happened
4. (none)
5. why Dora is calling me
6. who that man is
7. where Hank lives
8. (none)
9. What they are doing
10. (none)
11. what I should say
12. (none)

PRACTICE 3, p. 108

1. do they want
2. what they want
3. does Stacy live
4. where Stacy lives
5. what Carl likes
6. does Carl like
7. is Lina going
8. where Lina is going

PRACTICE 4, p. 109

1. Where does Lee live? **D**oes he live downtown?
2. I don't know where he lives.
3. What does Sandra want? **D**o you know?
4. Do you know what Sandra wants?
5. What Yoko knows is important to us.
6. We talked about what Yoko knows.
7. What do you think? **D**id you tell your professor
   what you think?
8. My professor knows what I think.
9. Where is the bus stop? **D**o you know where the bus
   stop is?
10. What did he report? What he reported is important.

PRACTICE 5, p. 109

1. how far it is
2. what that is on the table
3. how much it cost
4. What he said
5. when they are leaving
6. which road we should take
7. who called
8. what's happening
9. why they work at night
10. What they are trying to do
11. what kind of insects these are
12. whose keys these are

PRACTICE 6, p. 110

1. Who is that man?
   Noun clause: who that man is.
2. Where does George live?
   Noun clause: where George lives.
3. What did Ann buy?
   Noun clause: what Ann bought?
4. How far is it to Denver from here?
   Noun clause: how far it is to Denver from here.
5. Why was Jack late for class?
   Noun clause: why Jack was late for class.
6. Whose pen is that?
   Noun clause: whose pen that is.
7. Who did Alex see at the meeting?
   Noun clause: who Alex saw at the meeting.
8. Who saw Ms. Frost at the meeting?
   Noun clause: who saw Ms. Frost at the meeting?
9. Which book does Alice like best?
   Noun clause: which book Alice likes best.
10. What time is the plane supposed to land?
    Noun clause: what time the plane is supposed to land?

PRACTICE 7, p. 111

1. b
2. c
3. e
4. a
5. f
6. d
7. g, h

PRACTICE 8, p. 111

1. a, b, c, d, f
2. a, b
3. b, e

PRACTICE 9, p. 112

1. Do you know how much this book costs?
2. Do you know when Flight 62 is expected?
3. Do you know where the nearest restroom is?
4. Do you know if this word is spelled correctly?
5. Do you know what time it is?
6. Do you know if this information is correct?
7. Do you know how much it costs to fly from Toronto
   to London?
8. Do you know where the bus station is?
9. Do you know whose glasses these are?
10. Do you know if this bus goes downtown?

PRACTICE 10, p. 112

1. d
2. a
3. c
4. b
5. e
6. g
7. h
8. f

PRACTICE 11, p. 112

1. proud
2. angry
3. disappointed
4. aware
5. lucky
6. confident
7. worried ... relieved

PRACTICE 12, p. 113

1. a. is surprising
   b. nobody stopped to help Sam ... is surprising
2. a. is unfortunate that ... .
   b. people in modern cities are ... is unfortunate
3. a. is still true that people ... .
   b. people in my hometown ... help ... is still true.
4. a. is undeniably true that ...
   b. people need each other ... is undeniably true

5. a. seems strange to ... that people in cities often don't know their neighbors
   b. people in cities don't know their neighbors is strange to me

PRACTICE 13, p. 113

1. Millie said, "There's an important meeting at three o'clock."
2. "There's an important meeting at three o'clock," she said.
3. "There is," said Millie, "an important meeting at three o'clock."
4. "There is an important meeting today. It's about the new rules," said Millie.
5. "Where is the meeting?" Carl asked.
6. Robert replied, "It's in the conference room."
7. "How long will it last?" asked Ali.
8. "I don't know how long it will last," replied Millie.
9. "I'll be a little late," said Robert. "I have another meeting until 3:00 P.M. today."
10. "Who is speaking at the meeting?" asked Robert.
11. "I am not sure who is speaking," said Millie, "but you'd better be there. Everybody is supposed to be there."

PRACTICE 14, p. 114

1. was
2. needed
3. was having
4. had finished
5. had finished
6. to stay

PRACTICE 15, p. 114

1. if / whether she was planning
2. what time the movie begins
3. where she had been
4. what Kim's native language is
5. if / whether I was doing
6. why I hadn't called
7. if / whether we had been studying for the test
8. if / whether she had found her phone.

PRACTICE 16, p. 114

1. would arrive
2. was going to be
3. could solve
4. might come
5. might come
6. had to leave
7. had to leave
8. should go

PRACTICE 17, p. 115

1. if we could still get
2. how he could help
3. if / whether he could help
4. when the final decision would be made
5. what time he had
6. who she should give this message
7. where he / she might find
8. how long he / she had to wait
9. when we were going to get

PRACTICE 18, p. 115

Conversation 1
was going ... was ... asked ... would like ... had ... had ... was ... could ... were

Conversation 2
asked ... was ... told ... was ... said ... was ... had heard ... had ... was ... had been ... asked ... had been ... had not ... told ... had gone ... was

PRACTICE 19, p. 116

1. arrive
2. provide
3. get
4. be
5. apply
6. look

PRACTICE 20, p. 117

Part I.
get ... steps Sherri takes ... she gets ... her heart rate is ... whether ... whether or not

Part II.
"Can you help me find a fitness tracker?" Sherri asked.

Mark replied, "Absolutely! What features are you looking for?"

"I'm not sure," Sherri said. "Can you tell me what is available?"

"Sure," Mark answered. "The basic trackers count your steps and monitor your sleep. We also have more sophisticated models if you're looking for a heart rate monitor."

"I can't decide. I think I need to take a look at them," she said.

"Come this way, and I'll show you what we have."

CHAPTER 13: ADJECTIVE CLAUSES

PRACTICE 1, p. 118

When students begin their university studies, they often feel overwhelmed. Most college campuses have several places where students can seek help. The first place that a new student should look for is the advising office. An academic advisor is someone who answers questions that are related to course selection, degree plans, and academic progress. Students usually meet with the same advisor over the course of their university education. The student and advisor develop a relationship in which the advisor serves as a mentor or guide. Another helpful place that students can turn to is the counseling office. A counselor is someone who helps students with personal issues that may or may not be related to the student's academic life. Counselors help students who have trouble with time management, test anxiety, career selection, or similar issues. Both advisors and counselors play an important role in student success.

PRACTICE 2, p. 118

1. person   who fixes computers
2. man   who lives on a boat
3. woman   who speaks four languages
4. people   who are bilingual in the office
5. office   that is in an old building
6. buildings   that are in the neighborhood
7. trees   that were over 200 years old
8. trees   which were nearby
9. truck   that had broken down
10. truck   which caused the problem

PRACTICE 3, p. 118

1. a, b	3. c, d	5. b, c
2. a, b	4. a, b	6. b, c

PRACTICE 4, p. 119

1. man   that I met last night
2. woman   that Sandro is going to marry
3. people   whom we invited
4. book   which I just read
5. program   that Jason installed
6. house   we built in 1987
7. cake   I left on the table
8. book   my professor wrote

PRACTICE 5, p. 119

1. a, b, c, f	4. a, b, c, e
2. a, c, e, f	5. a, c, d, e
3. c, d, e	6. a, b, c, f

PRACTICE 6, p. 119

1. … I read was good
2. … I saw was very sad
3. … can live a long time
4. … we photographed
5. … does many things at the same time
6. … can trust
7. … the thieves stole was valuable

PRACTICE 7, p. 120

1. c, d, g, i
2. a, b, f, h

PRACTICE 8, p. 120

1. that / who / whom / Ø
2. who / that
3. that / which / Ø
4. which
5. that / who / whom / Ø
6. who / that
7. whom
8. that / which

PRACTICE 9, p. 121

1. That's a subject I don't want to talk **about**.
2. A person **who writes** with his left hand is called a lefty.
3. Our family brought home a new kitten that we **found at** the animal shelter.
4. What is the name of the podcast **to which** we listened last night? / What is the name of the podcast **that** we listened **to** last night?
5. The candidate for **whom** you vote should be honest.
6. Here's a picture of Nancy **that / which** I took with my phone
7. People **who** have high cholesterol should watch their diets.
8. Suzie is going to marry the man she has always **loved**.
9. There's an article in today's newspaper about a woman **that is** 7 feet tall.
10. Passengers **who / that** have children may board the plane first.

PRACTICE 10, p. 121

1. a. b		3. a. b
b. a		b. a
c. b		4. a. a
2. a. a		b. b
b. b		

PRACTICE 11, p. 122

1. Do you know the man **whose car** is parked over there?
2. I know a skin doctor **whose name** is Dr. Skinner.
3. The people **whose home** we visited were very hospitable.
4. Mrs. Lake is the teacher **whose class** I enjoy the most.
5. The teacher asked the parents **whose children** were failing to confer with her.

PRACTICE 12, p. 122

1. b, c	5. a, b
2. a, c	6. b
3. c	7. a, c
4. a, c	

PRACTICE 13, p. 123

1. a. where I grew up	b. in which I grew up
2. a. which I lived in	b. where I lived
3. a. where I lived	b. on which I lived
4. a. where I played	b. in which I played

PRACTICE 14, p. 123

1. a. that I go
   b. on which I go
   c. when I go
2. a. when I play tennis
   b. that I play tennis
   c. on which I play tennis

PRACTICE 15, p. 124

1. e	5. a
2. c	6. h
3. f	7. g
4. d	8. b

PRACTICE 16, p. 124

1. a, d	5. d
2. b	6. b, c
3. c, d	7. c, d
4. a, b, c	8. a

PRACTICE 17, p. 125

1. d	4. c
2. e	5. b
3. a	

PRACTICE 18, p. 125

1. no comma
2. I made an appointment with Dr. Raven, who is ...
3. Bogotá, which is the capital of Colombia, is a ...
4. no comma
5. South Beach, which is clean, pleasant, and fun, ...
6. no comma
7. ... Miranda Jones, who wrote ....
8. ... Nairobi, which is near several fascinating ...
9. no comma
10. no comma
11. no comma
12. no comma
13. A typhoon, which is a violent tropical storm, ...
14. no comma
15. Typhoon Haiyan, which destroyed parts of Southeast Asia, occurred in 2013.

PRACTICE 19, p. 125

1. a
2. b
3. a
4. b
5. b
6. a
7. b
8. a

PRACTICE 20, p. 126

1. I received two job offers, neither of which I accepted.
2. I have three brothers, two of whom are professional athletes.
3. Jerry is engaged in several business ventures, only one of which is profitable.
4. The two women, both of whom began their studies at age 40, have almost completed law school.
5. Eric is proud of his success, much of which has been due to hard work, but some of which has been due to good luck.
6. We ordered an extra-large pizza, half of which contained meat and half of which didn't.
7. The scientist won the Nobel Prize for his groundbreaking work, most of which was on genomes.
8. The audience gave a tremendous ovation to the Nobel prize winners, most of whom were scientists.

PRACTICE 21, p. 127

1. Mike was accepted at the state university, which is surprising.
2. Mike did not do well in high school, which is unfortunate.
3. The university accepts a few students each year with a low grade-point average, which is lucky for Mike.
4. The university hopes to motivate these low-performing students, which is a fine idea.
5. Mike might actually be a college graduate one day, which would be wonderful!

PRACTICE 22, p. 127

1. ~~who is wearing a green hat~~	wearing a green hat
2. ~~who is in charge of this department~~	in charge of this department
3. ~~which was painted by Picasso~~	painted by Picasso
4. ~~who are doing research~~	doing research
5. ~~which are in progress~~	in progress
6. ~~which are scheduled to begin in September~~	scheduled to begin in September
7. ~~which is the largest city in Canada~~	the largest city in Canada
8. ~~that orbit the sun~~	orbiting the sun
9. ~~which was formerly known as a planet~~	formerly known as a planet
10. ~~which means to "devalue someone or something"~~	meaning to "devalue someone or something"

PRACTICE 23, p. 127

1. Brasilia, officially inaugurated in 1960, is the capital of Brazil.
2. Rio de Janeiro, the second largest city in Brazil, used to be its capital.
3. Two languages, Finnish and Swedish, are spoken in Helsinki, the capital of Finland.
4. In Canada, you see signs, written in both English and French.
5. Libya, a country in North Africa, is a leading producer of oil.
6. Simon Bolivar, a great South American general, led the fight for independence in the nineteenth century.
7. Five South American countries, liberated by Bolivar, are Venezuela, Colombia, Ecuador, Panama, and Peru.
8. We need someone, holding a degree in electrical engineering, to design this project.
9. The project being built in Beijing will be finished next year.
10. A lot of new buildings were constructed in Beijing in 2008, the site of the summer Olympics that year.

PRACTICE 24, p. 128

Sample answers:

1. ... a lot of people waiting in ...
2. Students who are living on ... OR Students living on ...
3. ... the librarian who sits ... OR the librarian sitting ...
4. ... Anna whose birthday ...
5. ... Sapporo, which is ...
6. Patrick, who is my oldest brother, is married and has one child.
7. The person sitting next to me is someone I've never met.
8. ... is a small city located on ...
9. ... person to whom I wanted ...
10. Yermek, who is from Kazakhstan, teaches Russian classes at the college.
11. The people who we met on our trip last May ...
12. Dianne Baxter, who used to teach Spanish, has organized ...
13. ... since I came here, some of whom are from my country.
14. People who can speak English ...
15. Grandpa is getting married again, which is a big surprise.

CHAPTER 14: GERUNDS AND INFINITIVES, PART 1

PRACTICE 1, p. 129

Geocaching has become a popular outdoor activity in recent years. A geocache is a small container that someone has hidden outside. Participants use a GPS or a mobile device to find or hide geocaches. There are millions of geocaches around the world.

Ray and Isabel are looking for a geocache that someone has hidden. GPS coordinates have been posted on a website. Websites suggest leaving clues in addition to the coordinates, so Ray and Isabel are also using the clues.

The geocache contains a logbook for signing and dating. Some participants like to place a small trinket or toy in the geocache. After Ray and Isabel find the geocache, they will sign the logbook. Then they need to place the geocache back exactly where they found it.

Ray and Isabel enjoy finding these hidden surprises, but they aren't having much luck today. They have been looking for over an hour, but they can't seem to find it. Ray wants to quit. He's tired and hungry. Isabel prefers to continue searching. She doesn't like to give up.

PRACTICE 2, p. 129
1. playing
2. smoking
3. driving
4. paying
5. arguing
6. selling
7. having
8. reading

PRACTICE 3, p. 130
1. to cook
2. to transfer
3. to make
4. to fly
5. to paint
6. to work
7. to arrive
8. to tell

PRACTICE 4, p. 130
1. a
2. a
3. b
4. b
5. b
6. b
7. a
8. a
9. b
10. a
11. a
12. b

PRACTICE 5, p. 131
1. living
2. to be
3. to show
4. making
5. to be
6. being
7. humming
8. exercising
9. to exercise
10. to graduate

PRACTICE 6, p. 131
1. a, c
2. c
3. a, c
4. c
5. a
6. a, c

PRACTICE 7, p. 131
1. to work
2. me to work
3. to work / me to work
4. to work
5. to work / me to work
6. to work
7. to work
8. me to work
9. me to work
10. to work / me to work
11. to work / me to work
12. to work
13. to work / me to work
14. me to work

PRACTICE 8, p. 132
Part I.
1. to stay
2. to stay
3. him to stay
4. him to stay
5. staying
6. him to stay
7. to stay
8. to stay
9. him to stay
10. to stay

Part II.
1. traveling
2. traveling
3. to travel
4. traveling
5. to travel
6. traveling
7. traveling
8. traveling
9. traveling
10. traveling

Part III.
1. working
2. to work
3. to work
4. to work
5. to work
6. working
7. him to work
8. to work
9. to work
10. working

PRACTICE 9, p. 132
1. a. to turn
   b. meeting
2. a. to stop
   b. seeing
3. a. telling
   b. to talk
4. a. buying
   b. to tell
5. a. to learn
   b. to talk
3. c. speaking

PRACTICE 10, p. 133
1. b
2. a
3. b
4. a
5. b

PRACTICE 11, p. 133
1. a, b
2. a
3. a, b
4. a
5. a, b
6. a, b
7. a, b
8. b
9. b
10. a, b

PRACTICE 12, p. 134
1. taking
2. going
3. improving
4. flying
5. lowering
6. buying
7. drinking
8. hearing

PRACTICE 13, p. 134
1. b
2. b
3. c
4. c
5. a
6. c
7. a
8. c
9. c
10. b

PRACTICE 14, p. 134

1. about leaving
2. for being
3. from completing
4. about having
5. of studying
6. for not wanting
7. for washing ... drying
8. of stealing
9. to eating ... sleeping
10. for lending

PRACTICE 15, p. 135

1. about taking
2. in buying
3. to living
4. for not answering
5. about failing
6. about changing
7. for cleaning
8. from arriving
9. for writing
10. in saving ... from wasting

PRACTICE 16, p. 135

Part I.
1. go hiking
2. go sailing
3. go skiing
4. went birdwatching
5. went canoeing

Part II.
6. go dancing
7. go bowling
8. will go sightseeing
9. will go window shopping

PRACTICE 17, p. 136

1. playing
2. lying
3. locating
4. looking
5. doing
6. watching

PRACTICE 18, p. 136

1. It's
2. is
3. is
4. Is it
5. Going
6. It's
7. is
8. to jump
9. To see
10. Is

PRACTICE 19, p. 137

1. camping
2. to operate
3. getting
4. applying
5. to turn
6. sleeping
7. reading
8. to end
9. using ... speaking
10. watching
11. running

PRACTICE 20, p. 138

1. It's important **to keep** your mind active.
2. **Watching** TV is not good brain exercise.
3. I prefer **spending** time **playing** board games and computer games.
4. There is some evidence that older people can avoid **becoming** senile by **exercising** their brain.
5. Playing word **games is** one good way to stimulate your brain.
6. In addition, **it** is beneficial for everyone to exercise regularly.
7. Physical exercise helps the brain by **increasing** the flow of blood and **delivering** more oxygen to the brain.
8. Some studies show that **eating** any type of fish just once a week increases brain health.
9. Doctors advise older people **to eat** fish two or three times a week.
10. Everyone should try **to keep** a healthy brain.

PRACTICE 21, p. 138

1. Pedro is interested **in learning** about other cultures.
2. IIe has always wanted **to study** abroad.
3. He had difficulty **deciding** where to study.
4. He has finally decided **to live** in Japan next year.
5. He's excited about **attending** a university there.
6. Right now he is struggling **to learn** Japanese.
7. He has a hard time **pronouncing** the words.
8. He keeps on **studying and practicing**.
9. At night, he lies in bed **listening** to Japanese language-teaching programs.
10. The he dreams **about / of traveling** to Japan.

CHAPTER 15: GERUNDS AND INFINITIVES, PART 2

PRACTICE 1, p. 139

to be ... to remove, to be removed ... placing ... loosen up ... cleaning, to be cleaned ... to scrub ... Running ... to manage, manage

PRACTICE 2, p. 139

1. a
3. a, b
3. a, b
4. a, b
5. a
6. a
7. a, b
8. a, b
9. a, b
10. a

PRACTICE 3, p. 140

1. to
2. for
3. for
4. for
5. to
6. to
7. for
8. to
9. for

PRACTICE 4, p. 140

1. d
2. c
3. b
4. a
5. f
6. e

PRACTICE 5, p. 140

1. too
2. enough
3. too
4. too
5. too
6. enough
7. too
8. enough
9. enough
10. too
11. too
12. enough
13. too
14. enough
15. too … enough
16. too … enough

PRACTICE 6, p. 141

1. a
2. a, b
3. b
4. a

PRACTICE 7, p. 141

1. to be accepted
2. to be given
3. to be picked
4. being petted
5. to be held
6. being asked
7. being noticed
8. being invited
9. to be finished
10. to be submitted

PRACTICE 8, p. 142

1. b
2. a
3. b
4. b
5. a
6. b
7. a
8. b

PRACTICE 9, p. 142

1. b
2. a
3. b
4. b
5. a
6. b
7. b
8. a

PRACTICE 10, p. 143

1. to be called
2. being called
3. to call
4. to be elected
5. to be elected
6. being reelected
7. to elect
8. being understood
9. to understand
10. trying
11. to be left

PRACTICE 11, p. 143

1. a
2. c
3. b, c
4. b, c
5. b, d
6. c, d
7. a, b
8. a, c
9. c, d

PRACTICE 12, p. 144

1. a, c, d
2. a, c, d
3. a, b, c
4. a, b, d
5. a, c
6. b, c

PRACTICE 13, p. 145

1. practice / practicing
2. pass / passing
3. cry / crying
4. leave
5. win
6. arrive
7. rocking / rock
8. doing / do
9. talking / talk
10. reaching / reach

PRACTICE 14, p. 145

1. a
2. b
3. c
4. a, b
5. c
6. a
7. a, c
8. a

PRACTICE 15, p. 146

1. stand
2. fixed
3. beat
4. to stop
5. to clean
6. look
7. call
8. made … put

PRACTICE 16, p. 146

1. b
2. c
3. b
4. a
5. c
6. b, c
7. b
8. a

PRACTICE 17, p. 146

1. a. your
   b. you
2. a. his
   b. him
3. a. her
   b. her
4. a. their
   b. them
5. a. my
   b. me
6. a. our
   b. us

PRACTICE 18, p. 147

1. b
2. a
3. b
4. c
5. c
6. d
7. d
8. b
9. a
10. b
11. a
12. c
13. d
14. a
15. d
16. a
17. b
18. d

PRACTICE 19, p. 148

1. to buy
2. opening
3. being asked
4. having
5. to wear … dressing
6. jumping … falling
7. being taken
8. to stop delivering … to fill
9. gazing … to cheer
10. having

PRACTICE 20, p. 149

1. b
2. b
3. b
4. b
5. a
6. b
7. a
8. a
9. a
10. b
11. b
12. a
13. c
14. a
15. b
16. a
17. b
18. c
19. a
20. a
21. c
22. c
23. b
24. a
25. c

PRACTICE 21, p. 150

1. You shouldn't let children **play** with matches.
2. Maddie was lying in bed **crying**.
3. You can get there more quickly by **taking** River Road instead of the interstate highway.
4. Nathan expected **to be** admitted to the university, but he wasn't.
5. Our lawyer advised us not **to sign** the contract until she had a chance to study it very carefully.
6. John was responsible for **notifying** everyone about the meeting.
7. Apparently, he failed to **call** several people.
8. I couldn't understand what the reading said, so I asked my friend **to translate** it for me.
9. You can find out the meaning of the word by **looking** it up in a dictionary.
10. ... How can I make you **understand**?
11. Serena wore a large hat **to** protect her face from the sun.
12. We like to go **fishing** on weekends.
13. Maybe you can get Charlie **to take** you to the airport.
14. My doctor advised me not **to eat** food with a high fat content.
15. Doctors always advise **eating** less and exercising more.
16. Allen smelled something **burning**. ...
17. The player appeared to have been **injured** during the basketball game.
18. David mentioned **having traveled** to China last year.

CHAPTER 16: COORDINATING CONJUNCTIONS

PRACTICE 1, p. 151

1. thyme ... basil ... mint ... oregano
2. seasoning ... brewing ... making
3. herb ... vegetable ... flower
4. space ... knowledge
5. vegetables ... herbs ... hobby ... community ... connection

PRACTICE 2, p. 152

1. b
2. c
3. c
4. b
5. c
6. c
7. a
8. b

PRACTICE 3, p. 152

1. Conjunction: and
   sweet and fresh — a. adjective
2. Conjunction: and
   apples and pears — b. noun
3. Conjunction: and
   washed and dried — c. verb
4. Conjunction: and
   washing and drying — c. verb
5. Conjunction: and
   happily and quickly — d. adverb
6. Conjunction: but
   delicious but expensive — a. adjective
7. Conjunction: and
   Apples, pears, and bananas — b. noun
8. Conjunction: or
   apple or a banana — b. noun
9. Conjunction: and
   red, ripe, and juicy — a. adjective

PRACTICE 4, p. 153

1. c
2. e
3. a
4. g
5. f
6. d
7. h
8. b

PRACTICE 5, p. 153

1. (none)
2. ... calm, quiet, and serene
3. ... the ball, and they ran
4. ... kicking, passing, and running
5. ... rocks and insects, had a picnic, and flew kites
6. ... put their phones away, open their reading books, and review their notes
7. (none)
8. (none)
9. ... two cups of coffee, three glasses of water, one glass of orange juice, and three orders of eggs
10. (none)

PRACTICE 6, p. 154

1. I ~~he is honest~~, and honesty
2. C
3. I ~~quiet~~ quietly
4. C
5. C
6. I ~~to tour~~ touring
7. C
8. I ~~summarizing~~ summarize
9. C
10. C
11. I ~~they require~~
12. C

PRACTICE 7, p. 154

1. ... stopped. **T**he winds ...
2. ... stopped, and the winds ...
3. ... stopped, ... died down, ...
4. ... street. **H**is mother ...
5. ... street, and his mother ...
6. ... street. **H**is mother ...
7. ... coffee, and ...
8. ... coffee. **I**t is ...
9. ... ice cream, but ... .

PRACTICE 8, p. 154

1. Sherri's graduation was last week, **and now** she's looking for a job.
2. She completed her degree in nursing, **and she** also has a certificate in radiology. OR:
   She completed her degree in **nursing and also** has a certificate in radiology.
3. Sherri doesn't have any full-time work experience, **but she** completed a one-year internship at the hospital.
4. There is a job opening at Lakeside Hospital, **but it** requires five years of nursing experience.

PRACTICE 9, p. 155

1. My brother is visiting me for a couple of days. **We** spent yesterday together in the city, and we had a really good time.
2. **F**irst I took him to the waterfront. **W**e went to the aquarium. **W**e saw fearsome sharks, some wonderfully funny marine mammals, and all kinds of tropical fish. **A**fter the aquarium, we went downtown to a big mall and went shopping.
3. I had trouble thinking of a place to take him for lunch because he's a strict vegetarian, but I remembered a restaurant that has vegan food. **W**e went there, and we had a wonderful lunch of fresh vegetables and whole grains. I'm not a vegetarian, but I must say that I really enjoyed the meal.
4. In the afternoon it started raining. **W**e decided to go to a movie. **I**t was pretty good but had too much violence for me. I felt tense when we left the theater. I prefer comedies or dramas. **M**y brother loved the movie.
5. We ended the day with a delicious home-cooked meal and some good conversation in my living room. **I**t was an excellent day. I like spending time with my brother.

PRACTICE 10, p. 155

1. knows
2. know
3. knows
4. know
5. know
6. wants
7. like
8. has
9. agrees
10. are
11. realizes
12. are

PRACTICE 11, p. 156

1. a. Both Mary and her parents drink coffee.
   b. Neither Mary nor her parents drink coffee.
2. a. Either John or Henry will do the work.
   b. Neither John nor Henry will do the work.
3. a. Our school recycles not only trash but also old electronics.
   b. Our school recycles both trash and old electronics.

PRACTICE 12, p. 156

Part I.
1. I know both her mother and her father.
2. both the nurses and the doctor arrive
3. both bananas and mangos originated
4. both whales and dolphins are

Part II.
5. exports not only coffee but also oil
6. Not only Air Greenland but also Icelandair fly
7. not only a lime-green jacket but also lime-green pants
8. not only attended Harvard University but also Harvard Law School.

Part III.
9. Either Ricky or Paula knows
10. either to Mexico or Costa Rica
11. Either Jim or Taka's parents will take her
12. either salmon or tuna

Part IV.
13. neither Fred nor his children
14. neither she nor her children have
15. Luis has neither a family nor friends
16. neither hot nor cold

PRACTICE 13, p. 157

1. John will call either Mary or Bob.
2. Sue saw not only the mouse but also the cat.
3. Both my mother and father talked to the teacher.
4. Either Mr. Anderson or Ms. Wiggins is going to teach our class today.
5. I enjoy reading not only novels but also magazines.
6. Both smallpox and malaria are dangerous diseases.
7. She wants to buy a compact car. She is saving her money.
8. … snow tonight. The roads …
9. … we attended an opera, … ate at marvelous restaurants, and visited …

PRACTICE 14, p. 158

Across	Down
3. but	1. Neither
4. only	2. Both
6. either	3. and
7. nor	

CHAPTER 17: ADVERB CLAUSES

PRACTICE 1, p. 159

1. Before, As, Whenever, as long as
2. Now that, because
3. While, Even though
4. Whether or not, even if

PRACTICE 2, p. 159

1. as she was leaving the store
2. before we have breakfast
3. Since Douglas fell off his bike last week
4. Because I already had my boarding pass
5. if the workplace is made pleasant
6. After Ceylon had been independent for 24 years
7. as soon as she receives them
8. once he becomes familiar with the new computer program

PRACTICE 3, p. 160

1. … calm. Tom …
2. … calm, Tom …
3. … calm. **He** …
4. … fishing, the lake was calm. **He** …
5. … calm, so Tom went fishing. **He** …
6. … quiet, Tom …
7. … calm, quiet, and clear …
8. … poor, he …
9. … poor. He …
10. Microscopes, automobile dashboards, and cameras … people to use. **They** are designed … people. **When** "lefties" use these items, …

PRACTICE 4, p. 160

1. b
2. c
3. d
4. c
5. c
6. d
7. b
8. c
9. b
10. a
11. d
12. a

PRACTICE 5, p. 161

1. 1, 2
2. 2, 1
3. 1, 2
4. 2, 1
5. 2, 1
6. 1, 2
7. S
8. 1, 2

PRACTICE 6, p. 162

1. d
2. i
3. a
4. e
5. h
6. j
7. c
8. f
9. b
10. g

PRACTICE 7, p. 162

1. My registration was cancelled because I didn't pay the registration fee on time.
2. I'm late because there was lot of traffic.
3. Because Harry was on a strict weight-loss diet, he lost 35 pounds.
4. Since Mario's is closed on Sundays, we can't have lunch there tomorrow.
5. Now that Jack has a car, he drives to work.
6. Natalie should find another job since she is very unhappy in this job.
7. David will lead us because he knows the way.
8. Frank is looking for a job in a law office now that he has graduated from law school.

PRACTICE 8, p. 163

1. even though
2. because
3. Because
4. Even though
5. Because
6. Even though
7. even though
8. because

PRACTICE 9, p. 163

1. a. even though
   b. because
2. a. Because
   b. Even though
3. a. even though
   b. because
4. a. because
   b. even though

PRACTICE 10, p. 163

1. c
2. a
3. b
4. b
5. a
6. c
7. b
8. a

PRACTICE 11, p. 164

1. We won't go to the beach if **it rains** tomorrow.
2. If my car doesn't start tomorrow morning, I'll take the bus to work. *(no change)*
3. If I have any free time during my workday, I'll call you.
4. I'll text you if my phone **doesn't** die.
5. If we don't leave within the next ten minutes, we **will be** late for the theater.
6. If **we leave** within the next ten minutes, we will make it to the theater on time.
7. The population of the world will be 9.1 billion in 2050 if it **continues** to grow at the present rate.

PRACTICE 12, p. 165

1. a. so   b. does
   Meaning: If Asraf lives near you
2. a. so   b. are
   Meaning: If you are a resident of Springfield
3. a. not   b. don't
   Meaning: If you don't have enough money
4. a. so   b. are
   Meaning: If you are going to do the laundry
5. a. so   b. did
   Meaning: If I left the water running in the sink

PRACTICE 13, p. 165

1. don't approve ... approve
2. can afford ... can't afford
3. is raining ... isn't raining
4. don't understand ... understand
5. don't want to ... whether you want to

PRACTICE 14, p. 166

1. e
2. f
3. a
4. b
5. c
6. d
7. h
8. g

PRACTICE 15, p. 166

1. unless you can stand the heat
2. unless it is broken
3. unless you cooperate with your opponents
4. unless you help me
5. unless you stop digging

PRACTICE 16, p. 167

1. he wants something
2. she runs out of clean clothes
3. the temperature outside goes below 50 degrees F
4. it is absolutely necessary to get somewhere quickly
5. will you get into Halley College
6. could I afford a big house like that

PRACTICE 17, p. 167

1. pass
2. not going to go
3. rains
4. in case
5. only if
6. always eat
7. even if
8. whether
9. won't
10. don't wake
11. if
12. can we

PRACTICE 18, p. 168

1. h
2. g
3. a
4. f
5. b
6. d
7. e
8. c

PRACTICE 19, p. 168

1. b
2. b
3. d
4. a
5. b
6. c
7. d
8. b
9. c
10. a

CHAPTER 18: REDUCTION OF ADVERB CLAUSES TO MODIFYING ADVERBIAL PHRASES

PRACTICE 1, p. 170

Coloring books for children have always been popular, but lately many adults have been buying coloring books for themselves. It's not unusual these days to see an adult coloring pages <u>while waiting for a doctor's appointment or sitting on a bus</u>. <u>Looking for an easy activity to relieve stress</u>, some people turn to coloring. Research has shown that anxiety levels drop <u>when people color</u>. Coloring is similar to meditation <u>because it helps people focus on the moment</u> <u>while allowing the brain to switch off other thoughts or worries</u>. Other people enjoy coloring <u>because they feel that they can be creative</u> <u>even if they don't have the artistic ability to draw something from scratch</u>. Still others are looking for an escape from technology. <u>Constantly staring at screens all day</u>, adults need a chance to "unplug." Nostalgia is yet another reason for the sudden popularity of adult coloring books. <u>Wanting to feel like a kid again</u>, an adult might open up a coloring book. <u>Since becoming a trend</u>, adult coloring books have become widely available. They can be found in almost any bookstore and have even been included on bestsellers' lists.

PRACTICE 2, p. 170
Grammatically correct items:
2, 3, 4, 6, 8, 10

PRACTICE 3, p. 171

1. he opened   opening
2. I left   leaving
3. I had met   meeting / having met
4. I searched   searching
5. he was herding   herding
6. they marched   marching
7. she was flying   flying
8. they imported   importing

PRACTICE 4, p. 171

1. a. leaving
   b. left
2. a. invented / had invented
   b. inventing / having invented
3. a. working
   b. was working
4. a. flies
   b. flying
5. a. studied
   b. studying
6. a. learning
   b. learned
7. a. taking
   b. take
8. a. was driving
   b. driving

PRACTICE 5, p. 172
Subjects
1. (no change)
2. While driving to work, Sam had a flat tire.
3. Adv. clause: Nick; Main clause: son (no change)
4. Adv. clause: Nick; Main clause: he
   Before leaving on his trip, Nick gave his itinerary to his secretary.
5. Adv. clause: Tom; Main clause: he
   After working in the garden all afternoon, Tom took a shower and then …
6. Adv. clause: Sunita; Main clause: they (no change)
7. Adv. clause: she; Main clause: Emily
   Emily always clears off her desk before leaving the office at the end of the day.

PRACTICE 6, p. 172
Modifying Adverbial Phrases
1. Riding his bicycle to school   a
2. Being seven feet tall   b
3. Driving to work this morning   a
4. Running five miles on a very hot day   a, b
5. Having run for 26 miles in the marathon   b
6. Drinking a tall glass of refreshing iced tea   a, b
7. Clapping loudly at the end of the game   a
8. Speaking with her guidance counselor   a
9. Knowing that I was going to miss the plane because of heavy traffic   b
10. Having missed my plane   b
11. Waiting for my plane to depart   a

PRACTICE 7, p. 173

1. h
2. i
3. j
4. b
5. d
6. a
7. c
8. f
9. e
10. g

PRACTICE 8, p. 173

1. b, c
2. a, b, c
3. a, b
4. a, b
5. a, c
6. b, c
7. a, c

PRACTICE 9, p. 174

1. a. Upon receiving her acceptance letter for medical school, Sarah …
   b. On receiving her acceptance letter for medical school, Sarah …
2. a. Upon hearing the sad news, Kathleen …
   b. When she heard the sad news, Kathleen …
3. a. On looking at the accident victim, the paramedics …
   b. When they looked at the accident victim, the paramedics …

PRACTICE 10, p. 174

2. e. reaching the other side of the lake
3. c. discovering a burned-out wire
4. a. learning that the problem was not at all serious
5. b. being told she got it

PRACTICE 11, p. 175

1. d
2. a
3. f
4. i
5. j
6. h
7. g
8. b
9. e
10. c

PRACTICE 12, p. 175

1. (no change)
2. After finishing something very easy
3. (no change)
4. When doing or saying something exactly right
5. While working late in the night
6. After waking up in a bad mood
7. Having lost all my work when my computer crashed
8. (no change)

CHAPTER 19: CONNECTIVES THAT EXPRESS CAUSE AND EFFECT, CONTRAST, AND CONDITION

PRACTICE 1, p. 176

Parents often buy noisy electronic toys for their babies <u>because</u> these toys seem educational. <u>If</u> a toy talks or plays music, many parents believe that the toy is teaching the sounds and structure of language. <u>However</u>, some researchers believe electronic toys actually delay language development in small children. They believe this happens <u>due to</u> a lack of human interaction. <u>Because of</u> their busy schedules, parents often buy electronic toys to keep their children occupied. <u>Consequently</u>, these parents might spend less time talking to and interacting with their children. <u>While</u> electronic toys are entertaining, the most important skill for babies to learn is how to communicate with other people. <u>Even if</u> electronic toys sing the alphabet or say the names of shapes and colors, they do not promote communication. <u>On the other hand</u>, more traditional toys such as puzzles and blocks seem to encourage babies to communicate. Studies have found that books produce the most communication between parents and babies. <u>Whether or not</u> parents buy electronic toys, they should try to interact with their babies as much as possible.
1. because, due to, because of, consequently
2. however, while, on the other hand
3. if, even if, whether or not

PRACTICE 2, p. 176

1. b, c, f
2. a, d, e
3. a, c, e
4. b, d, f

PRACTICE 3, p. 177

1. because
2. because
3. due to / because of
4. because
5. due to / because of
6. because
7. because
8. due to / because of

PRACTICE 4, p. 177

1. heavy traffic
2. there was heavy traffic
3. he is getting old
4. his age
5. she is afraid of heights
6. her fear of heights
7. a cancellation
8. there was a cancellation today

PRACTICE 5, p. 177

1. Because she had a headache, she took some aspirin.
2. No change
3. Because of her headache, she took some aspirin.
4. No change
5. She had a headache. **T**herefore, she took some aspirin.
6. She had a headache. **S**he, therefore, took some aspirin.
7. She had a headache. **S**he took some aspirin, therefore.
8. She had a headache, so she took some aspirin.

PRACTICE 6, p. 178

Sentence 1
1. a
2. b
3. c

Sentence 2
1. a
2. b
3. a
4. b

PRACTICE 7, p. 178

1. b. Because the store didn't have any orange juice, I bought lemonade
   c. The store didn't have any orange juice. Therefore, I bought lemonade.
   d. The store didn't have any orange juice, so I bought lemonade.
2. a. Max has excellent grades. Therefore, he will go to a top university.
   b. Max has excellent grades. He, therefore, will go to a top university.
   c. Max has excellent grades. He will go to a top university, therefore.
   d. Max has excellent grades, so he will go to a top university.
3. a. Because there had been no rain for several months, the crops died.
   b. There had been no rain for several months. Consequently, the crops died.
   c. There had been no rain for several months. The crops, therefore, died.
   d. There had been no rain for several months, so the crops died.

PRACTICE 8, p. 179

Part I.
1. Because
2. Therefore,
3. because of
4. Therefore,
5. Therefore,
6. because of
7. Because
8. Because of

Part II.
9. Due to his poor eyesight, John
10. Since John has poor eyesight,
11. ... poor eyesight. Consequently,
12. ... heights. Consequently,
13. due to
14. ... overweight. Consequently,
15. Since

3. Edward missed the final exam. **He** simply forgot to go to it.
4. Because we forgot to make a reservation, we couldn't get a table at our favorite restaurant last night.
5. The server kept coming to work late or not at all. **Therefore,** she was fired.
6. The server kept forgetting customers' orders, so he was fired.
7. No change
8. The needle has been around since prehistoric times. **The** button was invented about 2,000 years ago. **The** zipper wasn't invented until 1890.
9. It is possible for wildlife observers to identify individual zebras because the patterns of stripes on each zebra are unique. **No** two zebras are alike.
10. When students in the United States are learning to type, they often practice this sentence: *The quick brown fox jumps over the lazy dog* because it contains all the letters of the English alphabet.

PRACTICE 10, p. 180

Sentence 1
 a. Because she ate some bad food, Kim got sick.
 b. Because of some bad food, Kim got sick.
 c. Kim ate some bad food, so she got sick.
 d. Due to some bad food, Kim got sick.

Sentence 2
 a. Adam had driven for 13 hours. Therefore, he was exhausted.
 b. Since Adam had driven for 13 hours, he was exhausted.
 c. Due to the fact that Adam had driven for 13 hours, he was exhausted.
 d. Adam had driven for 13 hours, so he was exhausted.

PRACTICE 11, p. 180

1. such		6. so
2. so		7. so
3. so		8. such
4. such		9. so
5. such		10. so

PRACTICE 12, p. 180

1. It was such a nice day that we took a walk.
2. Jeff was so late that he missed the meeting.
3. She talked so fast that I couldn't understand her.
4. It was such an expensive car that we couldn't afford to buy it.
5. There were so few people at the meeting that it was canceled.
6. Ted was so worried about the exam that he couldn't fall asleep last night.
7. The tornado struck with such great force that it lifted cars off the ground.
8. Joe's handwriting is so illegible that I can't figure out what this sentence says.
9. David has so many girlfriends that he can't remember all of their names.
10. There were so many people at the meeting that there were not enough seats for everyone.

PRACTICE 13, p. 181

Sentences 1, 3, 4, 5, 7, 8 express purpose

PRACTICE 14, p. 181

1. d		6. c
2. i		7. e
3. a		8. g
4. f		9. h
5. j		10. b

PRACTICE 15, p. 182

1. Rachel turned on the TV so that she could watch the news.
2. Alex wrote down the time and date of his appointment so (that) he wouldn't forget to go.
3. Nancy is taking extra courses every semester so (that) she can graduate early.
4. Amanda turned down the TV so (that) she wouldn't disturb her roommate.
5. Chris took some change from his pocket so (that) he could buy a snack from the vending machine.
6. I turned on the TV so (that) I could listen to the news while I was making dinner.
7. I turned off my phone so (that) I wouldn't be interrupted while I was working.
8. It's a good idea for you to learn keyboarding skills so (that) you'll be able to use your computer more efficiently.
9. Lynn tied a string around her finger so (that) she wouldn't forget to take her book back to the library.
10. Wastebaskets have been placed throughout the park so (that) people won't litter.

PRACTICE 16, p. 182

1. is		6. isn't
2. is		7. is
3. isn't		8. isn't
4. is		9. isn't
5. is		10. is

PRACTICE 17, p. 183

1. a. Even though
   b. Despite
   c. Despite
   d. Despite
   e. Even though
2. a. In spite of
   b. Although
   c. Although
   d. In spite of
   e. In spite of
3. a. Despite
   b. Although
   c. Despite
   d. Although
   e. Despite
4. a. In spite of
   b. Even though
   c. in spite of
   d. even though
   e. in spite of
   f. even though
   g. even though
   h. in spite of

PRACTICE 18, p. 184

1. e
2. c
3. b
4. g
5. a
6. i
7. d
8. j
9. h
10. f

PRACTICE 19, p. 184

1. a. Even though it was night, we could see the road very clearly.
   b. Although it was night, we could see the road very clearly.
   c. It was night, but we could see the road very clearly.
2. a. Despite the fact that Helena has a fear of heights, she enjoys skydiving.
   b. Despite her fear of heights, Helena enjoys skydiving.
   c. Helena has a fear of heights; nevertheless, she enjoys skydiving.
3. a. Though Millie has the flu, she is working at her computer.
   b. Millie has the flu, but she is working at her computer anyway.
   c. Millie has the flu, but she is still working at her computer.

PRACTICE 20, p. 185

Possible answers

1. Red is bright and lively, while gray is a dull color. OR While red is bright and lively, gray is a dull color.
2. Jane is insecure and unsure of herself. Her sister, **on the other hand,** is full of self-confidence.
3. **While** a rock is heavy, a feather is light. OR A rock is heavy, **while** a feather is light.
4. Some children are unruly. Others, **however,** are quiet and obedient. OR
   Some children are unruly; others, **however,** are quiet and obedient. OR
   Some children are unruly. Others are quiet and obedient, **however.**
5. Language and literature classes are easy and enjoyable for Alex. **On the other hand,** math and science courses are difficult for him. OR
   Language and literature classes are easy and enjoyable for Alex; **on the other hand,** math and science courses are difficult for him.
6. Strikes can bring improvements in wages and working conditions; **however,** they can also cause loss of jobs and bankruptcy. OR
   Strikes can bring improvements in wages and working conditions. **They can also cause loss of jobs and bankruptcy, however.**

PRACTICE 21, p. 185

1. I **should / had better / have to** call my mother. **Otherwise,** she'll start worrying about me.
2. The bus **had better** come soon. **Otherwise,** we'll be late for work.
3. You **should / had better / have to** make a reservation. **Otherwise,** you won't get seated at the restaurant.
4. Beth **should / had better / has to** stop complaining. **Otherwise,** she will lose the few friends she has.
5. You **have to / had better** have a government-issued ID. **Otherwise,** you can't get on the plane.

6. Louis **had better / has to** apply for his driver's license in person. **Otherwise,** he can't replace it.
7. You **have to be** a registered voter. **Otherwise,** you can't vote in the general election.
8. You **should** clean up the kitchen tonight. **Otherwise,** you'll have to clean it up early tomorrow.

PRACTICE 22, p. 186

1. e
2. h
3. d
4. g
5. b
6. f
7. a
8. c

PRACTICE 23, p. 186

1. exports
2. doesn't export
3. uses
4. is
5. originated
6. is

PRACTICE 24, p. 187

1. passes
2. doesn't pass
3. passes
4. passes
5. doesn't pass
6. passes
7. doesn't pass

PRACTICE 25, p. 187

1. the flowers bloomed
2. I took good care of the garden
3. my care
4. my care
5. , the flowers didn't bloom
6. … ; therefore, the flowers didn't bloom
7. ; however, the flowers bloomed
8. … garden. **Nevertheless,** the flowers did not bloom
9. … garden, so the flowers did not bloom
10. … garden, the flowers bloomed
11. … garden, the flowers didn't bloom
12. the flowers bloomed anyway
13. … garden, the flowers will bloom
14. … garden, the flowers will not bloom
15. … garden. **Otherwise,** the flowers will not bloom
16. … garden. **Consequently,** the flowers did not bloom
17. … garden. **Nonetheless,** the flowers bloomed
18. the flowers will bloom
19. will the flowers bloom
20. , yet the flowers did not bloom
21. the flowers won't bloom
22. or not you take good care of the garden

CHAPTER 20: CONDITIONAL SENTENCES AND WISHES

PRACTICE 1, p. 188

If you have ever been snorkeling or scuba diving, you may have seen a coral reef. Coral reefs look like rocks, but they are actually living creatures. Because reefs are so colorful and are home to such a large number of sea creatures, some people describe them as cities or rain forests of the ocean.

Unfortunately, coral reefs all around the world are dying. If a reef dies, so will a lot of the sea life around the reef. Coral reefs are an important part of the ocean food chain. They also provide shelter for many animals, such as fish, sponges, eels, jellyfish, sea stars, and shrimp. If there were no coral reefs, many species would simply not exist. If these creatures no longer existed, millions of people who depend on fish for their main food supply and livelihood would go hungry.

There are actions we can take to protect coral reefs. Pollution is one of the biggest problems for all sea life. If we choose to walk or bike instead of driving cars, there will be fewer pollutants. Another major problem is overfishing. If governments restrict or limit fishing around reefs, the reefs might have a chance of survival. Most importantly, we need to raise awareness. If more people were aware of the dangers of dying reefs, the reefs would probably not be in such bad condition. With greater awareness, more people will volunteer with beach and reef cleanup and be careful when swimming or diving near fragile reefs. If we follow these actions, we can keep our reefs around for future generations.

PRACTICE 2, p. 188

1. a. yes
   b. no
2. a. yes
   b. no
3. a. no
   b. yes
4. a. no
   b. no
   c. yes
5. a. no
   b. no
   c. yes
   d. no

PRACTICE 3, p. 189

Group 1
1. c
2. a
3. b

Group 2
1. c
2. a
3. b

Group 3
1. c
2. b
3. a

Group 4
1. a
2. c
3. b

PRACTICE 4, p. 189

1. heat ... boils
   heat ... will boil
2. forget ... look
   forget ... will look
3. pet ... purrs
   pet ... will purr
4. have ... will call
   have ... call
5. eat ... won't feel
   eat ... don't feel
6. is ... are
   is ... will be

PRACTICE 5, p. 190

1. b
2. a
3. b
4. a
5. b
6. b

PRACTICE 6, p. 191

1. were ... would be
2. had ... would travel
3. had ... would like
4. liked ... would cook
5. weren't ... could have
6. didn't have ... would go / 'd go

PRACTICE 7, p. 191

1. h
2. d
3. b
4. j
5. i
6. c

7. a
8. e
9. g
10. f

PRACTICE 8, p. 192

1. b
2. a
3. a
4. a
5. b
6. b

PRACTICE 9, p. 192

1. had not taken ... would not have met
2. had not forgotten ... could have paid
3. had known ... would have visited
4. had paid ... would not have cut off
5. had been ... would not have been canceled
6. had not discovered ... would not have developed

PRACTICE 10, p. 192

1. c
2. a
3. b
4. e
5. f
6. d

PRACTICE 11, p. 193

1. had ... could fly
2. could fly ... would get
3. get ... will have / 'll have
4. have ... will tell / 'll tell
5. had had ... would have told him
6. had told ... would not have been

PRACTICE 12, p. 193

1. I hadn't been sick yesterday, I would have gone to class.
2. Alan ate breakfast, he wouldn't overeat at lunch.
3. his watch had not been slow, Kostas would not have been late to his own wedding.
4. the bus were not always so crowded, I would ride it to work every morning.
5. Sara had known that Highway 57 was closed, she would have taken an alternative route.
6. someone had been there to help her, Camille could have finished unloading the truck.

PRACTICE 13, p. 194

1. If the wind weren't blowing so hard, we could go sailing.
2. If the wind had not been blowing so hard, we could have gone sailing.
3. If the water weren't running, I could hear you.
4. If the water had not been running, I could have heard the phone.
5. If the baby were not hungry, she wouldn't be crying.
6. If Jude had not been sleeping soundly, he would have heard his alarm clock.
7. If I had not been watching an exciting mystery on TV, I would have answered the phone.
8. If I weren't trying to concentrate, I could talk to you now.

PRACTICE 14, p. 194

1. a, c
2. b, d
3. a, d
4. b, c
5. a, d
6. a, d

PRACTICE 15, p. 195

1. If it weren't raining, we would finish the game.
2. If I had eaten lunch, I wouldn't be hungry now.
3. If Bob hadn't left his wallet at home, he would have money for lunch now.
4. If Bryce were not always daydreaming, he would get his work done.
5. If I hadn't played basketball for three hours last night, my muscles wouldn't hurt today.
6. If the band had not been playing so loud, I could have heard what you said.
7. If Diana had not asked the technician a lot of questions, she wouldn't understand how to fix her computer now.
8. If Sasha and Ivan had been paying attention, they would have seen the exit sign on the highway.
9. If the doctor had explained the test results to me, I would know what they mean.
10. If we had not been sleeping last night, we would have felt the earthquake.

PRACTICE 16, p. 196

1. Were I you,
2. Should you need
3. Had I known
4. Had I been offered
5. Should anyone call
6. Should the pizza need reheating
7. Should you feel
8. Were you really a lawyer

PRACTICE 17, p. 196

1. b
2. b
3. c
4. b
5. b

PRACTICE 18, p. 197

1. I hadn't forgotten to tell him that she needed a ride
2. you hadn't helped
3. I had opened the door quickly
4. he could have gotten time off from work
5. he had told his boss about the problem

PRACTICE 19, p. 197

1. d
2. a
3. c
4. d
5. c
6. d
7. c
8. b
9. b
10. a
11. c
12. d
13. b
14. d
15. c
16. b
17. b
18. b
19. a
20. c

PRACTICE 20, p. 198

1. b
2. b
3. a
4. b
5. b
6. b

PRACTICE 21, p. 199

1. were shining
2. had gone
3. had driven
4. could swim
5. had won
6. had gotten
7. hadn't quit
8. were

PRACTICE 22, p. 199

1. had gone ... could paint
2. hadn't moved ... had taken
3. would stop
4. hadn't invited
5. hadn't paid
6. A: would hurry
   B: would relax
7. A: hadn't been chosen
   B: had picked
8. A: weren't ... were
   B: were ... were
9. had told
10. would go

PRACTICE 23, p. 200

1. would get
2. would snow
3. would leave
4. would hang up
5. would end
6. would cook

PRACTICE 24, p. 201

1. allowed
2. had gotten
3. had thought
4. didn't have
5. could get
6. could take OR would take

PRACTICE 25, p. 202

1. would look
2. had had
3. hadn't been driving
4. would not have slid
5. steps
6. had known
7. would not have crashed
8. had not lost
9. would have had
10. had had
11. would not have to pay
12. would not have run into
13. would not be
14. were
15. would take
16. stay
17. would stay
18. were not
19. could go
20. will fly
21. will take
22. could drive
23. would be
24. had

APPENDIX: SUPPLEMENTARY GRAMMAR CHARTS

PRACTICE 1, p. 203

1. Airplanes have wings.

   S — V — O

2. The teacher explained the problem.

   S — V — O

3. Children enjoy games.

   S — V — O

4. Jack wore a blue suit.

   S — V — O

5. Some animals eat plants. Some animals eat other animals.

   S — V — O — S — V — O

6. According to an experienced waitress, you can carry full cups of coffee without spilling them just by never looking at them.

   S — V — O

PRACTICE 2, p. 203

1. Alice <u>arrived</u> at six o'clock. *VI*
2. We <u>drank</u> some tea. *VT*
3. I <u>agree</u> with you. *VI*
4. I <u>waited</u> for Sam at the airport for two hours. *VI*
5. They're <u>staying</u> at a resort hotel in San Antonio, Texas. *VI*
6. Mr. Chan is <u>studying</u> English. *VI*
7. The wind is <u>blowing</u> hard today. *VI*
8. I <u>walked</u> to the theater, but Janice <u>rode</u> her bicycle. *VI / VT*
9. Crocodiles <u>hatch</u> from eggs. *VI*
10. Rivers <u>flow</u> toward the sea. *VI*

PRACTICE 3, p. 203

1. Jack opened the <u>heavy</u> door <u>slowly</u>. *ADJ / ADV*
2. <u>Chinese</u> jewelers carved <u>beautiful</u> ornaments from jade. *ADJ / ADJ*
3. The <u>old</u> man carves <u>wooden</u> figures <u>skillfully</u>. *ADJ / ADJ / ADV*
4. A <u>busy</u> executive <u>usually</u> has <u>short</u> conversations on the telephone. *ADJ / ADV / ADJ*
5. The <u>young</u> woman had a <u>very</u> <u>good</u> time at the picnic <u>yesterday</u>. *ADJ / ADV ADJ / ADV*

PRACTICE 4, p. 204

1. quickly
2. quick
3. polite
4. politely
5. regularly
6. regular
7. usual
8. usually
9. well
10. good
11. gentle
12. gently
13. bad
14. badly

PRACTICE 5, p. 204

1. Ana **always takes** a walk in the morning.
2. Tim **is always** a hard worker.
3. Beth **has always worked** hard.
4. Carrie **always works** hard.
5. **Do you always work** hard?
6. Taxis **are usually** available ...
7. Yusef **rarely takes** a taxi ... .
8. I **have often thought** about ... .
9. Yuko **probably needs** some help.
10. **Have you ever attended** the show ... ?
11. Brad **seldom goes** out ... .
12. The students **are hardly ever** late.
13. **Do you usually finish** your ... ?
14. In India, the monsoon season **generally begins** ...
15. ... Mr. Singh's hometown **usually receives** around... .

PRACTICE 6, p. 205

1. Jim came to class <u>without</u> his books.
2. We stayed <u>at</u> home <u>during</u> the storm.
3. Sonya walked <u>across</u> the bridge <u>over</u> the Cedar River.
4. When Alex walked <u>through</u> the door, his little sister ran <u>toward</u> him and put her arms <u>around</u> his neck.
5. The two <u>of</u> us need to talk <u>to</u> Tom too.
6. Animals live <u>in</u> all parts of the world. Animals walk or crawl <u>on</u> land, fly <u>in</u> the air, and swim <u>in</u> the water.
7. Scientists divide living things <u>into</u> two main groups: the animal kingdom and the plant kingdom.
8. Asia extends <u>from</u> the Pacific Ocean <u>in</u> the east <u>to</u> Africa and Europe <u>in</u> the west.

PRACTICE 7, p. 205

1. <u>Harry</u> <u>put</u> the <u>letter</u> <u>in the mailbox</u>.

   S — V — O — PP

2. The <u>kids</u> <u>walked</u> <u>to school</u>.

   S — V — PP

3. <u>Caroline</u> <u>did</u> her <u>homework</u> <u>at the library</u>.

   S — V — O — PP

4. Chinese <u>printers</u> <u>created</u> the first paper <u>money</u> <u>in the world</u>.

   S — V — O — PP

5. Dark <u>clouds</u> <u>appeared</u> <u>on the horizon</u>.

   S — V — PP

6. <u>Rhonda</u> <u>filled</u> the <u>shelves</u> <u>of the cabinet</u> <u>with boxes</u> <u>of old books</u>.

   S — V — O — PP — PP — PP

PRACTICE 8, p. 205

1. honesty, fairness
2. school, class
3. her illness, her husband's death
4. jail, prison
5. ghosts, UFOs
6. my cousin, a friend
7. mathematics, sports
8. you, your children
9. smoking, cigarettes
10. magazines, a newspaper, websites

PRACTICE 9, p. 205

1. of
2. at
3. from
4. in
5. at
6. of
7. to
8. for
9. on
10. from

PRACTICE 10, p. 206

Situation 1:

1. to
2. to
3. of
4. to
5. with
6. to
7. to

Situation 2:

1. with / by
2. with
3. with
4. of
5. of
6. of, by

PRACTICE 11, p. 206

1. c
2. e
3. b
4. f
5. a
6. g
7. d

PRACTICE 12, p. 207

1. to
2. for
3. from
4. on
5. about
6. for
7. about
8. with
9. on
10. with
11. on
12. of

PRACTICE 13, p. 207

1. for
2. for
3. of
4. to ... for
5. with
6. to
7. on
8. for ... to
9. about
10. of
11. of
12. to / with
13. with
14. to

PRACTICE 14, p. 208

	Question word	Auxiliary verb	Subject	Main verb	Rest of question
1a.	Ø	Can	Chris	live	there?
1b.	Where	can	Chris	live	Ø?
1c.	Who	can	Ø	live	there?
2a.	Ø	Is	Ron	living	there?
2b.	Where	is	Ron	living	Ø?
2c.	Who	is	Ø	living	there?
3a.	Ø	Does	Kate	live	there?
3b.	Where	does	Kate	live	Ø?
3c.	Who	Ø	Ø	lives	there?
4a.	Ø	Will	Ann	live	there?
4b.	Where	will	Ann	live	Ø?
4c.	Who	will	Ø	live	there?
5a.	Ø	Did	Jack	live	there?
5b.	Where	did	Jack	live	Ø?
5c.	Who	Ø	Ø	lived	there?
6a.	Ø	Has	Mary	lived	there?
6b.	Where	has	Mary	lived	Ø?
6c.	Who	has	Ø	lived	there?

PRACTICE 15, p. 209

1. When are you going to the zoo?
2. Are you going downtown later today?
3. Do you live in an apartment?
4. Where does Alex live?
5. Who lives in that house?
6. Can you speak French?
7. Who can speak Arabic?
8. When did Ben arrive?
9. Who arrived late?
10. What is Ann opening?
11. What is Ann doing?
12. What did Mary open?
13. Who opened the door?
14. Has the mail arrived?
15. Do you have a bicycle?
16. What does Zach have in his hand?
17. Do you like ice cream?
18. Would you like an ice cream cone?
19. What would Scott like?
20. Who would like a soft drink?

PRACTICE 16, p. 210

1. How do you take your coffee?
2. What kind of dictionary do you have? (have you? / have you got?)
3. What does he do for a living?
4. Who was Margaret talking to? / To whom was Margaret talking?
5. How many people showed up for the meeting?
6. Why could none of the planes take off?
7. What was she thinking about? / About what was she thinking?
8. How fast / How many miles per hour (OR: an hour) were you driving when the police officer stopped you?
9. What kind of food do you like best?
10. Which apartment is yours?
11. What is Oscar like? (also possible: What kind of person / man is Oscar?)
12. What does Oscar look like?
13. Whose dictionary fell to the floor?
14. Why isn't Abby here?

15. When will all of the students in the class be informed of their final grades?
16. How do you feel?
17. Which book did you prefer?
18. What kind of music do you like?
19. How late is the plane expected to be?
20. Why did the driver of the stalled car light a flare?
21. Which pen do you want?
22. What's the weather like in July?
23. How do you like your steak?
24. How did you do on the test?
25. How many seconds are there in a year?

PRACTICE 17, p. 211
1. How much money do you need?
2. Where was Roberto born? / In what country / city was ...? / What country / city was Roberto born in?
3. How often do you go out to eat?
4. Who(m) are you waiting for? (very formal and seldom used: For whom are you waiting?)
5. Who answered the phone?
6. Who(m) did you call?
7. Who called?
8. How much gas / How many gallons of gas did she buy?
9. What does *deceitful* mean?
10. What is an abyss?
11. Which way did he go?
12. Whose books and papers are these?
13. How many children do they have? [British or regional American: How many children have they?]
14. How long has he been here?
15. How far is it / How many miles is it to Madrid?
16. When / At what time can the doctor see me?
17. Who is her roommate?
18. Who are her roommates?
19. How long / How many years have your parents been living there?
20. Whose book is this?
21. Who's coming over for dinner?
22. What color is Caroline's dress?
23. What color are Caroline's eyes?
24. Who can't go ... ?
25. Why can't Andrew go? / How come Andrew can't go?
26. Why didn't you / How come you didn't answer ... ? (formal and rare: Why did you not answer the phone?)
27. What kind of music do you like?
28. What don't you understand?
29. What is Janie doing right now?
30. How do you spell sitting? [you = impersonal pronoun]
31. What does Xavier look like?
32. What is Xavier like?
33. What does Ray do (for a living)?
34. How far / How many miles is Mexico from here?
35. How do you take / like your coffee?
36. Which (city) is farther north, Stockholm or Moscow? / Of Stockholm and Moscow, which (city / one) is farther north?
37. How are you getting along?

PRACTICE 18, p. 212
1. Did you find your keys?
2. Do you want some coffee?
3. Do you need help?
4. Are you leaving already?

5. Do you have any questions?
6. Are you going up?
7. Did you make it on time?

PRACTICE 19, p. 212
1. Haven't you seen ... ? No.
2. Don't you feel ... ? No.
3. Wasn't he ... ? No.
4. Didn't Dana tell ... ? No.
5. Don't Jill and you work ... ? Yes.
6. Isn't that ... ? Yes.
7. Wasn't she ... ? No.
8. Isn't she ... ? Yes.

PRACTICE 20, p. 213
1. don't you
2. have you
3. didn't she
4. aren't there
5. have you
6. don't you (also possible but less common: haven't you)
7. won't you
8. doesn't he
9. shouldn't we
10. can they
11. are they
12. isn't it
13. didn't they
14. aren't I
15. isn't it

PRACTICE 21, p. 213
1. He's	11. It's
2. Ø	12. It's
3. He's	13. Ø
4. Ø	14. Ø
5. She'd	15. We're
6. Ø	16. Ø
7. She'd	17. She's
8. Ø	18. She'd
9. We'll	19. She'd ... we'd
10. They're	20. he'd

PRACTICE 22, p. 214
1. I don't have any problems. I have no problems.
2. There wasn't any food on the shelf. There was no food on the shelf.
3. I didn't receive any letters from home. I received no letters from home.
4. I don't need any help. I need no help.
5. We don't have any time to waste. We have no time to waste.
6. You shouldn't have given the beggar any money. You should have given the beggar no money.
7. I don't trust anyone. I trust no one.
8. I didn't see anyone. I saw no one.
9. There wasn't anyone in his room. There was no one in his room.
10. She can't find anybody who knows about it. She can find nobody who knows about it.

PRACTICE 23, p. 214

1. We have no time to waste. or We don't have any time to waste.
2. I didn't have any problems. or I had no problems.
3. I can't do anything about it. or I can do nothing about it.
4. You can hardly ever understand her when she speaks.
5. I know neither Joy nor her husband. or I don't know either Joy or her husband.
6. Don't ever drink water from ... . or Never drink water from ... .
7. ... I could barely hear the speaker.

PRACTICE 24, p. 214

1. Hardly had I stepped out of bed ... .
2. Never will I say that again.
3. Scarcely ever have I enjoyed myself more ... .
4. Rarely does she make a mistake.
5. Never will I trust him again because ... .
6. Hardly ever is it possible to get ... .
7. Seldom do I skip breakfast.
8. Never have I known a more ... .

PRACTICE 25, p. 215

	Just add -ing	Drop the final -e	Double the final letter
1.		arriving	
2.	copying		
3.			cutting
4.	enjoying		
5.	filling		
6.	happening		
7.		hoping	
8.		leaving	
9.		making	
10.			rubbing
11.	staying		
12.			stopping
13.		taking	
14.			winning
15.	working		

PRACTICE 26, p. 215

	Just add -ed	Add -d only	Double the final letter	Change -y to -i
1.	bothered			
2.				copied
3.	enjoyed			
4.		snored		
5.	feared			
6.			occurred	
7.			patted	
8.	played			
9.	rained			
10.			referred	
11.				replied
12.	returned			
13.		scared		
14.				tried
15.	walked			

PRACTICE 27, p. 216

1. rains
2. visited
3. will win
4. is watching
5. will be flying
6. was thinking
7. will be working
8. went ... were sleeping
9. fell ... will help
10. are swimming

PRACTICE 28, p. 216

1. have
2. had
3. has been
4. was
5. will have been
6. have lived
7. had
8. have
9. had
10. had

PRACTICE 29, p. 216

1. have
2. has been
3. will have been
4. had
5. have
6. had
7. have been waiting
8. has
9. had

PRACTICE 30, p. 217

1. eats
2. ate
3. will eat / 'll eat
4. am eating / 'm eating
5. was eating
6. will be eating
7. have already eaten
8. had already eaten
9. will have already eaten
10. has been eating
11. had been eating
12. will have been eating

PRACTICE 31, p. 218

	L.VERB +	ADJ
1.	Ø (no linking verb in the sentence)	
2.	looked	fresh
3.	Ø	
4.	Ø	
5.	tasted	good
6.	grew	quiet
7.	Ø	
8.	Ø	
9.	Ø	
10.	smells	delicious
11.	Ø	
12.	got	sleepy
13.	became	rough
14.	Ø	
15.	Ø	
16.	sounded	happy
17.	turns	hot
18.	Ø	
19.	Ø	
20.	appears	certain
21.	seems	strange

PRACTICE 32, p. 219

1. clean
2. slowly
3. safely
4. anxious
5. complete
6. wildly
7. honest
8. thoughtfully
9. well
10. fair
11. terrible
12. good
13. light
14. confidently
15. famous
16. fine

PRACTICE 33, p. 219

1. raised
2. rises
3. sat
4. set
5. lay
6. lying
7. laid
8. lie

SPECIAL WORKBOOK SECTION: PHRASAL VERBS

PRACTICE 1, p. 223

1. a. after
   b. over
   c. up
   d. into
2. a. out
   b. into
   c. out
   d. out of
3. a. over
   b. through with
   c. out of
   d. back from
   e. off
4. a. off
   b. up
   c. on
   d. back
   e. in

PRACTICE 2, p. 224

1. passed out
2. Pick out
3. takes after
4. think ... over
5. puts up with
6. passed away
7. show up
8. get along with
9. turn in
10. pass out

PRACTICE 3, p. 224

1. our assignment?
2. a lie. / a story.
3. the city. / the banks.
4. your cigarette. / the lights. / the fire.
5. the war? / the crisis?
6. the problem? / the puzzle?
7. the lights? / the music? / the printer?
8. his classmate. / a girl.

9. chocolate. / smoking.
10. a friend. / a classmate.
11. high school. / college.

PRACTICE 4, p. 225

1. into
2. off
3. on
4. back
5. out
6. up
7. into ... out
8. up
9. up
10. on

PRACTICE 5, p. 226

1. away / out
2. up
3. off / out
4. up
5. off
6. up
7. about, on
8. out of
9. off
10. off ... in

PRACTICE 6, p. 226

1. out
2. back
3. by / in
4. on ... off
5. put ... out
6. up
7. up ... away / out
8. out ... back
9. up
10. on

PRACTICE 7, p. 227

1. up
2. over
3. after
4. up
5. out
6. down
7. up
8. out
9. off
10. up
11. out

PRACTICE 8, p. 228

1. back
2. up
3. out
4. over
5. on ... off
6. in ... out
7. on ... off
8. on ... off
9. up with
10. A: about / on
    B: along with
11. A: over ... in
    B: over